5.95

middle eastern cultures

Edited by
PAUL THOMAS WELTY

Coordinator - Asian Studies Program
Northeastern Illinois University

J. B. LIPPINCOTT COMPANY
PHILADELPHIA · NEW YORK

ABOUT THE EDITOR

Dr. Paul Welty is Coordinator of Asian Studies at Northeastern Illinois University. He has traveled and lectured extensively throughout the world. Besides editing *World Cultures Sourcebooks,* he is the author of *The Asians: Their Heritage and Their Destiny; Pageant of World Cultures; Man's Cultura¹ Heritage;* and *Readings in World Cultures.* Dr. Welty is a member of the Editorial Board of *World Affairs Magazine* and a member of a number of professional organizations including the American Historical Association, Association for Asian Studies, and the American Political Science Association.

THE LIPPINCOTT SOCIAL STUDIES PROGRAM

SUPERVISED BY

STANLEY E. DIMOND

Professor Emeritus, School of Education

University of Michigan

Dr. Dimond has served as Divisional Director, Department of Social Studies, Detroit Public Schools, and is Professor Emeritus of Education in the School of Education, University of Michigan. In addition to supervising the Lippincott Social Studies Program, Dr. Dimond is the author of *Schools and the Development of Good Citizens,* and co-author of *Our American Government* and *Civics for Citizens.*

BICENTENNIAL EDITION

Book and Cover Design by Nancy Earle
Map by Alan Young

Printed in the United States of America

ISBN-0-397-40225-2

5.7312.1

Culture is the collective intellectual achievement of a people and the embodiment of their values, their aspirations and their way of life.
—Saad Abdulbaki, Minister of Education, Iraq

Culture is a way of interpreting the world. Science ıs a way of transforming it. That is not sufficient reason for keeping them separate. In so far as science is a culture, it should be integrated, and one of the primordial tasks of cultural policy is to ensure that integration.
—Mehrdad Pahlbod, Minister of Culture and the Arts, Iran

The whole of humanity should be considered as a body, and a nation one of its organs. We should not say, What do I care if there is trouble in a remote corner of the world. If there is such trouble, we should be concerned with it as if it were our own. . . .
—Mustafa Kemal Atatürk, Turkey

The *World Cultures Sourcebooks* is a collection of observations, documents, and primary sources. The span of time covered by their readings ranges from prehistory, through the earliest known writings, and comes down to the most recent historical period. Each volume in the series explores the origins of the peoples in a cultural area, their creativity, and the evolution of their ideology. This series is dedicated to students who wish to evaluate sources and base conclusions upon firsthand evidence chosen from the ideas of inquiring minds.

Middle Eastern Cultures introduces the peoples of the Middle East. In most selections, Middle Easterners describe themselves, their concepts, and their values.

INQUIRY AND WORLD CULTURES

For many years anthropologists have emphasized the fact that investigations of other cultures require direct observation of the cultures being studied. Equally, historians have insisted upon the use of primary sources, of firsthand information.

Students, too often, are subject to the physical limitations of the academic process. You do not always have access to the raw materials on which your curriculum is based. The *World Cultures Sourcebooks* are presented in answer to this need. Through reading selections, students are invited to make inquiries into the history and cultural patterns of people in all parts of the world.

THE INQUIRY METHOD OF STUDY

Before beginning the serious study of any subject, there must be a reason, a purpose, for the study. This is the basis of the inquiry method, which combines the "content" approach with the "process" approach to education.

The editor and publisher of this book assume that it is natural for each member of a social group to be interested in other members of the same group as well as other groups. The readings have therefore been chosen to supply information about major aspects of the history and behavior of peoples in world culture areas. Each reading is preceded by one or more inquiry questions. Finding the answers to these questions is the assignment for each reading.

USING THE INQUIRY METHOD WITH THIS BOOK

The approaches to inquiry vary greatly, dependent upon the individual interests of teachers and students. However, certain features are common to most inquiry programs. First, a question or problem is posed and a certain body of material is chosen as the basis of the inquiry. In this book the inquiry problem or question is stated at the beginning of each reading.

The source material to be used for investigation of each inquiry problem consists of one or more readings. The readings are made up of written documents, interviews, or observations gathered from investigation and research.

In addition to the readings, each of the *World Cultures Sourcebooks* contains a map, a chronological table of major historical events for the area under study, and a list of further readings. The map makes it possible to establish spatial relationships: where is the country or area in relation to the rest of the world and in relation to its immediate neighbors? The chronological table provides information needed to establish the historical background and context of events mentioned in readings: what events or conditions led up to those described in the reading and what later developments took place? Further readings, listed at the end of the book, provide a carefully selected list of books for additional reading and reference. If a problem is to be studied in depth, or if the reader wishes more information, these books may be consulted.

All of these reference materials should be considered in finding answers to inquiry problems. Information related to the inquiry problem should be organized and evaluated. Finally conclusions or generalizations can be drawn, based upon evidence discovered in the course of the investigation.

BEHAVIORIAL GOALS

All students may not necessarily reach the same conclusions in answering questions. If so, the resulting differences may become the subject of discussion based upon observation of the facts presented. Through communication of this kind, it is possible to understand better the behavior and ideas of other people as well as your own behavior and ways of thinking.

A major aim of the inquiry or discovery method is to help you to understand your own patterns of behavior and thought processes. After answering the inquiry problems, you should analyze your own ways of thinking. How and why did you reach your conclusions? Did your own biases enter into the process? Did you have further information that was not available in the reading? Was the author of the selection also subject to his own biases? Did he have access to all the information needed? Might several different conclusions be justified?

This kind of appraisal of intellectual processes and attitudes is a logical basis for self-respect. It is also the basis of respect for the rights and ideas of other people.

CONTENTS

Locating the Middle East in Space

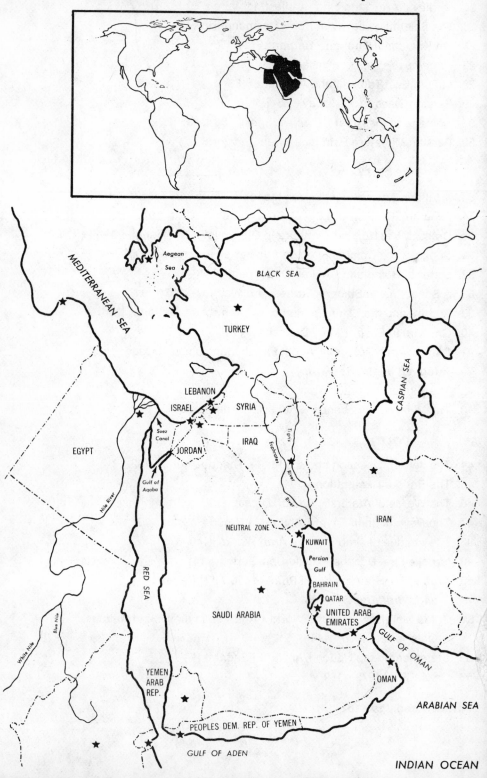

Locating the Middle East in Time

THE ANCIENT MIDDLE EAST

B.C.

10,000-8000	Middle Stone Age. Archaeological evidence indicates that man was domesticating the dog and beginning to cultivate plants in the Middle East. Remains of the first known town, Jericho (in Palestine) indicate existence of village life.
8000-5000	Neolithic period (New Stone Age). Further domestication of animals and increase in agriculture.
c.* 5000	Sumerians settle Tigris-Euphrates valley (modern Iraq). This region was later called Mesopotamia.
4241	Traditional date for beginning of Egyptian calendar.
c. 3100-2700	First and Second Dynasties in Egypt.
c. 3000-2500	Sumerian civilization at its height. The Sumerians invent a cuneiform writing, use a potter's wheel, plows, bows, and chariots. They work in copper, lead, and silver. Their chronicles describe a great flood. Their trade extends as far as the Indus River.
c. 3000	Assyrians live in Assur, a highland along the Tigris River. The Gilgamesh epic is composed.
2700-2200	Old Kingdom in Egypt; pyramids are built.
c. 2400	Akkadians conquer Sumerians. Qurti, forerunners of the Kurds, inhabit western and northwestern Iran.
c. 2400-2000	Mixed kingdom of Sumer and Akkad, first united kingdom in Mesopotamia. Chief city is Ur, from which Abraham led his family to Canaan on the Mediterranean coast.
2100-2050	First Intermediate Period in Egypt; invasions from south and east.
c. 2000-1200	Hittites are a great power in northern Asia Minor. Their knowledge of ironmaking gives them an advantage over their Bronze-Age neighbors. Highly developed civilization is centered on the island of Dilmun (possibly modern Bahrain).
c. 1894-1595	Under Amorite rule Babylon becomes major empire of Mesopotamia. Monasticism is practiced by women. Highly complex astronomical calculations are made.
c. 1750	Most famous Amorite king, Hammurabi dies. Hammurabi collected all laws and customs of his subjects and established a uniform legal code.
c. 1600	Glass is invented in Mesopotamia.
1570-1100	Egypt's Empire Period; expansion of Egyptian power.
c. 1230	Israelites, led by Moses, escape from Egypt.
1225-733	Peak of ancient Hebrew civilization in Canaan. The tribes of Israel are united under the rule of David and Solomon.
c. 1100-900	Height of Phoenician greatness. Centered in what is now Lebanon, the Phoenicians settle colonies along all the coasts of the Mediterranean. They explore and trade beyond the

---

*C. is an abbreviation for the word *circa* meaning *approximately*.

	Mediterranean Sea to lands along the Black Sea coast, and the Atlantic coast of Europe and Africa.
c. 940	Separate kingdoms of Israel and Judah.
612	Nineveh is destroyed, ending the power of the Assyrians in Mesopotamia.
612-539	Chaldean Empire becomes greatest power in Middle East.
c. 600	Zoroaster, a Persian prophet, founds Zoroastrian religion.
586	Nebuchadnezzar, king of the Chaldeans, rebuilds Babylon and destroys Jerusalem. He holds the Hebrews in captivity in Babylon.
c. 550-529	Reign of Cyrus the Great of Persia (modern Iran). The Achaemenian dynasty conquers Egypt.
521-486	Reign of Darius the Great. Persian Empire extends from Indus River to the Black Sea to Greece. Roads are built connecting cities such as Susa, Persepolis, Babylon, and Ecbatana. The 1600-mile Royal Road joins Susa, near Persian Gulf, to Sardis, near the Mediterranean.
332	Alexander the Great leads Macedonian conquest of Egypt.
c. 330	Alexander the Great of Macedonia defeats the Persians and invades Afghanistan.
323-30	Ptolemies rule in Egypt after death of Alexander the Great.
305	Seleucid dynasty begins rule of remaining part of Alexander's empire in Syria and Mesopotamia. Ptolemies rule in Egypt.
264-146	Punic Wars. Rome ends Phoenician power by destroying Carthage in North Africa.
c. 202	Trade is established between Persia and China.
190	Seleucids lose much of their empire to Rome.
30	Rome conquers Egypt.
c. 7-4	Jesus of Nazareth born in Palestine, a Roman province.

A.D.

70	Titus, later Roman emperor, destroys Jerusalem.
135	Beginning of the Diaspora. Roman Emperor Hadrian forbids Jews to enter Jerusalem, forcing them to disperse and live in various parts of the world.
216-276	Mani founds and spreads Manichaenism in Persia.
395-1453	Eastern Roman (Byzantine) Empire continues until Constantinople is captured by Ottoman Turks.
476	Fall of Roman Empire in West.
570	Muhammad is born.
640	Arab conquest of Egypt.
750-900	Arabs preserve, improve on, and make available Greek scientific knowledge to the world.

IRAN AND IRAQ

A.D.

600s	Kurds are converted to Islam.
1055	Seljuk Turks from Turkestan gain control of Baghdad (in Iraq) and are converted to Islam. The Seljuk Turks rule much

of Asia Minor for fifty years and threaten power of Byzantine Empire.

1220	Genghis Khan invades Persia (Iran). Mongol rule continues in Afghanistan until 1700s.
1221-1400	Mongols control Persia.
1243	Mongols defeat Seljuk Turks.
1300s	Ottoman Turks begin their rise to power in Middle East.
1502-1736	Safavid dynasty rules Persia.
1729-1747	Persians conquer Afghanistan until tribes unite and overthrow Persian rule.
1794-1925	Kjar dynasty rules Iran (Persia).
1908	Oil is discovered in southwestern Iran.
1921	Iraq (formerly Turkish territory) becomes separate kingdom, a British mandate.
1925-1941	Riza Khan Pahlevi modernizes Iran.
1932	Iraq becomes an independent kingdom.
1941	During World War II Britain occupies Iraq; Britain and Russia occupy Iran.
1955	Iraq, Iran, Turkey, Pakistan, and Great Britain sign an alliance known as the Baghdad Pact.
1958	Iraq is proclaimed a republic after military coup.
1959	Iraq withdraws from Baghdad Pact; the organization is renamed Central Treaty Organization (CENTO), headquartered in Ankara, Turkey. Membership includes Iran, Turkey, Pakistan, and Great Britain. U.S. is associate member.
1961-1962	Shah begins reforms in Iran: land distribution, end of serfdom, electoral reform.
1967	Iran signs $110 million agreement with Soviet Union primarily to buy arms. Mohammed Riza Pahlevi crowned Shah of Iran; he had actually been the ruler some years before the coronation.
1971	Iran receives backing for $1 billion defense program sponsored by the United States and Britain.
1972	Earthquake levels 50 villages and kills 5,000 people in Iran. Iraq and Syria expropriate the Western-owned Iraq Petroleum Company.
1973	Iraq sends men to aid Syria during war with Israel.

EGYPT

A.D.

640	Muslim Arabs conquer Egypt.
968-1171	Fatimid caliphate (from Tunisia) rules Egypt.
1171	Saladin adds Egypt to the Baghdad caliphate.
1250-1517	Mamelukes, a military class made up of former Turkish slaves, rule Egypt.
1517-1914	Egypt is part of Ottoman Empire.
1798	Napoleon invades Egypt.
1869	Suez Canal is completed.
1882	British invade Egypt.
1914	Egypt becomes a British Protectorate.

1922	Egypt gains independence.
1953	Egypt becomes a republic after King Farouk is overthrown.
1954	Gamal Abdel Nasser assumes power in Egypt.
1956	Egypt seizes Suez Canal; United Nations ends fighting after Britain, France, and Israel invade.
1958	United Arab Republic is formed by Egypt and Syria.
1961	Syria withdraws from United Arab Republic.
1967	Egypt and other Arab nations are defeated in Six-Day War against Israel. Israel occupies Sinai Peninsula and Gaza Strip.
1970	Nasser dies and is succeeded as president by Anwar Sadat. Soviet Union increases military aid to Egypt. Cease-fire along Suez Canal.
1971	Egypt, Libya, and Syria agree to confederate and no compromise with Israel.
1972	President Sadat orders Soviet military advisors to leave Egypt.
1973	Egypt and Syria attack Israel. Israel drives almost to Damascus, capital of Syria, and takes west bank of Suez Canal before cease-fire called.

LEBANON, SYRIA, AND TURKEY

A.D.

1000s	Seljuk Turks invade Turkey and threaten Byzantine emperor, who calls for crusades.
1096	Crusades begin.
1200s	Mongol invasions.
1300s	Ottoman Turks begin their rise to power.
1453	Constantinople is conquered by Ottoman Turks.
1517	Turkey invades and conquers Egypt.
1517-1918	Lebanon and Syria are part of Ottoman Empire.
1566	Ottoman Empire is at the height of its power.
1918	Ottoman Empire breaks up.
1920	Lebanon and Syria become a French mandate.
1923	Turkey becomes a republic; Kemal Atatürk modernizes country; women are given legal and social rights.
1941	Lebanon is proclaimed an independent republic.
1944	French proclaim Syria an independent republic.
1945	Arab League is formed.
1952	Turkey becomes member of NATO.
1955	Turkey, Iraq, Iran, Pakistan, and Great Britain sign an alliance known as the Baghdad Pact. Turkey becomes member of Central Treaty Organization (CENTO); headquarters of organization is established at Ankara, the capital of Turkey.
1958	United Arab Republic (UAR) is formed (Egypt, Syria and Yemen).
1961	Syria and Yemen withdraw from UAR.
1963	Coup brings Ba'ath Socialist Party to power in Syria. Turkey and Greece are involved in conflict between Turkish and Greek Cypriots.
1966	UN force is stationed in Cyprus to maintain peace.

1967	Al Fatah terrorist organization operates out of Syria against Israel.
1968	Turkish students demonstrate against presence of U.S. military forces.
1969	Government forces and Palestinian guerrillas clash in southern Lebanon.
1971	Political and economic unrest in Turkey leads military leaders to install a new premier.
1972	Syria and Iraq expropriate the Western-owned Iraq Petroleum Company.
1973	Heavy fighting between Lebanese government troops and Palestinian armed forces within Lebanon. Syria and Egypt attack Israel. Although aided by Soviet Union and other Arab nations, Syria loses territory to Israel.

ISRAEL, JORDAN, AND SAUDI ARABIA

A.D.

570-632	Muhammad, founder of Islam, teaches and spreads the Muslim faith in Arabia.
636	Palestine is conquered by Muslim Arabs.
700s	Most of Middle East is converted to Islam.
1096	Crusades begin. European Christians attempt to drive Seljuk Turks from Byzantine Empire and Holy Land.
1243	Mongols defeat Seljuk Turks.
1300s	Ottoman Turks begin their rise to power.
1517	Palestine is conquered by Ottoman Turks.
1700s	Saud family supports Wahabi religious group (Muslim reformers) and begins to rule in Arabia.
1800s	Turkey, aided by Egypt, defeats the Wahabis in Arabia.
1902-1925	Ibn Saud leads Wahabis in reconquest of Arabia.
1917	Balfour Declaration: Palestine to become a home for Jews.
1918	Ottoman Empire breaks up.
1921	Hashemite dynasty begins rule in Transjordan.
1926	State of Saudi Arabia is formed, with Ibn Saud as king.
1945	Arab League is formed, opposing creation of State of Israel.
1946	Transjordan becomes an independent kingdom.
1948	Israeli leaders proclaim Israel a nation. Neighboring Arab states attack Israeli forces. One million Arab refugees flee Israel.
1949	Fighting ends between Israel and Arab states with Israel gaining 50 per cent more land than originally held. Transjordan adopts official name "Hashemite Kingdom of Jordan."
1950s	Arab-Israeli fighting continues.
1950	Jordan annexes west bank of Jordan River.
1956	Egypt nationalizes Suez Canal. Israeli armies occupy Sinai Peninsula and Gaza Strip. French and English send troops into Suez Canal area. UN forces begin guarding Egypt-Israeli border, enforcing cease-fire.
1957	U.S. and Soviet pressure forces Israel, England, and France to withdraw from Egyptian territory.

1964	Crown Prince Faisal replaces Saud as chief of state in Saudi Arabia; abolishes slavery; reorganizes government ·
1967	In Six-Day War with Arab neighbors, Israel occupies Sinai Peninsula, Gaza Strip, east bank of Suez Canal, west bank of Jordan, and Golan Heights in Syria. Suez Canal is closed.
1968-1973	Friction continues between Israel and Arab nations.
1969	Mrs. Golda Meir becomes Prime Minister of Israel. Guerrilla activities of Palestinians increases.
1970	Martial law is proclaimed in Jordan as government troops battle Palestinian guerrillas.
1971	Bahrain on the Persian Gulf declares independence from England.
1972	Palestinian Arab terrorists kidnap and kill Israeli athletes at Olympic games in Germany.
1973	Israelis shoot down a Libyan airplane, leading to a new crisis with Arab nations. World energy crisis points up importance of vast oil reserves in the Middle East; Arab nations control 60 per cent of oil resources in western world. Syria and Egypt attack Israel. Israelis appear to be winning when UN-ordered cease-fire goes into effect. Arab nations led by Saudi Arabia, Libya, Morocco, and United Arab Emirates begin escalating embargo on oil shipments to nations friendly to Israel.

the environment

1.
Setting the Stage

In spite of the bleakness of the environment, humans developed and matured in the Middle East. They adapted to less than ideal living conditions and endured. The results of ability and perseverance were great civilizations and a remarkable heritage. The following article describes the geographic setting in which the people of this area developed from primitive societies to great civilizations.*

INQUIRY: What geographic features are shared by the countries described in this article? What differences are described? How does the author relate the geography of the Middle East to the development of civilizations there?

A hundred thousand years or so before Christ, while north Europe was still blanketed with snow and the mountains of south Europe were capped with glaciers, the Near East must have enjoyed more hospitable weather. It evidently received more rain than in historic times. Trees and bushes flourished where nothing but desert grass now struggles for growth. In the centuries preceding the dawn of history desiccation began as a result of the final retreat of the ice cap in Eurasia. River beds became the dry wadies we see today in the Egyptian desert, the Arabian peninsula and the Iranian plateau. Desiccation continued in historic times, but that was due partly to the destruction of irrigation works by wars or negligence and partly to the cutting down of trees by man and to promiscuous grazing by animals. Thus was the soil gradually deprived of plant roots to hold it together. Their loss facilitated erosion and the denudation of hillsides by winds and running rain water. Dried-up springs and deserted settlements on the fringes of the Syrian Desert, ruined villages bordering on neglected caravan routes in the Iranian plateau are produced by man rather than nature.

Mountain ranges along the western border of the area, from Turkey through Lebanon to Arabia, intercept the courses of the westerlies originating in the Atlantic or Mediterranean and bearing the prerequisite moisture for rain. As the mountains tap these resources, they leave the hinterland in a rain-shadow zone. The entire interior is therefore marked by dryness if not aridity. Other than the coastland only the river valleys receive sufficient precipitation in winter and relief from intensive heat in summer to warrant extensive agricultural activity. Whatever rain falls is normally crowded into December to February.

This twofold nature of the land is reflected in the two main categories into which the bulk of the population can be divided: settled farmers and

---

*Philip K. Hitti, A SHORT HISTORY OF THE NEAR EAST (Princeton, D. Van Nostrand Company, Inc., 1966), pp. 6-11. Courtesy of Van Nostrand Reinhold Company, a division of Litton Educational Publishing, Inc., Litton Industries.

wandering nomads. Accordingly Bedouins populate the desert interiors of Anatolia, Syria, Iran and Arabia as well as the fringes of Iraq and Egypt. The pattern in these two countries is changed because of their three rivers. Lebanon is so mountainous and narrow that it leaves no room for a barren interior or fringe. The Anatolian plateau rises 3000 to 3500 feet above the sea, that of Iran 1000 to 3000 feet and occupies about half of the land. Iran is shielded on the north by the Elburz Mountains and on the south by the Zagoras massif. Both plateaus experience relatively excessive cold in winter and intensive heat in summer (particularly July and August). The average January temperature in central Anatolia is 30° Fahrenheit, the July temperature 86°. Rainfall varies from 10 to 17 inches annually.

The Taurus and Anti-Taurus ranges in southern Anatolia retarded but did not stop communication with the Semitic, later Arab, world to its south. The mountains, together with the climate, however, did keep Anatolia un-Semitic, un-Arabic. Likewise the Elburz-Zagoras barriers kept Iranians from becoming Semitized or Arabicized, despite the fact that the bulk of the population has almost always gravitated westward and maintained closer cultural and commercial relations with the Fertile Crescent than with central Asia.

The Arabian pleateau is less elevated and more arid than the Iranian. Starting at a height of some 3000 feet, it dips as it extends eastward to the Persian Gulf. The entire Arabian peninsula is geologically an extension of the African Sahara; its sandy core is continued in the Syrian Desert and eastward through Iraq and Iran to central Asia.

The peninsula's western range stretches all along the Red Sea coast, attaining a height of 9000 feet in Hejaz, birthplace of Islam, and 14,000 feet in Yemen. So complete is the drainage of the moisture-bearing westerlies during their passage over the mountain that the entire hinterland is left almost rainless. The mean June temperature in Jeddah is 108° Fahrenheit. In all the peninsula only Yemen, the Arabia Felix of the Romans, receives enough precipitation to warrant extensive cultivation. Nejd, nursery of the Wahhabis headed by the Saud (Su'ud) royal family, constitutes the nucleus of the northern interior. The mean June to July temperature in Riyad is 108°F. The peninsula, largest of all Near Eastern countries, cannot boast a single perennial river that reaches the sea, nor does it have a body of water that could be called a lake. Its southern desert covers an area of 400,000 square miles and is appropriately called al-Rub' al-Khali (empty quarter). Treeless and waterless, it was not traversed by a European until the early 1930's.

At the eastern horn of the Fertile Crescent lies the valley of the twin rivers, the Tigris and Euphrates. At the extremity of the western horn lies the valley of the one river, the Nile. Both Egypt and lower Mesopotamia (present-day Iraq) are literally the gifts of the rivers that flow through them. Dry and rainless, they depend on river water for irrigation as well as drinking. Their richly fertile soil is the alluvium deposited through the centuries on a substratum of sand and rock, except at the river mouths, where the build-up has been on the sea. The site of a Sumerian seaport, Eridu, lies today about 150 miles from the head of the Persian Gulf.

In both Egypt and Mesopotamia spring and autumn are short, summers intensely hot and winters relatively mild. Any rain that falls in Egypt is limited to the coast and does not exceed eight inches. The mean July temperature in Cairo is 84°F.; the mean in January is 53°F. Baghdad receives an average rainfall of 5.5 inches and has a mean July temperature of 107°F. Both countries are almost stoneless and treeless (except for the date palm of Mesopotamia) necessitating incursions to Syria or Lebanon for the necessary supply of structural material. Egypt's dryness accounts for the remarkable preservation of its mummies and other buried treasures. It was these relics of antiquity that furnished Near Eastern archeologists with their earliest opportunity and enabled them to achieve some of the most sensational triumphs in the annals of archeology.

The valley of the Nile enjoys more regularity in climate and topography than that of Tigro-Euphrates. For thousands of miles its life-giving stream moves undisturbed on a generally level surface. Its counterparts in Mesopotamia rise in the Armenian mountains, wind their paths tortuously southward and part company. The Euphrates then suddenly turns southeast, belying its promise to continue toward the Mediterranean, while the Tigris flows close to the Zagoras. The Tigris gives no opportunity for considerable settlement between Mosul and Baghdad, and hardly any worth mentioning between Baghdad and the Gulf. The two rivers unite before emptying into the Gulf. Both have shifted their courses considerably within recorded time, a disturbing factor for settlers and archeologists. Their inundations at times have been so violent as to cause considerable damage. Moreover, Egypt is sheltered on all sides by deserts and waters. Mesopotamia is more exposed to invasions from Elam and Iran on the east, to migrations from Arabia on the south and to attacks from neighbors on the west.

These physical differences between the two valleys are reflected in the two civilizations cradled on their river banks. The Sumero-Babylonian society felt helpless vis-à-vis capricious forces personified in gods; it developed a pessimistic philosophy of life. Politically its country was not unified until the eighteenth pre-Christian century under the Semitic Hammurabi. The early Egyptian society felt more secure in its isolated land, enjoyed a long period of peace and became imbued with the sense of homogeneity. It developed a more optimistic outlook. Its gods, like its Nile, were generally beneficient. Egypt achieved political unity a thousand years before Mesopotamia. It experienced no serious invasion until the late eighteenth century B.C., when the Hyksos descended on it from Syria. It waited another thousand years to see another enemy on its soil—the Assyrians.

The mountain range along the eastern shore of the Mediterranean rises to about 5000 feet in Syria and 11,000 feet in Western Lebanon. Anti-Lebanon parallels Western Lebanon and culminates in Mount Hermon (Jabal al-Shaykh), overlooking Palestine. The two north-to-south Lebanons trap most of the precipitation of the maritime winds, leaving the Syrian hinterland but little. Whereas Beirut receives an annual average of 35 to 38 inches of rain, Damascus gets only 10 inches. In Beirut the mean annual temperature is 68°F., but its summers are more humid and less comfortable than Damascus with its higher temperature. The Lebanese coastal plain with the adjoining mountain slopes makes of the country a garden of the East.

Palestine is geologically a continuation of Lebanon, Transjordan a continuation of Anti-Lebanon and Syria. The Lebanese maritime plain becomes the plain of Sharon, which extends from Mount Carmel to connect with the littoral of Philistia. The highlands of Palestine attain a maximum elevation of only 3935 feet north of Safad. In Jerusalem, 2550 feet high, the average temperature in July is only 75°F., in January 47°F.

Such was the geographic setting of the stage on which our Near Eastern man played his role from primitivism to a dizzy height of civilization.

2.
The Bedouin

The Bedouin homeland is the desert and its fringes in the Arab world of the Middle East. Like their ancestors who roamed the Arabian and Syrian deserts long before historical records existed, the Bedouin of today lead a hard life in a harsh land. They must constantly search for those scarce desert oases where humans and animals can settle and live. Such an environment produces tough and hardened people.

The Bedouin prize the camel for it serves them in many ways. It is their means of transportation; it is their food and a source of milk and of covering for tents. It is often the substance of a Bedouin's wealth and the symbol of his status. He keeps horses, too, if he has the water and food for them. They are a part of his poetry and legend, and he frequently knows their genealogies as well as he knows his own. Bedouin herd goats and sheep and these also serve as food, clothing, and as a medium of exchange.

The Bedouin belongs to a family, a clan, and a tribe, and without this kinship unit, he is alone and insecure in a dangerous land. Historically, the Bedouin has been a raider and a fighter for in the desert only one law was and is truly respected—the law of self-preservation.*

INQUIRY: How do you believe increased industrialization in the Middle East might affect the way of life of the Bedouin?

The reported population of the Arabian peninsula exceeds 12 million. About half live in Saudi Arabia with most of the others in Yemen. There is no way of knowing how many are farmers, how many live in cities, and how many are nomads. It is doubtful whether more than 2 million Saudi are urban dwellers, even including towns, and the number of nomads may not be much larger, perhaps around 3 million. Since the area over

*From CROSSROADS, LAND AND LIFE IN SOUTHWEST ASIA by George B. Cressey. Reprinted by J. B. Lippincott Company. Copyright 1968.

which the Bedouin may roam takes in most of the country, there is a tendency to exaggerate their importance. There is no question, however, that they constitute a dramatic and significant element in the cultural landscape, one whose importance was doubtless greater in the past. The importance of the Bedouin, even today, is shown by the fact that Arabian livestock surpasses date palms as a source of wealth.

The Arabs divide themselves into two main categories. Those who dwell in permanent houses, that is to say the townsfolk, are the *hadhar*. Those who dwell in black, haircloth tents and live a nomadic existence are the *badia;* from this comes our word Bedouin. In the latter group are numerous seminomads who either have houses in a town or camp near its borders in summer, and during winter move a hundred miles or less into the desert. There is a further distinction between the proper Bedouin, who have their own camels and range widely, and tribes which care for sheep which may belong to wealthy town dwellers or even to other Bedouin tribes. Camels can survive longer periods without water than sheep and thus have a longer grazing radius.

The proper Bedouin breed only camels and regard themselves as the salt of the earth. This is particularly true of the *Sharif* tribes who claim descent from the Patriarchs Qahtan and Ishmael. The Anaiza tribes of central Arabia consider themselves to be the aristocrats of the desert, and in their numbers are included the rulers of Saudi Arabia, Kuwait, Bahrein, and Qatar. Other Sharif tribes are the Ruwala, Shammar, Harb, and Mutair.

Formerly, there were established areas for each tribe and its subdivisions; today, many groups are found hundreds of miles away from their traditional area. These are clearly decades of major sociological as well as economic change, but tribal animosities still run deep and change slowly.

Bedouin have a remarkable ability to find their way across the desert. There is an Arab saying that a Murra tribesman can be taken on a three-day journey across trackless country, blindfolded, and then told to bury a coin in the sand at night. A decade later he will be able to return and locate his coin.

Bedouin hospitality is proverbial. A stranger will always find a welcome, and may even remain for three days before revealing his objective. When important guests are to be received, the women, who are behind a curtain at the other end of the tent, roast some coffee beans on a long-handled pan held over a fire of desert brush or camel dung. The beans are then pounded to powder in an iron mortar. The coffee is mixed with cardamom seeds and freshly brewed in a small pot. Any coffee left over after the guests have been served is put in a larger pot for use later in the day, and coffee which remains after that is poured into a still larger pot for the women's use the following day. The coffee is drunk from small cups, a thimble-full at a time. After several rounds of coffee, heavily sweetened tea is served in small glasses and then more coffee. If this is a formal affair, the termination of the visit will be politely signalized by passing around a small charcoal brazier on which incense is burning, or drops of perfume may be placed on one's hands.

* * *

3.
The Northern Tier:
Turkey, Iran, Afghanistan

Much attention has been focused on the Arab world and the Arab-Israeli conflict in recent years. We sometimes tend to forget about the other peoples—Turks, Iranians (Persians), and Afghans—that have played historic roles in the cultural and political development of the Middle East. These people continue to play their vital roles today. There can be no real understanding of the Middle East without some knowledge about Turkey, Iran, Afghanistan, their people, and their landscape.*

INQUIRY: Does the author of this article describe the people chiefly in terms of their differences in culture, in terms of the influence of geography on their customs, or in terms of their historical backgrounds?

The Northern Tier as defined in this study comprises Afghanistan, Iran, and Turkey. The area as a whole stretches from the borders of Bulgaria and Greece in Europe to those of Pakistan and the People's Republic of China in Asia. Afghanistan is landlocked, bounded on the north by the Soviet Union and Chinese Sinkiang, on the east and south by Pakistan, and on the west by Iran. Iran is bounded on the north by the Soviet Union and the Caspian Sea, on the east by Afghanistan and Pakistan, on the south by the Arabian Sea (Gulf of Oman) and the Persian Gulf, and on the west by Iraq and Turkey. Turkey is separated into two parts, European and Asiatic, by the Straits of Dardanelles, the Sea of Marmara, and the Bosporus, which together form the only sea link between the Black Sea and the Aegean Sea. In Europe, Turkey is a neighbor of Bulgaria and Greece and in Asia it is bounded by Syria, Iraq, Iran, and the Soviet Union.

The Northern Tier extends over one million square miles. This vast area is about one-third the size of the United States and one half of Western Europe. Every one of these three Northern Tier states is larger than France, and they all compare favorably in size with various states of the United States. Afghanistan is about as large as Texas (250,000 square miles). Iran is four times the size of California (628,000). And Turkey is about the size of Texas and South Carolina (296,500).

THE REGION

The Northern Tier is usually considered as part of the Middle East. Iran and Turkey are included within the region by most writers, but Afghanistan is included only by some. . . .

---

*From THE NORTHERN TIER: AFGHANISTAN, IRAN, AND TURKEY by Rouhollah K. Ramazani © 1966 Litton Educational Publishing, Inc. Reprinted by permission of Van Nostrand Reinhold Company.

The Iranian plateau roughly comprises Afghanistan as well as Iran. Furthermore, Afghanistan as well as Iran and Turkey share common geographic proximity to the Soviet Union. . . .

Physical Separation

The Northern Tier is effectively separated from the rest of the Middle East. Afghanistan, Iran, and Turkey generally form part of the enormous Middle East landmass of over 2.5 million square miles that is penetrated by the arms of the Mediterranean Sea, the Persian Gulf, and the Red Sea. But the Anatolian and Iranian plateaus are marked off from the rest of the Middle East by the Taurus-Zagros mountain system. These mountain ranges distinguish the plateaus from the valleys and plains of the Fertile Crescent, roughly coinciding with the cultural division of the area between the Arab and non-Arab countries. . . .

PEOPLES AND CULTURES

The population of the Northern Tier is one of the most hetero-geneous in the world. In spite of its gigantic mountain barriers and barren deserts, its geographic location has served as a crossroad for the migration of peoples ever since early man began to disperse throughout the world. Almost all the major races of mankind are represented in the area. But the national boundaries of none of the three states of the area correspond with the racial characteristics of its people. The Mediterranean, or brown, race, which is generally characterized by long-headedness, relatively small stature, and wavy hair, and the Armenoid race, marked by round-headed-ness, dark hair and eyes, and "frizzy" hair, are both represented in Turkey. The eastern part of the country is dominated by the Armenoid type, whereas toward the west extreme heterogeneity prevails. Furthermore, the Arme-noids extend into northwest Iran, where they are intermixed not only with the Iranian race but also with Turk (Turanian) elements. The most im-portant example of this Armenoid addition to the Iranian element is the Bakhtiari tribes of the central Zagros, and the best example of the Arme-noid-Iranian intermixture with Turki element is the Qashqa'i tribes of the central Zagros.

In northeastern Iran the intermixture of Turki and other races becomes prominent. But this racial stock does not stop on the frontiers of Iran. It continues into Afghanistan as well as Turkistan of the Soviet Union. Furthermore, in these countries they are significantly intermixed with other elements, such as the Mongoloid races which show affinities with the Turki stock. In Afghanistan, however, other racial characteristics are also present, as evidenced by the Iranian and the Proto-Nordic (Indo-Aryan) elements.

Folk Islam

Regardless of the public attitude toward religion, folk Islam is still a powerful force among most of the people of the Northern Tier. Popular Islam is universally prevalent among the peasantry in Turkey as well as in Afghanistan and Iran. Religious attitudes and practices permeate the lives of most of the village and small-town people from birth to death.

Marriage, divorce, inheritance—in short, the overall attitudes toward the universe and the place of man in it—are influenced by Islamic standards, precepts, values, and customs, sometimes mingled with even older pre-Islamic patterns of life. In the urban centers, agnostic attitudes are found, particularly in Turkey, but less so in Iran and hardly at all in Afghanistan, where western-educated individuals continue to practice Islam as they understand it.

Although all the major groups and most of the minor groups of people in the Northern Tier are Muslim, they do not share the same language and sentiment. The three major groups are the Turks, the Persians, and the Afghans. Of the three Northern Tier countries, Turkey has the largest number of Turks, Iran the largest number of Persians, and Afghanistan the Afghans. The problem is how to define these peoples. Who is a Turk? Who is a Persian? And who is an Afghan?

The Turks

. . . the Turks thoroughly immersed themselves historically in Islam. For this reason all that was pre-Islamic Turkish was forgotten. Even the name Turk is "in a sense Islamic." In the pre-Islamic inscription it refers only to one among the related steppe peoples. But in the late fourteenth century the real Turkish element was revived when the Ottomans expanded into eastern Anatolia. Here they encountered large groups of Turkish nomads, with their tribal organization intact. In the fifteenth century the signs of Turkish consciousness appeared, Turkish poetry flourished, and a literary school tried to write in pure Turkish language without excessive use of the Persian and Arabic words which were already a part of the Turkish literary heritage.

This movement was greatly forwarded in the course of extensive reforms of Kemal Atatürk. The Turks, as well as the Persians, had adopted the Arabic script, but the new Turkey decided to do away with it. In 1928 the Latin alphabet was introduced. This was followed by intensive research for the revival of the Turkish language and the eradication of Arabic and Persian words and expressions. Mustafa Kemal himself signaled the attack upon the Arabic script on August 9, 1928, when he demonstrated the new letters on a blackboard to a group of Turkish statesmen.

This historic assertion of Turkishness in both language and sentiment is the hallmark of Turkish identity. The Turks were Islamized fully, wrested new domains for Islam, and defended its banners over centuries. But they were not Arabized. They kept their own language and have attempted to link themselves to the Hittites. . . .

The Persians

Another large group of people in the Northern Tier are the Persians. The Persian identity is rooted in a long history and rich language and literature. The Persians were an ancient group who settled in the province of Fars, then known as Parsa or Persis. In 553 B.C. Cyrus, the subking of Parsa, asserted the Persian independence from the closely related Medes, and launched the military campaigns that gave rise to the first "world empire." The ancient Persian Empire extended from Armenia and the

Caucasus in the northwest to the borders of Sind in the southeast; from the Tigris-Euphrates basin in the southwest to the River Jaxartes (Syr Darya) in Central Asia, and from the eastern limits of Asia Minor in the west to the Hindu Kush in the east. . . . pre-Islamic Iran was also the abode of the great ancient religion of Zoroaster.

However, neither Zoroastrianism nor the military power of the Sassanian Empire proved effective against Islam and the Arabs who invaded Iran in the seventh century. Over the centuries the people of Iran were Islamized, but were not Arabized. During the ninth and tenth centuries a number of "Persian kingdoms," such as the Tahirids, the Safarids, the Samanids, and the Buwayhids, asserted their independence vis-à-vis the Arabs. These political uprisings were accompanied by a Persian literary "renaissance." Outstanding Iranian philosophers and writers such as al-Ghazzali, al-Razi, and Avecina had written in Arabic, but now others, such as the poets Rudaki and Daqiqi, wrote in the Persian language. The consolidation of a new Iranian state was delayed as the Northern Tier was hit by the waves of Turkish and Mongol invasions between the eleventh and fifteenth centuries. The Persian literary assertion continued, however, as evidenced by the rise of such literary giants as Ferdawsi, Umar Khayyam, Sa'di, and Hafiz.

Unlike the Turks, the Persians continue to use a modified Arabic alphabet, but the language and the sentiment are Persian. During the rule of Reza Shah, the pre-Islamic heritage of Iran was much emphasized, and attempts were made to "purify" the language from Arabic loanwords and expressions. But the Iranian excesses, like the Turkish ones, have prompted some of the more thoughtful educators of Iran to warn against indiscriminatory "purges" of "foreign" words from the Persian language.

The Afghans

The name "Afghan" was historically used to describe the Pushtuns, but it is now used to denote any native of the land area of Afghanistan. The Pushtuns constitute an estimated fifty to sixty percent of the present population of Afghanistan. The origins of the Pushtuns are obscure. Pushtu, a literary as well as a spoken language, seems to have come into being during the first Muslim centuries. However, the seventeenth century produced the two greatest and most influential of the Pushtu poets, Rahman Baba and Khushhal Khan Khattak. But the literary and linguistic history of the Afghans is much intertwined with that of the Persians. Pushtu and the Persian account for about four-fifths of the population; and Persian predominates in the capital. . . .

Since the Pushtun element scarcely dominates the scene in Afghanistan and since their language is rivaled by Persian, the nationalist element in Afghanistan is inclined to use the Pushtu as a unifying force in the country. Afghanistan is a relatively new country, its independence dating back to 1747. Before that time it had been either a congeries of small states under nominal Arab rule, part of Mongol or Mogul empires, or dismembered among India, Iran, and the Uzbeks. Pushtu was declared the official language of the country in 1936, despite its definitely limited vocabulary as a medium of expression in the age of science and technology. The new Constitution of Afghanistan makes both Pushtu and Dari (Persian) the *official* languages of the country, but only Pushtu is the *national* language.

THE MINORITIES

The Northern Tier is the abode of many other peoples. Although Afghans, Turks, and Persians constitute the major groups in the area and are generally the dominant elements in their respective countries, they are by no means the only inhabitants of the countries in which they live or of the Northern Tier as a whole. Side by side with these three already discussed are approximately forty to fifty distinctly different groups in the Northern Tier. They are distinguished from the majority of the population of the country in which they live by their religious beliefs, racial characteristics, sectarian orientations, languages and dialects, and in short by any one or combination of these elements.

* * *

To attempt to identify the peoples of the Northern Tier by racial characteristics alone is hazardous. This is the case not only because of the far-reaching intermixtures that have occurred throughout time, but also because the paucity of anthropological studies, particularly in regard to the peoples of Afghanistan, makes it impossible to speak of racial origins of the peoples of the Northern Tier with any degree of finality. One must, therefore, search for other criteria as well in order to describe the composition of the peoples of the Northern Tier. This is all the more important in an area where such ancient peoples as the Hittites, the Phrygians, the Lydians, the Scythians, the Dravidians and the Persians lived; where such peoples as the Greeks, the Romans, the Arabs, the Turks, and the Mongols ruled; and where great civilizations such as the Iranian, and the Turkish flourished. Hence, the cultural as well as the racial elements must be considered in discussing the peoples of the Northern Tier.

4.
The Kurds

The Kurds speak an Indo-European language that is related to Persian. They are located mostly in three countries of the Middle East—Turkey, Iraq, and Iran. Over the centuries, they have preserved a strong spirit of independence and the desire to govern themselves. They consider themselves separate from the other inhabitants of these countries. Historically there have been clashes between the Kurds and the rulers of their host countries. In modern times, the conflict of the Kurds with the military forces of Iraq have been well publicized.*

**INQUIRY: How have a minority people such as the Kurds suc-
ceeded in preserving their customs while living in countries dominated
by other groups?**

There are many tribes living in various regions of Iran. These are fiercely proud freedom-loving people who seem to be madly in love with nature, the vastness of the country in which they live and the formidable mountains where they hunt and make their living.

The Kurds are one of the most important Iranian tribes. They are descendants of the Guti, or Qurti, people who inhabited western and north-western Iran from about 2400 to 2300 B.C. The Kurds are of purest Iranian-Aryan stock, who, during their long history have not been mixed with non-Aryan races and have kept their true characteristics and racial purity.

The Iranian Kurdistan (pronounced Kord-es-tan) there live many Kurdish tribes, including the Golbaghi, Sanjabi, Feizollah-Beigi, Nagsh-bandi, Zand, Javan-Rudi, Kalhor, Tileku, Khor-Khoreh, and Abassi. Other Kurdish tribes live in Turkey and Iraq and some in Soviet Armenia.

The inhabitants of Iranian Kurdistan are fiercely patriotic and have on numerous occasions demonstrated their love and devotion for their country.

The surface of Kurdistan is traversed by lofty mountain ranges, mostly wooded, with summits reaching above 10,000 feet in altitude. The mountains are covered with forests of oak and other hard timber. The valleys are lush and idyllic, their beauty breath-taking. Many of these valleys are under regular cultivation. The Kurds are very good farmers, considering their great love for riding, hunting and fishing. The crops produced by the Kurds include wheat, cotton, barley and tobacco.

The Kurds raise a variety of fine livestock. They breed excellent horses and cattle and keep sheep and goats in large numbers.

Many Kurds live a seminomadic life, migrating seasonally from the highlands to the lowlands with their herds of cattle, sheep and goats. The rest live in villages or tend their farms and orchards. During the winter months many engage in rug weaving and making beautiful blankets.

Although largely isolated by the mountainous terrain of their country, they do some trading in the cities bordering their region.

Kurdish women are much less restricted than women in other Moslem communities. Kurds speak a western Iranian language, which in fact is a dialect of the ancient Pahlavi language.

In the 7th century they were converted to Islam by the Arabs. Although still Moslems, they have adapted the religion to their own way of life and ancient traditions. The Kurd is noted as much for his bravery as for his

---

*"Iranian Tribes: Kurds—An Ancient People of Purest Iranian Stock," *Iran Today*, 1963. Reprinted by permission.

generosity and hospitality. In certain areas there are mystics who live in seclusion and practice a religion of self-denial and constant prayer and devotion. However, their basic religious philosophy is that of ancient Persians: "Decent speech, decent thoughts and decent deeds."

They have also observed throughout centuries ancient Iranian customs and traditions, including the annual observance of the Iranian New Year, or No-Ruz. That day, March 21, marking the advent of spring, is observed by the Kurds in communal feasts and picturesque group dances performed by young boys and girls. Their costumes, too, are reminiscent of ancient Iranian apparel.

On holidays the Kurds go out in the country on community picnics. There people from various villages get together in good fellowship to feast, sing and dance.

As was said before, the Kurd is a good farmer; he produces abundant food, not only for himself and his family, but also for the surrounding urban centers.

Iranian Kurdistan produces annually: 200,000 tons of wheat; 40,000 tons of barley and 1,250 tons of fine tobacco.

An interesting event in a Kurdish village is a wedding. Once a dashing young man chooses his bride, a group of village leaders bearing presents, go to visit the parents of the girl. If the young lady and her parents see no objection to the proposal a date is set for the big event. However, several days before the actual wedding, parties and receptions are held in honor of the young couple in which the whole village—or the two villages, if the bride and groom happen to be from different villages—take part.

The wedding feast continues for three, five or seven consecutive days and nights depending upon the economic or social stature of the principals. All day long and most of the night they eat, drink, sing, dance and make merry. On the last day of the festivity, early in the morning a group of young men lead the happy groom to the house of the bride, where they are treated to a sumptuous feast by the bride's family. After performing traditional rites such as formally thanking the bride's parents for their consent to the marriage, the groom formally takes leave and together with his companions returns to his own homestead.

Meanwhile, a group of men and women, belonging to the groom's family, form a procession to go to the bride's house and invite her to her husband's home. As the procession approaches the house, inside the entire family of the bride start singing and dancing and when the groom's folks arrive they are greeted with loud cheers and clapping. After partaking refreshments, the procession starts on its return trip, this time with the bride, wearing a scarlet veil of fine tule. She is escorted by two women holding her by the arms. The bride, as other members of the procession walk if the distance is not too great. If the groom comes from another village, then the bride rides a horse.

Before the procession leaves, the bashful bride bids his family goodbye. She kisses her mother and her father's right hand, who then says a few words of prayer and blesses his daughter and son-in-law, wishing them happiness, long life, prosperity and many children.

Meanwhile, the bridegroom, accompanied by his companions, comes out to meet the bride. As the two groups approach, the groom takes a big red apple and throws it to the bride who catches it deftly and coyly kisses it and hands the groom a piece of candy. The broom breaks a bottle of rose water at the feet of the bride and unties a long, silk sash which the bride wears around her slender waist.

With this and the piece of candy, the groom hurries back in order to be home when the bride arrives.

As the procession approaches, people rush out of their houses bearing gifts for the bride—mostly fine fabrics for dresses, curtains, table cloths, etc.

As the bride enters her husband's home, the groom, who is standing on the roof, stamps firmly on the roof with his right foot. This indicates that he shall be the master of the family. Then he rushes down to greet his beloved and participate in the rejoicing.

Gifts showered on the young couple include generous sums of money to help them establish their new household.

5.
Historical Setting

The history of civilization is a chronicle filled with unique contributions from that part of the world known as the Middle East. The following article describes man's creative experiences in the Middle East and how they have benefited people elsewhere in the world.*

INQUIRY: Which contributions of the Middle East to western culture does the author think are most important? Do you think that writing, astronomy, mathematics, and metal working were developed independently in other parts of the world?

In the length of its recorded history, in the variety and richness of its experience, and in its contribution to human progress the Near East stands unique among the areas of the world. This is the area comprising what is today Turkey in Asia (Anatolia), Iraq and Iran (Persia), Syria, Lebanon, Israel and Jordan, Arabia and Egypt. It is also called currently the Middle East. . . . The unparalleled historic experience of the Near East is, of course, based upon its temperate climate, strategic situation at the intercontinental meeting place of Europe, Asia and Africa and its interoceanic position between the Mediterranean Sea and the Indian Ocean.

History began with writing, and writing began in the Near East. For five thousand years the area has been a going concern. But centuries before the curtain rose on written records, Near Easterners had developed urban life

---

*Philip K. Hitti, A SHORT HISTORY OF THE NEAR EAST (Princeton, D. Van Nostrand Company, Inc., 1966), pp. 1-3. Courtesy of Van Nostrand Reinhold Company, a division of Litton Educational Publishing, Inc., Litton Industries.

with political, economic and social institutions. Still earlier they had discovered metal, particularly copper, and worked it into tools and weapons that gave them advantage over their stone-using neighbors. Even earlier, some Near Easterner had learned through long and sustained experience, initiated by chance, that certain wild plants growing in his land could be domesticated and that certain wild animals could be tamed. He thereby lifted himself from the status of a food gatherer, roaming from place to place in quest of food, to that of a food producer. This made settled life, with its agricultural pursuit, accumulation of property and increase of population possible. Luckily the area provided the kind of climate, vegetation and animal life without which transition from a nomadic life of grazing and hunting to a settled one could not have been achieved.

What enhances the importance of such history-making prehistoric events is their transmission to regions other than their original. As they passed on to the European mainland they served as a prelude to the classical Greco-Roman civilization, the parent of our European-American. The extent of the material debt Europe owes the Near East was hardly realized until a century ago. The ancestor of the early European wheat and barley, archeologists and botanists assert, should be sought in the wild cereals that still grow in Syria, Lebanon and Palestine. The ancestor of the domesticated European sheep is the one that once roamed the plateau extending from Anatolia to Iran. Early Cretan metallurgy follows Egyptian and Syrian traditions. Primitive eastern European ceramics display similarity to western Asian products. Migration, invasion and trade provided the means of passage. Anatolia, Phoenicia (Lebanon) and Egypt served as bridges. Crete in the Mediterranean and Mycenae in southern Greece were the stepping stones.

Domestication of plants and animals, metallurgy, pottery and other material objects were not the only gifts from the Near East. Embedded in our daily cultural lives are relics of a different kind of legacy. Our seven-day week stems from the Genesis story of creation, itself based on a Semitic system of numeration in which the number seven figures. The early Semites of Mesopotamia (Babylonians) believed in seven planets, to the first of which, the sun, they dedicated the first day of the week. Hence our Sunday. To the second planet, the moon, they dedicated the second day—our Monday. The seventh planet, Saturn, gave us our Saturday. Our division of the hour into 60 minutes, the minute into 60 seconds and the circle into 360 (a multiple of 60) degrees is likewise an inheritance from early Mesopotamia. Our solar calendar was inherited from ancient Egypt through Rome.

Still greater than these cultural strands interwoven into the fabric of our culture are the varied intellectual and spiritual elements from Phoenicia and Palestine. The Phoenicians, ancient Lebanese, perfected the alphabetic system of writing which they bequeathed to the rest of the civilized world. The Mesopotamians (strictly, Sumerians) and Egyptians after them had originated a pictorial system of writing, but it was the Phoenicians who evolved out of pictures the few, simple signs prized everywhere among the most precious and effective tools of intellectual life.

On the spiritual side the Palestinian heritage is unexcelled. Both Judaism and Christianity were born and nurtured therein. Their daughter, Islam, the third great monotheistic religion, was cradled in an adjoining territory.

All three religions are the products of the spiritual experience and genius of the same people, the Semites. The recording and dissemination of their sublime message and ethical doctrines were facilitated by the Phoenician alphabet.

In medieval times Moslem Arabs, heirs of the Semitic tradition and to a less extent of the Hellenic, held aloft the torch of enlightenment throughout a large portion of the civilized world. From their Syrian capital Damascus, they ruled an empire extending from the Atlantic to central Asia. From their subsequent capital Baghdad, they spread their translations and renditions of Greek, Persian and Indian philosophy, science and literature throughout that vast domain. From Moslem Spain, Sicily and Crusading Syria, some of these intellectual treasures passed on to Europe to become a vital force in its modern renaissance. Among other words the following testify to the extent of Arab impact: algebra and zero in mathematics; zenith, nadir, Arab and other star names in astronomy; alcohol, alkali and alchemy in medicine; sugar, coffee, orange, lemon, atlas, satin and damask in agriculture and industry; divan, mattress, sofa and jar in everyday vocabulary.

6.
The Key to the Ancient Mediterranean: Syria, Lebanon, and Israel

The region that lies between the peninsula of Asia Minor on the north and the Nile on the south is the key to understanding the past and present history of the Mediterranean. This is the thesis of the distinguished teacher and author Michael Grant in the following reading.

The countries that occupy this area on the eastern shores of the Mediterranean are Syria, Lebanon, and Israel. From the earliest itmes to the present, these shores have been a meeting ground for numerous ethnic groups and cultures. The results of their visits have influenced the cultural heritage of people on all shores of the Mediterranean and beyond.*

INQUIRY: Do you believe that cultures become mingled in modern times in the way that they were mingled in ancient Syria, Lebanon, and Israel?

The key to the ancient history of the Mediterranean, and to a great deal of its modern history as well, is the easternmost of all its shores—

---

*"The Key to the Ancient Mediterranean: Syria, Lebanon, and Israel" by Michael Grant, *Mankind*, April 1969. Reprinted by permission of Michael Grant Publications, Ltd. and *Mankind*.

the region extending between the peninsula of Asia Minor on the north and the valley and delta of the Nile on the south.

Those two countries which it spans and joins are well defined and labeled. The one, with its hinterland, is Asiatic Turkey (Anatolia) and the other is Egypt. But the vital area in between has no single name or identity. From top to bottom on the map, it nowadays comprises the Hatay (an appendage of Turkey), most of Syria, Lebanon, and Israel in its current enlarged form. The whole region was known comprehensively to the ancients as Syria and was described more recently by Arab Nationalists as Greater Syria—and sometimes it is vaguely known as the Levant, though that designation normally covers the shores of Anatolia as well.

Yet, for all this ambiguity, the region preeminently deserves study in its own right, as a single unit. And this it has very rarely received—partly because large portions of the territory have usually been inaccessible to travelers, and partly also because students of the Mediterranean, other than Biblical specialists, have generally been motivated by a conscious or unconscious pre-Western prejudice which has caused them to underestimate the significance of the most easterly coasts of that sea.

To the ancients the land seemed destined for prosperity by nature. In spite of the southern latitude and the dangers of unpredictable drought, there were rainfalls in late autumn and early spring, and the plains beside and between the mountains were fertile. "Figs there were in it, and grapes," said an Egyptian visitor. "It had more wine than water. Its trees bore every fruit. Barley was there and wheat. There was no limit to the kinds of cattle. Plentiful was its honey, abundant its olives."

And yet Syria and Lebanon and Israel, so greatly blessed by nature, were also visited with a special curse. On the map, this area looks clearly definable by Turkey, Egypt, the Mediterranean, and—to the east—the desert. But the long Mediterranean coastline is vulnerable, and the eastern approaches to the region show that its apparent definition and unity is an illusion. It did not need three modern Israeli-Arab wars to point out the territory is, in fact, grievously lacking in the natural unity which enabled other Mediterranean countries such as Italy, Greece, Egypt, or Spain to grow at different times into defensible national states.

The whole large area of Syria-Lebanon-Israel contains a series of uplifted limestone ridges which, instead of forming its boundaries, run straight through it parallel to the coast. At the northern extremity there are Mounts Amanus and Casius, followed by Bargylus (Jebel Ansariya), and next comes the Lebanon range which is the most imposing of the coastal massifs. South of Lebanon are the Galilee hills, and after them Mount Carmel, the northern-most point of the Samaritan plateau, succeeded by the Judaean plateau which stretches down as far as Sinai.

The lowlands beside and between these folds are long funnels open to every sort of influence and invasion from the north and south by external peoples covetous of all this wealth and fertility. The two principal tubular areas inviting such encroachments are the coastal regions and then—beyond the first ranges and parallel to them, from 20 to 60 miles distant from the sea—a continuous depression running through the valleys of the Orontes, Litani (Leontes), and Jordan and on through the Dead Sea, deepest of all subsidences in the earth's crust, to the Gulf of Eilat or Akaba.

THE ENVIRONMENT

17

But it is not only through the extremities of these funnels that the coast-land is vulnerable, for the mountains are also broken by passes that have eternally served as passages for acquisitive armies. And behind the openings, through further uplands and deserts, stretch back the classic routes into the sources of the aggressions—and civilizations—which it was the destiny of these lands to receive and absorb.

Accordingly this area never became a single national state but remained a conglomeration of small units. This was also true of Greece, and yet it achieved greatness. But Greece, except for occasional dramatic events, was left alone for centuries to work out its destiny. The small states of Syria, Lebanon, and Israel, on the other hand, were almost never free of invasions by the giants of Asia and Egypt—and so the territory, for all its resources, remained in turmoil, an amorphous political and cultural quicksand.

"To me," said Paul Morand, "the Mediterranean is a pit surrounded by tiers of seats over which the nations are leaning, all crowded together. The same piece has been played for thousands of years." In Syria and Lebanon and Israel the scenery of this theatre was built of elements that were peculiarly inflammable—also peculiarly creative, since out of the conflagrations came a mixture which exercised a gigantic influence upon developments throughout the Mediterranean world.

The movement of external and alien peoples into this region began at an exceedingly early date. Men and women living in caves on Mount Carmel in the tenth millennium B.C., who made use of reaping knives or sickles, may well have come from the more northerly foothill (Tauros-Zagros) area where decisive developments were made possible by the presence of wheat, barley, sheep, and goats—all vital aids to civilization—in their wild and natural forms which gradually gave way to domesticated varieties.

Then, before 6000 B.C., a comparatively advanced culture developed in the extreme northwestern corner of Syria. Here, on the lower Orontes, the various advances in agriculture and stock-breeding registered during the previous millennia were concentrated in the nearly 400 square miles of the Amik plain, which was close to the great westward curve of the Euphrates and therefore accessible to movements of population and culture from the east.

However, it was not by the land route from the east but by the sea route from the west and south that the most decisive early influences came to bear upon the region. This was because of Egypt, which gradually achieved a national unity wholly beyond the capacity of the Syria-Lebanon-Israel area. This unity was made possible, indeed necessary, by the Nile—which simply had to be controlled and irrigated in a coordinated fashion if the people on its shores were to survive. The Sumerians in southern Mesopotamia had been presented with a similar problem by the erratic Tigris and Euphrates, and had partially solved it by an efficient city-state organization. Egypt went much further, in two stages.

First, two kingdoms were established—Lower Egypt, which was the Nile delta, and Upper Egypt, which lay south of it and stretched down towards the Sudan. Then, by the initiative of the latter they were united (around 3200 B.C.), becoming immeasurably the strongest state which the region, and probably the world, had seen thus far. Yet although they learned how to navigate the Nile, it remained, apparently, for the people of the Syrian coast to teach them how to build effective seagoing ships. Egypt was exceedingly interested in this coast because its own homeland was very short of timber, the local woods not being very serviceable for building ships. The Egyptians were therefore eager to obtain the fir, cedar, pine, cypress, and juniper with which northern Syria and Lebanon were once rich—though nowadays erosion and human devastation have long since stripped their slopes.

The town which provided the necessary harbor and expertise was Byblos, on the coast of what was later called Phoenicia beneath the Lebanon range. Byblos stood at the northernmost point of Egypt's normal sphere of influence and virtually possessed a monopoly of trade with that country. Indeed, during the third millennium B.C. this city of rectangular houses and cobbled streets even had an Egyptian temple, measuring over 80 and later over 90 feet long. The construction of a shrine of this considerable size suggests the presence of a substantial commercial colony from Eygpt. Byblos acted as a distribution center for Egyptian exports of papyrus, for which indeed "byblos" (Bible) became the standard name. The city also exported copper and other metals brought in by caravan from the north.

The people of the Lebanese and Syrian coastal lands were experts at every kind of woodwork, and it was probably they who both constructed and to a large extent manned the first Egyptian seagoing ships, thus becoming the first professional Mediterranean shipbuilders and sailors. "The seaman," said Joseph Conrad, "looks upon the Mediterranean as a man may look at a vast nursery in an old, old mansion, where innumerable generations of his own people have learned to walk. It has led mankind gently from headland to headland, from bay to bay, from island to island, out into the promise of worldwide oceans." And the earliest initiatives seem to have been taken by these sailors from Byblos who created and navigated the seagoing vessels seen on Egyptian monuments.

Byblos, and the coast extending to the south of it, was colonized by peoples speaking a north Semitic dialect. They had already arrived by 2500 B.C.—and perhaps a good deal earlier since Lebanese and Syrian mountains and rivers mostly possessed names of early Semitic origin. Peoples speaking this sort of language, already profoundly mixed in race, had long been prominent in Mesopotamia; but a tradition, which may be right, held that these arrivals on the Levantine shores had come overland not from the east but from more primitive territories in western Arabia.

Copper statuettes of the period indicate that they were a herdsman type, familiar over large areas of the Near East—short stocky people with pronounced chins, trim beards and swept-back plaited hair, clothed in short kilts and broad belts fastened with tasseled cords. They called their new homeland Canaan, a name which later came to be used for territories extending over a much wider area.

But they were not to remain undisturbed, since Syria was deeply vulnerable to the great wanderings of many peoples who devastated Mesopotamia and the rest of the Middle East towards the end of the third millennium B.C. In *circa* 2100 the Egyptian temple at Byblos was burned down, and the city's life and culture changed abruptly. Perhaps this event was part of the convulsions which at about this time inundated Syria with a further wave of Semitic invaders.

These newcomers, the Amorites, were induced by the advanced prosperity of the land they now occupied to adopt some of its culture and to form highly developed though small and inevitably precarious city-states. These included Aleppo between the Orontes mouth and the Euphrates, Carchemish on the present Turco-Syrian frontier, Qatna (Mishrife) behind the Lebanon range, and the commercial center of Mari (Tell Hariri) on the Euphrates near the border of Syria and Iraq.

The 20,000 surviving documents of Mari's archives, written in old Babylonian cuneiform (wedge-shaped) characters, display in startling detail how complex the international position in this part of the world had already become. Dating from the 18th century B.C. onwards, they mention more than 30 separate states linked or divided, in modern style, by the diplomatic interactions of intrigue, commercial and cultural exchanges, and warfare. The civilization of this area was a blend of many influences, and certain architectural and artistic features were imitated by the far-off Cretans whose own distinctive civilization was now reaching its zenith.

One Amorite was Shamsi-Adad I (circa 1814-1782) who ruled over the Assyrians (distant relatives of his own people), and created a powerful state in the undulating, well-watered pasture lands of the upper Tigris. The Assyrians were masters of a formidable blend of first-class archery, administrative ability, and cold-blooded diplomacy; and they drew much of their power from outposts in Asia Minor which provided them with copper. Mixed with tin, this made the bronze that gave them better weapons and agricultural tools than had been known before.

When, therefore, Shamsi-Adad set up his own son at Mari and established close relationships with Qatna, Aleppo, and Carchemish, and above with the other great power, Egypt, was inevitable. For the monument was in an area which was normally within the sphere of the Egyptians, who had been using Byblos as a center of expansion. Their exports reached Qatna and they exercised some sort of control, perhaps economic more than political, over most of the Lebanon coast and Bekaa plain.

Assyria, as it turned out, was unable to compete with Egypt at this junction since it was eclipsed by Babylonia—which was too remote to be active so far west. But, instead, a perilous new threat now came upon Egypt and its Syrian dependencies from the mountainous territories north of Mesopotamia. From these regions a people of uncertain linguistic affinities, the Hurrians, extended their influence and power over huge areas, which they kept under control by the mounted warriors and chariots that were their specialty. Although these people possessed little art of their own (except a fine type of pottery), they absorbed the Mesopotamian and other cultures which they brought into the areas they infiltrated.

By the 16th century the Hurrians had established the powerful kingdom of Mitanni in northwestern Mesopotamia, and this directly or indirectly controlled most of Syria. Perhaps there was even an outpost as far south as Gaza, where excavations have disclosed burials of men with their horses which suggest the influence of Mitanni. But the kingdom's principal capital on the Syrian shore was at the other extremity of the coastline—at Alalakh (Tell Atchana) near the mouth of the Orontes. In this terminal region of trade routes to the Mediterranean from the east, Alalakh (a little inland from the later Antioch) had already been the site of 15 cities, and its temple had been rebuilt and dedicated to different gods as many times. The names of the population were mostly Semitic, but in mid-second millennium their ruling class was Mitannian.

Between the spheres of influence of Egypt and Mitanni, there was still an uneasy border zone of small Syrian city-states which sought to play off the one great power against the other. In the 16th century B.C., Egypt engulfed many of the coastal neighbors of Byblos, cities in the area later to be known as Phoenicia which were now heard of for the first time. But the most formidable reckoning for the minor Levantine states came a century later from the armies of Thothmes III.

The prince of Kadesh—a fortress which commanded the passage between Lebanon and Anti-Lebanon at the point where this route widens into the broad plains of north Syria—had instigated a confederacy to resist Thothmes. Kadesh was joined by a southerly city, Megiddo. Commanding the Jezreel (Esdraelon) gap which separates the hills of Galilee to the north from those of Judaea to the south, Megiddo was of such strategic importance that its name has earned a grim reputation in the form of Armageddon. But the Egyptians, operating by land and sea from their fortified base at Gaza, crushed the confederate armies beneath the walls of Megiddo itself. As the king of Egypt complained, they failed to take the city although "its capture is equal to the capture of a thousand cities," because they were so eager to pick up the plunder of the battlefield.

However, Megiddo fell three weeks later, and the insatiably aggressive Thothmes III seems ultimately to have conquered almost the whole of western Syria, placing its towns under vassal princelings and establishing, at the price of freedom, a unity of rule and communications which the area had never seen before and was not to see again for nearly a thousand years.

Much weakened by this Egyptian expansion in their southern flank, Mitanni succumbed during the 14th century to a power which had arisen to their northwest in Asia Minor; the kingdom of the Hittites. Originating somewhere between the Carpathians and the Caucasus, these people had arrived in Asia Minor shortly before 2000 B.C., their migration forming part of that huge wave of assaults from the north which extended from India to western Europe and affected the destinies of the entire Near and Middle East. The Hittites cremated their dead, used iron—eventually smelting it into a metal stronger than bronze—and employed formidable horse chariots.

For three centuries Syria became a battleground between Hittites and Mitannians, until under Suppiluliumas I (*circa* 1380-40) the Hitties were wholly victorious. The prince of Byblos appealed desperately to Pharaoh Akhenaten of Egypt; but he was a visionary who did not concern himself with foreign affairs, and the numerous appeals were ignored.

One of the most important towns which was obliged to note the change of political wind was Ugarit (Ras Shamra, "fennel") on the north Syrian coast not far from the modern Latakia. Ugarit profited from its central position upon the trade routes to become one of the great ports of the Mediterranean. During its climax, between 1400 and 1200 B.C., it dispatched Mesopotamian, Hurrian, Hittite, Egyptian, Syrian, and Aegean products far and wide.

The city had very close links with Crete and other islands, and also with the Greek mainland where Mycenae had become a dominant power. Cretans and Mycenaeans had their own trading settlements at Ugarit, with separate living quarters and burial palaces in town and harbor. There were also groups of commercial travelers from other coastal cities, as well as from Cyprus and Egypt; a passport has been found authorizing a man and his son to use the routes to Egypt and Hittite territories. The manufactures and cultures of all these countries were on the move, and the center most largely responsible for their diffusion was Ugarit.

The royal palace, consisting of 70 rooms, five courtyards, a park and ornamental lake, also possessed a furnace for baking the clay tablets which scribes used to write on. These writings include not only the local government's extensive and varied records but at least four cycles of epic history, describing—in a western Semitic dialect akin to Hebrew—the exploits and rivalries of the gods with a diversity of subject matter which reflects the blend of the various racial and cultural elements at Ugarit.

The epics were written in a variation of the old wedge-shaped curniform script of Mesopotamia, which was in the process of being adapted to novel alphabetic purposes. Formerly each of these signs had represented a syllable, but this system was inconvenient since it needed far too many signs. From early in the second millennium, therefore, there had been Syrian experiments making them denote not only a whole syllable, as hitherto, but the first sounds of a syllable.

However, the old wedge-shaped imprints were only suitable for clay and stone, which were clumsy media, and by 1500 various places in Syria and Israel had instead taken the Egyptian pictorial, linear script and adapted it, radically, to the new sort of phonetic notation; and then the direction was moved from vertical to horizontal. And so, finally, a Byblos inscription of 1000 shows a real (though still vowel-less) alphabet. Writing had now become a very great deal easier to learn, and was accessible to enormously increased numbers of people.

However, in relation to the great powers of the day—the Hittites and Egyptians—these Canaanite people were middlemen in the most literal and comfortable sense, sandwiched between the great powers. They finally clashed in around 1286 when Mutawallis the Hittite fought Rameses II of Egypt at Kadesh. Egyptian propaganda, already in those days very active, claimed a victory, but probably the Hittites really won. After further fighting, however, the two powers (unprecedentedly) made peace, fixing relative spheres of influence in Syria—which had, therefore, to stop its perilous tightrope trick of maintaining a precarious balance between the two empires.

But now furious onslaughts descended upon both sides from many backward peoples who were on the move over a vast area. Desperate emergencies which descended upon the Egyptians shortly before and after 1200 were in the end successfully fought off, though at a terrible cost, and Egypt was not, after all, engulfed. But the Hittite empire crumbled and collapsed—and in Syria, too, there was chaos. Excavations show that Aleppo, Carchemish, Alalakh, and Ugarit all fell to the invading hordes, and so did a whole series of recently emerged towns and fortresses of Judaea.

Who were the people who spread these massive devastations far and wide? There was a gigantic series of migratory waves extending all the way from the Danube valley to the plains of China. Their causes cannot be determined nor can it be confirmed whether, as has been suggested, drastic changes played a part. Egyptian sources call the invaders Peoples of the Sea, and relate them to "the northern countries which are in their isles" or shorelands. The same records also refer to specific peoples or tribes, but their names, unfortunately, can be interpreted in a variety of ways. Probably they included dispossessed Anatolians and Aegeans; and swords, brooches, cremation rites, and probably also ships of European type now appear. The rocky southern coasts of Asia Minor, which had always served as nurseries and havens for pirates, are very likely to have been used as bases, and the invaders may well have been coastal peoples who had learned their techniques of warfare while serving the great powers as sailors and mercenary soldiers.

One of these Sea Peoples established itself at the lower extremity of the seaboard in present-day Israel. This was the tribe of the Philistines, who had finally come to occupy important positions in the Egyptian army and then, during the 12th century, subdued the Canaanite population throughout the coastal region between Mount Carmel and Gaza. The northern half of this strip was the Plain of Sharon, but it was the southern part, subsequently called Philistia, which contained the chief towns of their confederacy. The principal center seems to have been Ashdod, situated in a commanding position three miles from the sea, not above a harbor since there were only straight beaches in that area, but adjoining the road which led from Egypt and the Philistine border town, Gaza, up to the Sharon plain and Syria beyond.

The Philistines (whose name means "migrants" but now has an abusive significance because 19th-century German students called the non-University youth by this name) were a formidable people who during the mid-11th century B.C. temporarily reduced all their neighbors (including the Hebrews) to impotence. It was the Philistines, furthermore, who bequeathed to the Holy Land its historic name of Palestine.

One of the Hebrew prophets indicated that the Philistines had come originally from Caphtor—a term which, though it may cover various east Mediterranean areas, seems to refer particularly to Crete. The Philistines certainly possessed strong links with the Cretans and even stronger ones with the Mycenaeans. The distinctive wine jars of Philistia display a series of imitations of Mycenaean styles interpreted in local clays and techniques. The armor of the Philistines' champion Goliath was Aegean in character. Although nothing of their speech and script has survived except a few proper names, they seem to have spoken a language that was not Semitic like that of their Hebrew neighbors but Indo-European, or at least connected with that family of tongues. However, the Canaanites who became their subjects evidently exercised a reciprocal influence, since Philistine towns generally retained Canaanite names.

Their strength lay partly in their high-prowed ships, which are depicted by Egyptian artists, and partly also in horses and chariots—but principally in their use of iron which, under efficient monopolistic control, became a common, everyday metal. The Egyptians were impressed by the huge round shields and stout swords of the Philistines, and iron also began to be used for the tips of plows, which thus became better able to turn over the heavier soils where corn, vines, and olives were cultivated. A further new technical aid of a different sort consisted of the camel, which was domesticated in about the 12th century and inaugurated the great caravans from Philistia to Mesopotamia.

But behind this coastal area occupied by the Philistines lay the stretch of Judaean uplands into which groups of Hebrews, taking advantage of the widespread convulsions, gradually came from Egypt (where they had sojourned since the time of Joseph), apparently joining up with other tribes which they found in the region. According to recent research this Exodus is likely to have taken place in the 13th century B.C. (though it may have occurred somewhat earlier).

The Israel of Saul, David, and Solomon began two centuries later and this is the only part of the entire history of the Syria-Lebanon-Israel area which may be described as well known and does not need repeating here. But two facts are peculiarly significant to the present account. One of them is that the Jewish religion, which now took shape, was outstanding among all the heritages diffused from this area of many diffusions, outlasting *ad infinitum* the political background against which it grew. Secondly, the kingdom which reached its climax under Solomon (*circa* 974-937 B.C.) was more powerful than any which was ever formed in the Syria-Lebanon-Israel region throughout ancient times; and it has only been approached again, or equalled, by the Israel of A.D. 1967-8.

Jerusalem, enjoying a judicious blend of accessibility and isolation, dated back to around 2600 B.C., having been founded—as recent excavations show—on a site to the southeast of the Old City in order to guard an essential spring in the valley. The Canaanite tribe of the Jebusites, from whom David took over the city, had performed a major town-planning operation, and Solomon employed the resources of his coastal ally, Tyre, to endow it with a splendid temple. The excavation of 450 well-built horse-boxes at Megiddo, though of slightly later date, shows the Philistine-style chariotry on which he relied.

The further large-scale development of Philistine metal-working, too, is shown by finds at Ezion-geber near the northern end of the Gulf of Eilat, which have disclosed Solomon's elaborate, unique plants for the smelting and refining of copper and iron. In order to generate the maximum heat, these metal-works were situated at a place where the wind is strongest—and not too far away from woods which could supply the refinery with fuel. Both metals were amply exploited. At Cartan in the Jordan valley many bronze objects of the tenth century have been discovered, and the increased use of iron made for greater efficiency in agriculture. So, also, did a new and rapidly extended practice of lining cisterns with waterproof lime-plaster for the conservation and storage of rainwater.

Yet the political strength of the Hebrews rapidly declined because after Solomon it proved impossible to maintain national unity, and the country split into two parts. The ten northern tribes established a new dynasty to form the kingdom of Israel, which after two changes of capital established its royal residence at Samaria, a central observation point near the plains of Sharon and Jezreel. The single tribe of Judah, later enlarged by border rectifications, retained its capital at Jerusalem, under the house of David.

Both states flourished in the eighth century B.C.—Israel with a ruling class of aristocrats and wealthy merchants and Judah with a more homogeneous population. Neither kingdom was large or strong enough to exert independent political influence, or was even able for very long to survive. In 721 Samaria was conquered by the Assyrian king Sargon II. The more compact state of Judah held out until 597, but then Jerusalem succumbed to the Babylonian army of Nebuchadnezzar. A subsequent revolt was followed by two years' siege, at the end of which the city was captured and razed to the ground in 586.

Massive deportations, after each kingdom fell, led to the widespread dispersion which in due course spread the influence of the Jews, and the religion they so remarkably retained, throughout the Mediterranean area. Yet it was not long after the fall of Jerusalem that a partial return to their homeland began. Captivity ended when Persia, which had succeeded to Babylon's empire (539), allowed 42,000 Jews to go back to a small area around Jerusalem, and a new temple was built (516). Subsequent Mediterranean empires allowed or encouraged the existence of small local principalities of Hebrew faith, but it was not until the most modern times that a state comparable in strength with that of David and Solomon has been reestablished.

The north of Syria had remained outside their influence, and in other hands, and in the 13th century B.C., when everything was in a state of collapse, the downfall of the Hittites had caused a vacuum throughout Asia Minor. But throughout the peninsula's Mesopotamian and Syrian borderlands, Hittite influence though adulterated was not destroyed, and a network of small kingdoms formed a "strange Hittite afterglow" which lasted for nearly 500 years. These little states are often called "Neo-Hittite," but the Hittite-descended rulers only formed a veneer over populations containing complex racial mixtures in which the Canaanite strain predominated. The survival of the communities was due to the strength of their hilltop towns, which were often round or oval in shape and possessed massive walls, sometimes in two concentric circles.

Most of these states were based on centers in the interior of Syria, including Zincirli (Mt. Amanus), towns in the Amik plain (lower Orontes), and Hamath. Every minor principality of this kind was in constant danger from the Assyrians, but the spectacular invasions by the latter were punctuated by respites when they temporarily fell into political decline.

One of these setbacks, in the 12th century B.C., had been caused by yet another fresh wave of Semitic-speaking immigrants, the Aramaeans. The invasions and infiltrations of these originally uncouth nomads continued from the 14th century onwards for 200 years, a period when the whole of the eastern Mediterranean was suffering from upheavals.

Overwhelming Assyria and Babylonia, the Aramaeans broke shortly after 1200 into the central latitudes of Syria, where their tribes eventually consolidated into a series of small states which became neighbors and enemies of the Neo-Hittite kingdoms. At first the frontier between these two distinct and hostile groups passed south of Hamath through Lebanon, but then the Aramaeans struck north and conquered Hamath and Zincirli, so that in all Syria only the lower Orontes valley and its hinterland were left under Neo-Hittite control.

The Aramaeans were landsmen, skilled in caravan traffic and controling the trade routes from east to west and south to north which crossed in their territories. Yet these small states had no easier passage than their predecessors in a world of larger powers.

This was even true of the strongest of them, Damascus, situated beyond Anti-Lebanon—between Israel and Hamath—in a 30-mile-wide plain famous for its grainfields, orchards, gardens, and olive groves. The princes of Damascus had to look vigilantly in both directions. First they were obliged to contend with their momentarily powerful, and indeed dominant, Hebrew neighbors during the successive reigns of Saul, David and Solomon. Then Damascus became an ally of Israel and tried to resist the Assyrians, but the coalition it led against them in around 853 B.C. was defeated at Qarqar northwest of Hamath.

The next disastrous threat to the Aramaeans occurred during the following century, when many of their states became the vassals of a new power formed by the rulers of Urartu. These were a people of horsemen and herdsmen, perhaps speaking a language derived from the area of the Caucasus. They derived most of their art from Assyria but displayed peculiar expertise in metal work, engineering, and irrigation. The Urartian capital was far to the east on Lake Van, but they established protectorates over the Neo-Hittite territories along the lower Orontes valley and seacoast, and pushing south through Syria reduced a number of Aramaean principalities also.

At the end of the eighth century, however, the power of Urartu was broken by the Assyrians. These now proceeded to annex the Neo-Hittite kingdoms which the Urartians had controlled—before long we hear of a ruler in the Hatay being executed—while the Aramaean states resumed their efforts to maintain an independent existence. Sometimes they prospered, but it was not very long before Damascus and its allies succumbed finally to Tiglath-Pileser III of Assyria (*circa* 733), and soon afterwards a similar confederacy, under the leadership of Hamath, was again overwhelmed (*circa* 721).

Following the immemorial custom of the region the Aramaeans were not so much cultural innovators themselves as borrowers of elements from other people's cultures and religions. These borrowings included a simple practical script modified from Phoenician models. And yet, by a strange chance, it was these Aramaeans who were destined to impose their language upon the entire Near-Eastern world. By the time of Jesus, who himself spoke Aramaic, its dialect reigned unchallenged as the common speech of all Near-Eastern peoples.

On the coast to the west of Damascus, the great ports of Phoenicia were concentrated within easy reach of one another. Their Semitic-speaking inhabitants were Canaanites who had escaped absorption by the more recently arrived Aramaeans owing to the protection afforded by the limestone Lebanon massif, which rises steeply in the immediate hinterland. Certain passes, it is true, were inviting to enemies, notably at either extremity of the range the Litani (Leantes) and the Nahrel-Kelb (Eleutheros), of which the Hanles still bear the inscriptions of many invaders. Yet the passes brought not only occasional conquerors but also more frequent traders along the reopened camel-caravan routes.

And these gaps in the mountains, with their perennial streams, also brought down a more reliable supply of rainwater than the temporary rivers in between. With the help of this water, each community had its own strip of cultivable land, small but fertile enough to grow vines and olives and breed sheep, goats, and cattle. Nevertheless, the towns did not face landwards; from their two-way facing harbors on bold headlands and adjoining islets, they looked out to sea.

In around 1100 Tiglath-Pileser I of Assyria extorted tribute not only from Byblos but also from two other cities, Sidon and Arvad (Arados). Sidon is 40 miles south of Byblos, Arvad 50 miles away to the north. This admission of suzerainty meant that, temporarily, the timber and other resources of the cities were in Assyrian hands. But during the period of great stress which followed, neither Assyria nor Egypt could maintain control, and Phoenicia had its chance.

To begin with, Byblos still exercised some sort of dominance over Sidon and Tyre, but before long both these cities in turn profited from the long maritime experience of the Byblians to take the lead themselves. The rise of Sidon ("Fishery") came suddenly in around 990-80 B.C. when the victories of the Israelites under David had neutralized the Aramaean peril in the hinterland. Tyre (Sur, "the Rock"), 20 miles from Sidon and separated from it by a gully, was called "its daughter." Probably this means that its population included Sidonian immigrants, in addition to sea-raider settlers and coastal Cannanites. As elsewhere in Phoenicia, tombs show mixtures of different kinds of burial rites.

Under David and Solomon, whose temple was built by Tyrians, these people took the lead, and for a time at least their king, Hiram I (*circa* 970-36), ruled Sidon as well. Air and submarine archaeology has revealed the partially submerged quays of Tyre, and the turrets and battlements of the town appear on an Assyrian relief. In the ninth and eighth centuries trade continued to mount and multiply in the crowded many-storied houses of Tyre, "the crowning city," said Isaiah, "whose merchants are princes, whose traffickers are the honorable of the earth."

As in the most antique past, many of these cargoes consisted of the timber of Lebanon, to which the Old Testament refers in detail. But an even more important export consisted of clothing and textiles, colored with the dyes which Phoenicians extracted from the spiny-shelled *murex* (rock-whelk) caught in baskets off their coast.

Each *murex* secretes two precious drops of a yellowish liquid from which tones ranging from rose to dark violet could be extracted in the boiling vat. In the absence of mineral dyes, this was the only fast and firm dye the ancients possessed, not needing to be treated with the alum or fixatives which had to be added to vegetable colorings. The hills of shells on the outskirts of Tyre and Sidon (the refuse of factories located on the lee sides of the town owing to their unpleasant smell) recall the vast scale of the exploration.

The inhabitants of this coast may well have owed their national name of dark or purple men (Phoinikes) to the lucrative monopoly which transformed their robes into these colors. They were also excellent weavers and embroiderers, and superb metallurgists, working and then exporting silver brought from Cilicia, and copper imported from Cyprus and refined with fuel from their own Lebanese hills. The Phoenicians were also famous for gold-working techniques of *repousse* and granulation which they had learned from Mycenae and Egypt. And from the Egyptians again they had mastered the art of converting their fine, flinty river sand into popular and exportable glass.

Like earlier peoples in this cultural melting pot, the Phoenicians gained their aesthetic ideas from a great number of sources. For example, their ivory work resembles the ivories produced in other parts of Syria (as well as by Syrians working in Israel and Assyria) in its facile synthesis of Egyptian, Canaanite, Aramaean, and Cypriot models into neat and delicate masterpieces—which in turn gave many ideas to the Greeks.

An even stronger influence was exercised by the Phoenician and Syrian alphabet which before about 800—serving a literature of which we have little knowledge—developed from Canaanite models into a mature form which only needed the addition of vowels (by the Greeks) to turn into the alphabet used by the ancient Indo-European speaking peoples from whom we ourselves derive our writing.

The maritime enterprise of the Phoenicians exceeded even that of the far-ranging Mycenaeans. They are said to have been the first people to navigate by observing the stars, to travel beyond sight of land, to sail at night, and to undertake voyages in wintertime. Representations have survived showing their trading ships with curved prows and sterns and two banks of oars below a raised deck.

Since, unlike the Egyptians, they had no great river to serve as a navigation school, for them it was the open Mediterranean, sink or swim; no shelter was available nearer than Cyprus, which developed through their colonization a strange, fantastic culture, part Phoenician and part Mycenaean. The Phoenicians extended the great Mycenaean heritage of exploration, trading, and colonization throughout the Mediterranean. Most notable of all was their establishment of Carthage (*circa* 814) which diffused the ideas and institutions of Tyre and Sidon in many parts of the west, and only finally succumbed to Rome nearly 700 years later.

But the recovery of Assyria in the ninth century B.C., which brought heavy pressure upon the Neo-Hittite and Aramaean states, bore heavily upon the Phoenicians as well. Tyre and Sidon were among the cities which bowed before the storm and paid successive Assyrian monarchs their tribute of gold, silver, fine many-colored cloths, and ivory.

They also had to accept Assyrian governors (around 742), and although still allowed to fell timber in the Lebanon, they were taxed when it was brought down to the warehouses. This provoked riots, but Sargon II "gave peace" to Tyre; Sennacherib like others used its sailors; and Esarhaddon (681-69) laid waste rebellious Sidon, and allowed artists to represent him holding the prince of Tyre (as well as the king of Egypt) upon a leash.

Assyria's position, however, began to weaken when its neighbors the Medes, in what is now northwestern Persia, asserted their independence in about 620. Soon afterwards, they jointly attacked and destroyed the Assyrian capital Nineveh. Their allies in this enterprise were the Babylonians, who took over the Assyrian heritage and drove out an Egyptian army which had again penetrated from end to end of the Levant.

This victory, at Carchemish, was won by the king's son Nebuchadnezzar, who during his own subsequent reign captured not only Jerusalem but then

Tyre, which fell after a seige of 13 years (*circa* 571). Sidon, which apparently gave in without a struggle, was restored to its ancient position as the chief town in Phoenicia.

A quarter of a century later, the overthrow of Babylon by the Persians brought to an end the vast phase of Near Eastern history which had been dominated by Mesopotamia (Sumeria, Assyria, Babylonia). Yet, Sidon and Tyre still displayed greater powers of survival than their masters, for although they too passed into the Persian empire for more than two centuries, they continued to provide the conquerors with their seamen and their fleets.

The period in ancient history when there were independent states in Syria and Israel had gone forever. But their contribution to the history of the Mediterranean, through the Mediterranean to our own development, had been gigantic. The same circumstances which had brought countless invasions, immigrations, and infiltrations down upon these lands had filled them with a vast variety of cultures. And the next thing that happened was that these diverse cultural influences spread extensively toward the west.

This was partly due to the seafaring of the Phoenicians and their colony of Carthage. But it was also due to the fact that the Greeks, at the most formative stage of their cultural and artistic development (eighth-seventh centuries B.C.), had just reestablished contact with Syria, particularly through their commercial settlement at Al Mina (Posidium); and the Greeks drew an immense amount of inspiration from what they learned in that area. Admittedly they transformed what they learned in an inspired fashion all their own.

All the same, it was this territory of Syria-Lebanon-Israel which had provided the basis for Greek cultural development. Greek "orientalizing" art (and its Etruscan offshoot in Italy) is full of modified Neo-Hittite and Syrian and Phoenician themes, and Assyrian and Urartian and Babylonian motifs that had come through Syria.

It was also from Syria and Phoenicia that the Greeks borrowed many of their myths and learned their alphabet; and it was through these countries again that the Hellenistic monarchies learned the systems and organizations of the great Mesopotamian monarchies of the past, and handed on this knowledge to Rome. And it was along the roads and sea routes of Rome that the outstanding religious creations of this same area, Jewish monotheism and Christianity, spread over the western world. Our debt to the nameless, explosive rectangle of territory which includes Israel, Lebanon, and Syria is incalculable.

7.
Evidence of Early Contacts

Meeting peoples from different cultures and backgrounds has always been profitable. Different groups mix their ideas, goods, and language with each other. Sometimes from the giving and taking there emerges something new that is mutually valuable. It is apparent that such was the case in the Middle East where the inhabitants met with those who lived to the east of them. There were probably more exchanges between people in ancient times than we can document. The following two readings indicate that there were connecting links between people in the Middle East and those farther to the east in Asia.*

INQUIRY: How do you think an invention, such as glassmaking, could have spread from the Middle East to China in ancient times? What kinds of transportation might have been used?

A FORGOTTEN CIVILIZATION

Bahrain Island, halfway down the Persian Gulf from the delta of the Tigris and Euphrates rivers, has been known to archeologists and grave robbers as an island of the dead. The yellow sand of the island is covered with uncounted large grave mounds—an estimated 100,000 of them. . . .

The wonder of the grave mounds became a mystery when several archeological expeditions came to the island after the turn of the century and found no trace of towns or cities. Inevitably the expeditions tended to concentrate on the excavation of the larger mounds. These proved to have been already visited by robbers in remote antiquity. But the gold, copper and ivory objects that still remained here and there in the massive tomb-chambers bore witness to the wealth they once contained, and indicated that the graves were at least as old as the Bronze Age—earlier than 1000 B.C. The fact that no settlements were discovered gave rise to the theory that Bahrain was solely a burial island, a cemetery for peoples dwelling on the mainland of Arabia.

This theory had an essential weakness: The island has a plentiful water supply and a soil that is productive where it is watered, while nearby Arabia is sandy and waterless. Accordingly in 1953 the Prehistoric Museum of Aarhus in Denmark dispatched a small expedition, comprising the two authors of this article, to Bahrain. Our objective was to reconnoiter the island as a whole and to resolve the mystery of the grave mounds by locating, if we could, the settlements of their builders.

This limited objective was achieved in the course of the first season's work. We discovered one large city, a number of smaller settlements and an extensive temple-complex, all dating to the period of the grave mounds and representing a hitherto unknown civilization. From this auspicious beginning, the work has continued on an expanding scale for the past seven years. . . . In the 1960 season the expedition consisted of 27 Scandinavian archeologists and was operating over a front of 600 miles, from Kuwait at the head of the Persian Gulf to Abu Dhabi and Buraimi in the east. Bahrain has proved to be the legendary Dilmun referred to in the cuneiform texts

---

*From "A Forgotten Civilization of the Persian Gulf," by P. V. Glob and T. G. Bibby. Copyright © 1960 by Scientific American, Inc. All rights reserved; Sir Leonard Woolley, "Birth of Glass." Reprinted from the UNESCO COURIER (June 1963).

of Sumer, the bridge between that primary seat of the urban revolution and the civilization of the Indus Valley in what is now Pakistan.

* * *

. . . near the village of Barbar on the northwestern coast . . . a large block of hewn stone, projecting above the surface, tempted investigation. A trial trench laid bare a stone-flagged court surrounded by the lowest courses of a wall of cut limestone. In the center of this court the trench exposed part of a double circle of curved blocks. A widening of the trench showed these to be a plinth that must have borne statues or cult objects. To the east of the plinth two stone slabs stood upright, with a recess in the upper edge to take a seat top. . . . We had uncovered the holy of holies of a temple. The statuette evidenced unmistakable Sumerian affinities— secure evidence for an early date. Moreover, several of the lapislazuli pendants were of a type found in the cities of the Indus Valley.

Now, after seven seasons of work on the temple of Barbar, the central area has been completely cleared. The square temple has been shown to stand upon a terrace supported by walls of finely cut and fitted limestone. A ramp leads down to the east to an oval enclosure full of charcoal from extensive and repeated burnings and containing stone foundations, perhaps blocks on which animals were sacrificed. To the west a flight of steps leads down from the terrace to a small tank or bathing pool. The temple is thus reminiscent in its layout of the temples of Early Dynastic Sumer, but, with its bathing pool, it also recalls the ritual baths of the Indus Valley cities. We have found the structure to be only the final stage of three successive building phases, each representing additions to the terrace and to the temple above it.

A wealth of small objects has been discovered within the complex—axes and spears of copper, a magnificent bull's head that calls to mind those that adorned the harps in the Early Dynastic royal graves at Ur of the Chaldees and eight circular soapstone seals. These seals are of a type well known to archeologists and much discussed. Among the thousands of cylindrical seals found in Mesopotamia there are a mere 17 of these round seals. They were not native to Mesopotamia, and appeared to date to the period be tween 2300 and 2000 B.C. Several bore inscriptions in the unknown language of the Indus Valley civilization. Moreover, three examples of the same type of seal had actually been found in the prehistoric Indus Valley city of Mohenjo-Daro. But they were obviously not native to the Indus Valley, where large square seals, found by the hundreds, had been shown to be the native type. It was now apparent to us that the round seals were native to Bahrain. The temples at Barbar could thus be placed in the third millennium B.C.; they belonged to a people who traded with both Mesopotamia and India and had a culture distinct from both.

* * *

It now seems clear that Bahrain was a center of urban life for at least 3,000 years before the Christian era. In the centuries around 2000 B.C. it was a place of considerable wealth and power. Its unique civilization was in close cultural contact with the Sumerians of Mesopotamia 150 miles up the Persian Gulf to the north and with the cities of the Indus Valley, 1,000 miles across land and sea to the east.

References to such a center of civilization turn up again and again in the extensive literature dug up in the cities of Mesopotamia over the past century. Commercial documents describe trading voyages down the Persian Gulf from the cities of Ur, Larsa, Lagash and Nippur. The historical accounts of the campaigns of the kings of Sumer, Babylon and Assyria tell of tribute and submission received from the countries of the "lower sea." Three lands down the Gulf are named with particular frequency: the kingdoms of Dilmun, Makan and Meluhha. They are always named in that order, presumably the order of their distance from Mesopotamia.

Henry Rawlinson, the British colonial official and scholar who deciphered cuneiform more than a century ago, was also the first to suggest that Bahrain might be the site of Dilmun. He based his theory on the discovery on Bahrain of a cuneiform inscription naming the god Inzak, who is cited in the god lists of Mesopotamia as the chief god of Dilmun. With the discovery of the rich cities and temples of Bahrain this theory may now be regarded as confirmed. Dilmun is described in the cuneiform records of Mesopotamia as an island with abundant fresh water lying some two days' sail, with a following wind, from Mesopotamia. Ships are frequently recorded as sailing to Dilmun with cargoes of silver and woolen goods to be exchanged there for the products of Makan (copper and diorite) and those of Meluhha (gold, ivory and precious woods). This would suggest that Meluhha was none other than the Indus Valley civilization, and that Makan must be sought between Bahrain and India. Dilmun is also named as supplying products of its own: dates and pearls. Clearly, however, Dilmun's main importance was as a clearing house for goods from farther east, the abode of merchants and shippers engaged in widespread commerce. This view agrees closely with the new archeological evidence.

BIRTH OF GLASS

From a very early date the Egyptian potter had, as a side-line to his ordinary business, practised the making of vessels in glazed frit. Glaze had been known at the beginning of the Dynastic Age and was applied to small objects cut out of steatite or moulded in frit (or siliceous paste) and soon vases were made in the same way; the technique spread quickly, and beads of glazed frit occur freely in Sumer in the Early Dynastic period.

The glaze, was, of course, glass, and about a dozen objects (nearly all small beads) made of real glass can be assigned to relatively early times—in Egypt to the Eleventh and Twelfth Dynasties and in Mesopotamia to about 2100 B.C.—and on the whole it seems that Mesopotamia may here have been the first in the field, especially as an example of glass from Eridu is a fair-sized lump, unshaped, a piece of the manufacturer's raw material.

But shortly before 1600 B.C. the discovery was made that slender rods of coloured glass, half-melted, could be twisted round a core into the form of a bottle, then re-heated so that the rods should coalesce, and then polished; during the second stage the soft surface could be "combed" so as to produce waves in the rods, thus variegating the pattern at the craftsman's pleasure;

the result was a little polychrome vase, lustrous and semi-translucent, unlike anything else known and certain to command a high price.

The earliest examples of such come from Syria, to which country the invention may be credited, but by the beginning of the Eighteenth Dynasty the Egyptians had taken it over and were making vases finer in quality than the Syrians had ever made. The same technique was used for manufacturing beads, large balls with polychrome inlay in the form of "eyes" or rosettes.

These gaily attractive ornaments, easily portable and not too fragile, were ideal objects of trade with the peoples of less civilized or of barbarous lands, and they were exported widely, westwards to Italy and across the European continent, to come to light again in graves in Britain, while the eastern trade took them to China and to Indonesia—"eyebeads" from Loyang (the Chou capital) are proved by spectrographic analysis to be identical with others from Qau in Egypt.

The Chinese imitated such imported beads with great success—so much so that the polychrome beads made in South China are only to be distinguished from the foreign examples by their marked barium content, whereas the Egyptian and Syrian glass contains no trace of barium, and also by the presence of lead, which in the west is not found in glass until shortly before the Christian era.

The facts seem to show that lead glass—"flint glass" as it is often called—was a Chinese invention; it is an invention that has had far-reaching results in glass manufacture, but it was due to experiments prompted by the beads of silica-soda-lime glass coming from the Middle East.

religion

8.
The Book of the Dead

Prehistoric people in all parts of the world searched for reasons for the things that happened to them and for protection against harm. When they couldn't find any natural explanations, they turned to the supernatural. They believed that they had found the divine in many forms— in the fertility of the earth, in the light and warmth of the sun, in the stars of the night, in the wind and the rain, and in animals.

The Egyptians were among the earliest people to arrive at a belief in divine beings. Gradually they came to a belief in the promise of eternal life for all people who had lived a good moral life. When the soul appeared after death before Osiris, the Supreme Judge, he was required to make a number of declarations which indicated the good moral and ethical content of his life while on earth. Following are a selected few of these declarations taken from The Book of the Dead, which was composed around 1500 B.C.*

INQUIRY: Which ideas in this selection are similar to religious teachings that you know? Which are different?

Homage to Thee, O Great God, Lord of the city of MAᴀTI, I have come unto Thee, O my Lord, and I have brought myself hither that I may gaze upon Thy beauties (or beneficence).

I know Thee, I know Thy Name, I know the name[s] of the Forty-two gods who are with Thee in this Hall of MAᴀTI, who live as the warders of sinners [and] who swallow their blood on that day of reckoning up the characters (or dispositions of men) in the presence of UN-NEFER (i.e. OSIRIS). In truth 'REKHTI-MERTI-NEB-MAᴀTI' is Thy Name.

Verily I have come unto Thee, I have brought unto Thee MAᴀT (i.e. TRUTH, or the LAW), I have crushed for Thee SIN.

1. I have not acted sinfully towards men.
2. I have not oppressed the members of my family.
3. I have not done wrong instead of what is right.
4. I have known no worthless folk.
5. I have not committed abominable acts.
6. I have not made excessive work to be done for me on any day (?).
7. I have [not made] my name to go forth for positions of dignity.
8. I have not domineered over servants.
9. I have not belittled god [or the God].
10. I have not filched the property of the lowly man.
11. I have not done things which are the abominations of the gods.
12. I have not vilified a servant to his master.

---

*E. A. Wallis Budge, FROM FETISH TO GOD IN ANCIENT EGYPT (London, Oxford University Press, 1934), pp. 296-300. Courtesy of University College, Oxford and Christ's College, Cambridge.

13. I have not inflicted pain (or caused suffering).
14. I have not permitted any man to suffer hunger.
15. I have not made any man to weep.
16. I have not committed murder (or slaughter).
17. I have not given an order to cause murder.

9.
Monastic Life in Ancient Babylonia

Monastic life usually brings to mind vivid images of the monks of medieval Europe toiling in the fields, copying old manuscripts, and chanting their prayers in candle-lit chapels. Nuns, praying and working within the cloistered walls of convents are also part of the history of western religious life. Christians, however, were not the first to follow a monastic way of life.

Centuries before the Christian era, Buddhist men and women founded monasteries in India, Ceylon, Southeast Asia, and elsewhere. Buddhist monasteries were centers of quiet meditation and prayer. They were storehouses of books and places where scholars came to discuss the mysteries of Buddhism. Later, when Buddhism spread to China, Korea, and Japan, monasteries became a familiar part of the landscape of these countries. Buddhists, however, were not the first to follow a monastic way of life.

As long ago as 1894 B.C. there were women who followed a monastic way of life in ancient Babylonia. Hundreds of clay documents have survived to tell the story of Babylonian women who found the monastic life a rewarding one. In the following article Dr. Rivkah Harris describes some aspects of the life of the first known monastics.*

INQUIRY: What might have been the motives for joining a monastery in ancient times? Do you think people have the same motives today?

Monasticism is found among Hindus, Buddhists, and Christians. But the earliest known form of monastic life appeared in the second millenium B.C. in the ancient Near East, in Mesopotamia, the land between the Tigris and Euphrates Rivers.

The Hammurapi Age, more technically termed the Old Babylonian period, a relatively short span of 300 years (1894-1594 B.C.), witnessed the establishment, flowering and sudden disappearance of a unique *cenobitism*.[1] Because of the need of Babylonians to record all private and public transactions, along with their use of an almost imperishable material, clay,

---

*"The Monastic Life in Ancient Babylonia" by Rivkah Harris. *Synergist*, Winter 1969.

---

[1]Cenobitism means living in a religious community.

hundreds of documents remain which inform us, though in a limited way, of the lives of these celibates.

One point must be stressed at the very onset, the only group of monastics known to date from Mesopotamia were women. These women were called *nadītu*'s in Akkadian which means, "the ones who are left fallow." (The comparison of women to fields is common throughout the ancient Near East.) The girl who became a *nadītu* was to remain "fallow" throughout her life, prohibited from all sexual relations. There were several kinds of *nadītu*'s dedicated to various gods and, therefore, living under different regulations. We will here discuss only the best known group which was probably the most numerous and most prestigious of all, the *nadītu*'s dedicated to the god Shamash. Shamash was the sun god, the judge of heaven and earth and the patron god of Sippar, a city some sixty five miles northeast of the capital Babylon

Here in the midst of Sippar surrounded by a wall was the cloister (*gagū* in Akkadian) where some two hundred *nadītu* women and the cloister officials lived. The young Babylonian girl would be brought by her father at an age when girls ordinarily married, in her early teens. Here she would live, behind its walls away from the "outside" (as the world was referred to by the *nadītu*'s) until her death when she would be buried in the *gagū* cemetery alongside her sister *nadītu*'s. Though there were times when a *nadītu* might have the freedom to leave for short family visits or have her relatives visit her she had to live until death in the cloister, later thought of as a gloomy place, almost a prison.

But the life of the *nadītu*'s was by no means a passive one. In some crucial and striking ways the cloister and its *nadītu*'s do not at all resemble the Christian nunnery and its nuns. Each *nadītu* lived in her own private house within the cloister compound which she might own or rent from a sister *nadītu*. She had her slaves and slavegirls to take care of the household tasks. A life of poverty was not demanded of the Babylonian nun. On the contrary, many, if not most of them, were born into the wealthiest and most respectable families of their society. Among them were to be found princesses, even a sister of King Hammurapi, the daughters of the temple, military, and cloister officials, members of the top echelon of the bureaucracy. Some were daughters of city administrators, of wealthy scribes, judges, physicians and diviners. Some were related to affluent artisans such as the goldsmith. When these girls were brought to the cloister they did not come empty handed. Most were given fields, houses, plots of lands, slaves, jewelry, precious household furniture and utensils as their dowry. The Code of Hammurapi stipulates that the *nadītu* of Shamash was to receive a full share of the inheritance, equal to that of her brothers! This is an astonishing provision considering that theirs was a patriarchal, agricultural society.

Herein, we believe lies one of the major reasons for the establishment of the cloister in this particular period of Mesopotamian history. Celibacy was not unknown before the Hammurapi age. There was the Sumerian institution of the *entu*-priestess, a royal princess who remained unmarried for life who participated in the annual sacred marriage ritual upon which the fertility of the land depended. But this is the first and only period in which a group of women lived as celibates. This age is remarkable for being the first time in this country when business and wealth are in the hands of private individuals, when there exists what in a fully developed capitalistic society is termed a middle class. Ordinarily when the daughter of a "middle class" family married she received a substantial dowry which she took away from her family. But the dowry which the girl brought with her into the cloister though it was hers for her lifetime returned *to* her brothers on her death. That the economic consideration was a major motivation for the establishment of the cloister institution is clearly demonstrated by the fact that successive generations of women in certain families became *nadītu*'s. There are many examples of a great aunt, aunt and niece, as well as cousins, living in the cloister and in all cases the relationship is patrilineal. Undoubtedly the aim was to maintain the integrity of the patrimony.

But the *nadītu* was not only to enjoy the usufruct of her share of the inheritance it was apparently her responsibility to invest her assets wisely in order to insure a high return. Thus we find that hundreds of the *nadītu* texts are business documents: contracts of sale, lease and hire. With few exceptions it is the *nadītu* who buys houses and fields, leases out fields, houses and plots, and hires out her slaves as farm hands to Sipparian farmers or as menials in their households. What emerges is the amazing picture of a group of women celibates acting early in this period as a major economic power in their community. Though they did not leave the walls of their cloister, these various transactions were conducted on their behalf by business agents or relatives who communicated with them by letter, it was they who must have advised and considered the possibilities. Frequently we can trace the affairs of a *nadītu* for some thirty years or more for many were long-lived avoiding as they did the hazards of child-bearing and exposure to the epidemics of those living "outside." Over and over again we find them reinvesting their capital derived from lending silver and barley, from the rents of their real estate and the hire of their slaves in more fields, houses and slaves. We even note the tendency of some *nadītu*'s to concentrate their investments in one special area whether in land holdings or in slaves. That their interest lay in expanding the paternal estate is seen from the many examples in which the real estate purchased is adjacent to family-owned properties.

But though economic considerations must have loomed large, we realize, of course, that as significant if not more so was the religious dynamic which must underlie the unique institution of the *gagū*. But as is so often the case with Mesopotamian civilization religious factors are the most elusive and incomprehensible to discover and understand. In the case of the cloister and its *nadītu*'s we have two "key" documents and indirect evidence on this question. There are no records detailing the rites or rituals which the *nadītu*'s performed. And perhaps due to characteristic Babylonian reticence about such matters there exist no text which could provide us with insight into the religious committments and attitudes of the *nadītu*'s. We must perforce read between the lines of letters and search for cues to the religious background of a significant institution of an alien and polytheistic people.

Our two "key" texts are both administrative accounts of the expenditures incurred by the cloister administration in the course of a girl's initiation as a *nadītu* and from these much is learned. The young girl accompanied by her father (the mother is not mentioned) would arrive at the beginning of a three day religious festival. Offerings of meat and jars of oil would be presented on her behalf. The cloister administration would present the father with a betrothal gift consisting of jewelry and comestibles. From this we infer that the girl dressed in bridal dress became the "bride" of the god Shamash. The second day of the festival called "the day of the dead" was the highlight of the festival for all *nadītu*'s. On this solemn day, once a year, the living *nadītu*'s remembered the dead ones by performing for their "spirits" the necessary funerary services ordinarily performed by the progeny of the deceased. But these celibates had no offspring to carry out these vital rituals and so the living *nadītu*'s did so. The young initiate was probably brought to the cloister cemetery on that day to witness her guarantee of eternal care in the afterlife. During this festival, too, she may have been brought into the awesome presence of the images of Shamash and his consort, the goddess Aya, a privilege few others were granted. In one letter a *nadītu* describes her emotion at this sight as one of extreme joy.

From the second crucial text we learn that at the initiation the "rope of Shamash" was placed on the arm of the neophyte, an act which must have symbolized her new and intimate relationship to the god.

Another index of the religious dimension is found in the names of the *nadītu*'s. Most of them contain the name of either Shamash or Aya. The most commonly found name is that of Amat-Shamash, "Servant-girl of Shamash." Often names are composed of the verb meaning "the one who is demanded (by the deity)." It seems quite probable that many, though not all, of the novices assumed a new name at their induction, the usual practice of Christian monks and nuns.

Letters written by (more accurately dictated by) *nadītu*'s are easily detected. Their standard salutation is, "May my Lord (Shamash and my Lady (Aya) keep you well." They abound in pious phrases, unlike the letters of ordinary persons. Some refer to ritual ablutions, offerings, and prayers which must have been part of their daily lives.

We know that *nadītu*'s as well as cloister officials, were obligated to bring offerings of meat, beer and flour, the repast for the images and temple priests on the occasion of the festivals of Shamash, an obligation they often passed on to the lessees of their real estate as part of the rental.

In order to understand the religious significance of the cloister and its *nadītu* inhabitants we would suggest the following. Just as the temple of Shamash in Sippar, maintained and provided for with lavishness and magnificence by the Sipparians, insured the city of prosperity and happiness so, too, did the cloister with its chaste women dedicated for life to this god further guarantee this god's continuing concern for its well being.

Before concluding an unusual practice of the *nadītu*'s should be mentioned. Often an older *nadītu* adopted as her daughter another *nadītu* either related to her or a friend, or else a slave, usually female, as her child. Strangely enough, the cloister administration though it kept records of the business transactions and lawsuits (a frequent occurrence) and concerned itself with the legal affairs of the *nadītu* was not obligated to look after her in old age. Each *nadītu* had in some way or another to provide for her old age security. Though it was the responsibility of the *nadītu*'s brothers to provide her with the basic necessities for life the long years of seclusion and separation from her family apparently made it advisable for the *nadītu* to look to someone with whom she did have years of contact. The *nadītu* who was adopted would receive a substantial bequest at the death of her adoptive mother; the slave his or her outright freedom. In the rare case where a *nadītu* became seriously ill without having made arrangements beforehand, the cloister administration would step in and appoint a younger *nadītu* as nurse and heiress.

Even before the vigorious dynasty of the kings of Babylon came to a sudden end one can detect a gradual diminution of the economic importance of the *nadītu* women. Whether this change may be correlated with the greater centralization and control from the capital which made for a general decline in private ownership is difficult to say. But we do know that the end of this era brought an end, too, to the institution of the cloister and the *nadītu*'s. Never again was this institution revitalized probably because it did not meet the needs of the future generations.

Nevertheless, the memory of the *nadītu* did live on though in a strange and distorted way. In a late text, a paean to the greatness of Babylon and its god Marduk, we read of "the *nadītu* who skilfully heals the fetus." Of the fine women of Babylon it is the *nadītu* who is praised for her skill, perhaps even her magical power, to save the fetus which would otherwise have died. The *nadītu* then who was prohibited from bearing children was later associated with the saving of infants! More ironic is the view found in the late Babylonian scholarly vocabulary lists where the *nadītu* is equated with the prostitute and the harlot. This view died hard, held as it was by modern Assyriologists until recently. But the data proves that the *nadītu* lived and died as the chaste "bride" of Shamash.

10.
Zoroastrian Scriptures

The Persians expressed their beliefs in a religion known as Zoroastrianism, which takes its name from a prophet called Zoroaster, who is believed to have lived in the seventh century B.C. He believed that a powerful battle was being waged between two great forces for the control of the universe and man. One was the creator of goodness and light, Ahura Mazda; the other was the maker of evil and darkness, Ahriman. Here are a few verses from the *Zend-Avesta*, the sacred book of this religion.*

INQUIRY: Compare the ideas expressed in this reading with those in reading 8 *(The Book of the Dead)*. What concepts do they have in common?

(*And Ahura Mazda answered:*) O well-disposed believer,
Hearken not to the followers of the Evil One,
For these seek to wreck houses,
Raze villages,

---

*Reprinted with permission of The Macmillan Company from THE WORLD'S GREATEST SCRIPTURES by Lewis Browne. Copyright 1946 by Lewis Browne.

Despoil clans and provinces;
They can cause only disaster and death.
So fight them with all your weapons!

The righteous alone shall be saved
From destruction and eternal darkness,
From foul food and the worst curses,
At the time of the End of Days.
But ye wicked ones, beware,
For to these will ye be delivered,
Because of your evil spirit!

He who serveth Ahura Mazda in mind and deed,
To him shall be granted the bliss of divine fellowship,
And fullness of Health,
Immortality,
Justice and Power,
And the Good Disposition.

The man who is well-disposed, he comprehends this,
Even as does Mazda, who is All Wise.
It is such a one who weds justice to authority,
It is the well-disposed man who most surely prospers,
And is a companion to Ahura Mazda.

11.
Selections From the Old Testament

For almost four thousand years the ancient Hebrews and their descendants, the Jews of today, have spoken and written with love and reverence of one God whom they called Yahweh. The Hebrew Bible, or Old Testament, forms the Holy Scripture of Judaism, as well as being part of the sacred Scriptures of Christianity and Islam. All three religions were born in the Middle East and grew out of the Hebrew belief in one God. The following are two readings from the Old Testament.*

INQUIRY: Which of the commandments proclaimed by Moses have been incorporated into the civil laws of many western countries? Why do religious and civil rules often deal with the same problems?

THE SECOND BOOK OF MOSES, CALLED EXODUS

So Moses went down unto the people, and spake unto them.
And God spake all these words, saying, "I am the Lord thy God, which have brought thee out of the land of Egypt, out of the house of bondage.

---

*From the King James Version of the Bible.

"Thou shalt have no other gods before me.

"Thou shalt not make unto thee any graven image, or any likeness of any thing that is in heaven above, or that is in the earth beneath, or that is in the water under the earth; thou shalt not bow down thyself to them, nor serve them: for I the Lord thy God am a jealous God, visiting the iniquity of the fathers upon the children unto the third and fourth generation of them that hate me; and showing mercy unto thousands of them that love me, and keep my commandments.

"Thou shalt not take the name of the Lord thy God in vain; for the Lord will not hold him guiltless that taketh his name in vain.

"Remember the sabbath day, to keep it holy. Six days shalt thou labor, and do all thy work: but the seventh day is the sabbath of the Lord thy God: in it thou shalt not do any work, thou, nor thy son, nor thy daughter, thy manservant, nor thy maidservant, nor thy cattle, nor thy stranger that is within thy gates: for in six days the Lord made heaven and earth, the sea, and all that in them is, and rested the seventh day: wherefore the Lord blessed the sabbath day, and hallowed it.

"Honour thy father and thy mother: that thy days may be long upon the land which the Lord thy God giveth thee.

"Thou shalt not kill.

"Thou shalt not commit adultery.

"Thou shalt not steal.

"Thou shalt not bear false witness against thy neighbor.

"Thou shalt not covet thy neighbour's house, thou shalt not covet thy neighbor's wife, nor his manservant, nor his maidservant, nor his ox, nor his ass, nor anything that is thy neighbour's."

ISAIAH

"Comfort ye, comfort ye my people," saith your God. "Speak ye comfortably to Jerusalem, and cry unto her, that her warfare is accomplished, that her iniquity is pardoned: for she hath received of the Lord's hand double for all her sins."

The voice of him that crieth in the wilderness, "Prepare ye the way of the Lord, make straight in the desert a highway for our God. Every valley shall be exalted, and every mountain and hill shall be made low: and the crooked shall be made straight, and the rough places plain: and the glory of the Lord shall be revealed, and all flesh shall see it together: for the mouth of the Lord hath spoken it."

The voice said, "Cry." And he said, "What shall I cry?"

"All flesh is grass, and all the goodliness thereof is as the flower of the field: the grass withereth, the flower fadeth: because the spirit of the Lord bloweth upon it: surely the people is grass. The grass withereth, the flower fadeth: but the word of our God shall stand for ever."

O Zion, that bringest good tidings, get thee up into the high mountain; O Jerusalem, that bringest good tidings, lift up thy voice with strength; lift it up, be not afraid; say unto the cities of Judah, "Behold your God!"

Behold, the Lord God will come with strong hand, and his arm shall rule for him: behold, his reward is with him, and his work before him. He shall feed his flock like a shepherd: he shall gather the lambs with his arm, and carry them in his bosom, and shall gently lead those that are with young.

12.
From the Gospel of St. Matthew

Christianity grew from the worship of the God of the Jews. Its founder was Jesus of Nazareth, a Jew who was born in the land of Israel almost two thousand years ago. He grew to manhood in a place called Nazareth and, at about thirty years of age, began what might be called his public life. For the next three years he wandered among the people of this land and spoke to them about their God, about the way God wanted men to act toward one another, about mercy and kindness, about life and death, and about many other matters of divine and human importance. The story of Jesus and his teachings is told in four books called Gospels (good tidings) which make up the first part of the New Testament. Here are a few selections of his teachings taken from *The Gospel According to St. Matthew.**

INQUIRY: Jesus grew up practicing the religion of Judaism. Do the teachings given here conflict with those in reading 11? If so, how? If not, are there any differences between them?

And seeing the multitudes, he went up into a mountain: and when he was set, his disciples came unto him: and he opened his mouth, and taught them, saying,
"Blessed are the poor in spirit:
For theirs is the kingdom of heaven.

Blessed are they that mourn:
For they shall be comforted.

Blessed are the meek:
For they shall inherit the earth.

Blessed are they which do hunger and thirst after righteousness:
For they shall be filled.

Blessed are the merciful:
For they shall obtain mercy.

Blessed are the pure in heart:
For they shall see God.

Blessed are the peacemakers:
For they shall be called the children of God.

Blessed are they which are persecuted for righteousness' sake:
For theirs is the kingdom of heaven.

Blessed are ye, when men shall revile you, and persecute you, and shall say all manner of evil against you falsely, for my sake.

*From the King James Version of the Bible.

Rejoice, and be exceeding glad: for great is your reward in Heaven: for so persecuted they the prophets which were before you."

* * *

"Lay not up for yourselves treasures upon earth,
    Where moth and rust doth corrupt,
And where thieves break through and steal:

But lay up for yourselves treasures in heaven,
    Where neither moth nor rust doth corrupt,
And where thieves do not break through nor steal."

* * *

"Judge not, that ye be not judged. For with what judgment ye judge, ye shall be judged: and with what measure ye mete, it shall be measured to you again. And why beholdest thou the mote that is in thy brother's eye, but considerest not the beam that is in thine own eye? Or how wilt thou say to thy brother, 'Let me pull out the mote out of thine eye'; and, behold a beam is in thy own eye? Thou hypocrite, first cast out the beam out of thine own eye; and then shalt thou see clearly to cast out the mote out of thy brother's eye."

13.
Christian Teaching

With Saul of Tarsus, baptized Paul, Christianity began to reach out to the gentiles, or those who were not Jews. Paul, the product of a Greek and Hebrew background, was a Roman citizen. A convert himself, he converted many others to Christianity as he moved from city to city. To encourage the new Christians after he had gone and to further instruct them in Christian teachings, he wrote them letters.

The Gospels, Acts of the Apostles, Epistles, and the Apocalypse, concerning the end of the world and first written in Greek, form the Books of the New Testament. Following is a selection from the First Epistle of Paul to the Corinthians, which gives his views on charity, or Christian love.*

INQUIRY: Why do you think that teachings such as these would have been considered dangerous to the state of Rome? Why are religious reformers often considered a threat to the government or to the majority?

Though I speak with the tongues of men and of angels, and have not charity, I am become as sounding brass, or a tinkling cymbal. And though I have the gift of prophecy, and understand all mysteries, and all

*From the King James Version of the Bible.

knowledge; and though I have all faith, so that I could remove mountains, and have not charity, I am nothing. And though I bestow all my goods to feed the poor, and though I give my body to be burned, and have not charity, it profiteth me nothing. Charity suffereth long, and is kind; charity envieth not; charity vaunteth not itself, is not puffed up, doth not behave itself unseemly, seeketh not her own, is not easily provoked, thinketh no evil; rejoiceth not in iniquity, but rejoiceth in the truth; beareth all things, believeth all things, hopeth all things, endureth all things. Charity never faileth: but whether there be prophecies, they shall fail; whether there be tongues, they shall cease; whether there be knowledge, it shall vanish away. For we know in part, and we prophesy in part. But when that which is perfect is come, then that which is in part shall be done away. When I was a child, I spoke as a child, I understood as a child, I thought as a child: but when I became a man, I put away childish things. For now we see through a glass, darkly; but then face to face; now I know in part; but then shall I know even as also I am known. And now abideth faith, hope, charity, these three; but the greatest of these is charity. . . .

14.
The Koran

The one God of the Jew and of the Christian is also the one God of the Muslim. Muslims, the followers of the religion of Islam, believe that there is only one God, called Allah. They believe that Allah is the creator of all things. They believe that this is the same God who spoke through the voices of the prophets Abraham and Moses, as well as through Jesus and their own special prophet, Muhammad.

Muslims believe that Muhammad (c. 570–632 A.D.) was chosen to complete and to seal the long series of revelations, and they call him "the Seal of the Prophets." Muhammad dedicated his life to proclaiming the truths which had been revealed to him. These truths are recorded in a holy book called the Koran. The Koran is for the Muslims the written word of God. Following are a few selections from the Koran which indicate some of the basic beliefs of the Muslims.

INQUIRY: Do the teachings of Muhammad conflict with those of Moses and Jesus given in previous readings? If not, why do you think there should have been so many conflicts between followers of Islam, followers of Judaism, and followers of Christianity? Are "religious wars" likely to be about actual religious differences or is war more often an extension of political aims?

SūRA II.

In the name of God, Most Gracious, Most Merciful.

* * *

2. This is the Book;
   In it is certain guidance
   To those who fear God;

3. Who believe in the Unseen,
   Are constant in prayer,
   Give out of what God
   Has provided for them;

4. And who believe in the Revelation
   Sent to thee. . . .

* * *

SECTION 8.
62. Those who believe (in the Qur-ān),
    And those who follow the Jewish (scriptures),
    And the Christians and the Sabians,—
    All who believe in God
    And the Last Day,
    And work righteousness,
    Shall have their reward.

* * *

SECTION 11.
87. God gave Moses the Book
    And followed him up
    With a succession of Apostles;
    God gave Jesus the son of Mary
    Clear Signs and strengthened him
    With the holy spirit. Is it
    That whenever there comes to you
    An Apostle with what you
    Do not desire, you are
    Puffed up with pride?—
    Some you called imposters,
    And others you slay!

* * *

125. Remember God made the House (the Ka'ba)
     A place of assembly for men
     And a place of safety;
     And hold the Station
     Of Abraham (within the House) as a place
     Of prayer; and God made a covenant
     With Abraham and Ismā'īl,
     That they should sanctify
     His House for those who
     Surround it, or use it
     As a retreat, or bow, or
     Prostrate themselves (therein
     In prayer).

* * *

136. Proclaim: "We believe
      In God, and the revelation
      Given to us, and to Abraham,
      Ismā'īl, Isaac, Jacob,
      And the Tribes, and that given
      To Moses and Jesus, and that given
      To (all) Prophets from their Lord:
      We make no difference
      Between one and another of them:
      And we bow to God (in Islam)."

                                    *   *   *

SECTION 22.
177. It is not righteousness
      To turn your faces
      Towards East or West;
      But it is righteousness—
      To believe in God
      And the Last Day,
      And the Angels,
      And the Book,
      And the Messengers;
      To spend of your substance,
      Out of love for Him,
      For your kin,
      For orphans,
      For the needy,
      For the wayfarer,
      For those who ask,
      And for the ransom of slaves;
      To be steadfast in prayer,
      And practice regular charity;
      To fulfill the contracts
      Which you have made;
      And to be firm and patient,
      In pain (or suffering)
      And adversity,
      And throughout
      All periods of panic.
      Such are the people
      Of truth, the God-fearing.

                                    *   *   *

280. If the debtor is
      In a difficulty,
      Grant him time
      Till it is easy
      For him to repay.
      But if you remit it
      By way of charity,

That is best for you
If you only knew.

* * *

286. On no soul doth God
Place a burden greater
Than it can bear.
It gets every good that it earns,
And it suffers every ill that it earns.
(Pray:) "Our Lord!
Condemn us not
If we forget or fall
Into error; our Lord!
Lay not on us a burden
Like that which You
Laid on those before us;
Our Lord! lay not on us
A burden greater than we
Have strength to bear.
Blot out our sins,
And grant us forgiveness.
Have mercy on us.
You art our Protector;
Help us against those
Who stand against Faith."

creativity

15.
Folk Music: "Hora Hanegev"

Israel has been long known for music. Books of the Old Testament describe music used in religious ceremonies as well as songs of love. This modern Israeli folk song celebrates the blooming of the Negev. By irrigating this semidesert land, the Israelis have turned it into farmland. The "hora" is a round dance popular in Romania as well as in Israel.*

INQUIRY: How does the rhythm of this song compare with other music for folk dances that you have heard?

Ze-mer ze-mer lach, ze-mer ze-mer lach,
We shall sing a song, We shall sing a song,

ze-mer lach me-cho-ra-ti me-cho-ra-ti.
We shall sing a song to you, my fa-ther-land.

Ha-ra-ra-ich he-ma yis-ma-chu
Then will glad-ness cov-er your moun-tains

et me-chol ha-ho-rah yis-ar; e-lef pra-chim le-
While the ho-ra wild-ly we dance; A thou-sand flow-ers

fe-ta yif-ra-chu vi-chu-su et pne ha-mid-bar.
will bloom from foun-tains cov-er-ing the dry des-ert sands

*HORA HANEGEV
English lyric by Herbert Haufrecht & David Gerlich
Based on a traditional Israeli song
TRO—© Copyright 1963 HOLLIS MUSIC, INC.,
New York, N.Y.   Used by permission

52

16.
Folk Music: "Kouh Beh Kouh"

The Iranian folk song "On the Road" describes the singer's joy at seeing his sweetheart, the beautiful Hadjar.*

INQUIRY: Do popular songs that you know still use many of the ideas of folk music? Why do you think music can be called an international language?

1. *Kouh beh kouh__ mi - gar - di - dam, dom - ba - lé   khar - gousch,*
1. On the road__ the moun-tain side, Chas - ing rab - bit in fast stride,

yâ - ré khod - ra man di - dam gousch - va - ré   dar ___ gousch,
There my sweet-heart did ap - pear Wear- ing gold ring in __ her ear,

gousch - va - ré   dar _____ gousch Hoi! __ hoi! __ hoi!
Wear - ing gold ring in __ her ear. Hoi! __ hoi! __ hoi!

Ha - djar gra - schang é,   mast - o ma - lang é! _____
Ha - djar so__ love - ly, Joy - ful and __ hap - py! _____

2. *Kouh beh kouh migardidam,*   2. On the road the mountain side,
   az peiyé âhou,   Hunting reindeer running wild,
   yâré khodra man didam   There my sweetheart did appear
   pahlou beh pahlou,   Filled my heart with boundless cheer.
   Djân! djân! djân!   Hoi! hoi! hoi!
   Hadjar gaschang é,   Hadjar so lovely,
   masto malang é!   Joyful and happy!

17.
Folk Music: "Üsküdar"

A popular folk tune from Turkey, "Üsküdar" tells of the joys of love. The modern city of Üsküdar was known as Chrysopolis in ancient times. It was founded by Greek colonists.*

INQUIRY: Compare this Turkish song with the Iranian song "Kouh Beh Kouh." What are their similarities and differences?

2. Üsküdar' a ğider iken
bir mendel buldum, } (2)

Mendilimin içinede
locum doldurdum. } (2)

3. Katibimi arar iken
yanimada buldum; } (2)

Katip benim ben katibim,
el ne karişir } (2)

2. On that road I later found
A kerchief of finest cloth, } (2)

Cleaning it with tend'rest care,
Surely 'twas his, I thought. } (2)

3. Anxiously I looked for him,
When he appeared near me; } (2)

Promising to wander no more,
Mine he'll forever be. } (2)

18.
Wheels and Man

As early as 3250 B.C. the Sumerians were using wheeled wagons and carts. The Sumerian use of the wheel spread into the Middle East, North Africa, Asia, and Europe. (Perhaps others discovered the wheel independently in other parts of the world.) The invention of the wheel eased life and expanded people's horizons. It enlarged trade, quickened travel, and made work more efficient. It is difficult to conceive of life without the wheel, but people have been without it for more years than they have possessed it. The wheel has been of great importance in establishing civilizations.*

INQUIRY: Very complex cultures (such as the Mayan, Aztec, and Inca) have existed without the use of the wheel, and their accomplishments were remarkable. Do you think wheels would have been as useful if the Sumerians had not had draft animals available?

The vehicular wheel, which revolutionized transportation, is basically a disc equipped with bearings to allow it to spin freely. The manufacture of a disc requires in itself the performance of another rotary motion, namely tracing a circle. Tracing a true circle can be accurately executed only with an appropriate instrument. A length of string, one end of which is fixed, or by a forked stick or bone, one prong of which is rotated on the other as a fixed point can serve as such an instrument. As a matter of fact, the wishbone of a bird may well have been the first, accidentally discovered "compass," which many used successfully to draw a perfect circle in the sand. Once the concept of a free-spinning disc was developed, the next step toward the invention of the wheel and its application to vehicular transport was logical.

The earliest known vehicular wheels were probably made of horizontal cross-sections of fallen tree logs. In the Near East the use of solid spokeless wooden wheels most probably coincided with the domestication of draft animals: the oxen, the mule and the horse. The first wheeled vehicles were clumsily built four-wheeled wagons or two-wheeled carts. Each wheel consisted of three wooden discs, held together by wooden, copper or bronze clamps. The existence of such disc-wheeled vehicles is known to us primarily through pictographic symbols and miniature terracotta replicas. Such replicas, employed probably in magico-religious contexts, are first found in Mesopotamian tombs and burials and would indicate that massive wheeled wagons and carts were used as early as 3250 B.C. by the Sumerians, and were soon followed and imitated by other cultures between the Tigris and Euphrates Rivers, on the Indus River and in Anatolia. Then their use gradually diffused into North Africa and through the Caucasus to Europe,

---

*"Wheels and Man" by Stephen F. Borhegyi. Reprinted from ARCHAEOLOGY, Volume 23, No. 1, Copyright 1970, Archaeological Institute of America.

the Middle Danube area, and to northern and western Europe. By 1500 B.C. wheeled vehicles were used as far east as China.

Meanwhile, by 3000 B.C., lighter and fast-moving two-wheeled mule and horse drawn chariots made their appearance in Mesopotamia, Anatolia and Egypt. They changed the military history of the Middle East, spurring nations to conquer foreign lands and establish far-reaching empires. The first spoked wheels appeared around 2000 B.C. in Mesopotamia, and then in Egypt. By 1000 B.C. they were universally in use around the shores of the entire eastern Mediterranean. Meanwhile, the earlier wooden wheels and wooden chariots were rapidly being replaced by more durable ones plated with or made entirely out of metal, first of bronze, and later on of iron. And so the wheel was rolling on its way to revolutionary success all over the Old World.

The ultimate success of equipping wheels with comfortably bouncing rubber tires or tubes was not possible until after the sixteenth century, when the discovery of the New World brought inventors of wheels and horse- and oxen-drawn vehicles face to face with the discoverers of solid and liquid rubber in Mexico. The natives of Mesoamerica were first stunned by the unfamiliar horses and vehicles. The Spaniards were awed by the Indians' bouncing rubber balls. The Indians soon took to the horses, mules and carts while the Spaniards began experimenting with rubber. And so, the rubber covered wheel came into use, to the mutual benefit of the Old and New World.

19.
The Invention of Writing

Around 3000 B.C. people began to write beginning what is properly called history. Passing events and the endless varieties of human behavior could be recorded and described. People could now bequeath their legacy of thought and deeds to the future as well as to the present. And others could build on their speculations and experiences, ensuring the continuing progress toward greater knowledge. The invention of writing was vital to the birth and growth of civilizations.*

INQUIRY: What advantage does script writing have over the use of pictographs? With new means of communication, do you think reading and writing might become less important? Imagine and try to describe a modern society that might use recording devices, radio, and television more than reading and writing.

The Sumerians in Lower Mesopotamia rank with the Egyptians, the Cretans and the Chinese as the earliest inventors of an efficient system

---

*"Cuneiform Script." Reprinted from the UNESCO COURIER (August-September 1969).

of writing. They took the first step from the pictographic to the syllabic system and thus helped to develop writing as we know it today. About 3000 B.C., the Sumerians made seals, used as property marks, and then employed word-signs picturing the object referred to. These original "pictographs" were then given phonetic values resulting in a greater descriptive precision. This was now a "rebus-writing," a word that was difficult to render pictorially being shown by the sign for another word with the same or similar sound. It thus became possible to write almost any combination of spoken words. By 2500 B.C., the writing had evolved into a few wedge-shaped strokes from which the name "cuneiform" is taken. It was written on tablets of damp clay with a stylus—often the sharpened point of a reed. Babylonians and Assyrians—and later the Hittites and Persians—took over the cuneiform script from the Sumerians and adapted it to their own languages. Sometimes an explanatory picture was included in the writing to guide the illiterate. But pictures and script now had no need of each other. Reading and writing began to spread throughout Mesopotamia.

20.
The Code of Hammurabi

The Amorite king, Hammurabi (1728-1686 B.C.), ruled over an empire in Mesopotamia from his capital city of Babylon. In an attempt to bring some unity to his many conquests, Hammurabi codified the varying laws and customs of his lands. Centuries later some provisions of Hammurabi's code continued in use influencing Arabic and Islamic law. A few selections from this code follow.*

INQUIRY: Why were many of Hammurabi's laws concerned with property, money, prices, buying, and selling? In what ways are these laws different from the laws expressed in reading 11?

3.   If a man has borne false witness in a trial, or has not established the statement that he has made, if that case be a capital trial, that man shall be put to death.
6.   If a man has stolen goods from a temple, or house, he shall be put to death; and he that has received the stolen property from him shall be put to death.
8.   If a patrician has stolen ox, sheep, ass, pig, or ship, whether from a temple, or a house, he shall pay thirtyfold. If he be a plebeian, he shall return tenfold. If the thief cannot pay, he shall be put to death.
14.   If a man has stolen a child, he shall be put to death.

*BABYLONIAN AND ASSYRIAN LETTERS, CONTRACTS AND LAWS by C. H. W. Johns. Charles Scribner's Sons (1902).

15. If a man has induced either a male or female slave from the house of a patrician, or plebeian, to leave the city, he shall be put to death.

21. If a man has broken into a house he shall be killed before the breach and buried there.

22. If a man has committed highway robbery and has been caught, that man shall be put to death.

23. If the highwayman has not been caught, the man that has been robbed shall state on oath what he has lost, and the city or district governor in whose territory or district the robbery took place shall restore to him what he has lost.

25. If a fire has broken out in a man's house and one who has come to put it out has coveted the property of the householder and appropriated any of it, that man shall be cast into the selfsame fire.

* * *

48. If a man has incurred a debt and a storm has flooded his field or carried away the crop, or the corn has not grown because of drought, in that year he shall not pay his creditor. Further, he shall post-date his bond and shall not pay interest for that year.

53, 54. If a man has neglected to strengthen his dike and has not kept his dike strong, and a breach has broken out in his dike, and the waters have flooded the meadow, the man in whose dike the breach has broken out shall restore the corn he has caused to be lost. [54.] If he be not able to restore the corn, he and his goods shall be sold, and the owners of the meadow whose corn the water has carried away shall share the money.

55. If a man has opened his runnel for watering and has left it open, and the water has flooded his neighbor's field, he shall pay him an average crop.

100. [If an agent has received money of a merchant, he shall write down the amount] and [what is to be] the interest of the money, and when his time is up, he shall settle with his merchant.

* * *

108. If the mistress of a beer-shop has not received corn as the price of beer or has demanded silver on an excessive scale, and has made the measure of beer less than the measure of corn, that beer-seller shall be prosecuted and drowned.

109. If the mistress of a beer-shop has assembled seditious slanderers in her house and those seditious persons have not been captured and have not been haled to the palace, that beer-seller shall be put to death.

* * *

128. If a man has taken a wife and has not executed a marriage-contract, that woman is not a wife.

* * *

138. If a man has divorced his wife, who has not borne him children, he shall pay over to her as much money as was given for her bride-price and the marriage-portion which she brought from her father's house, and so shall divorce her.

141. If a man's wife, living in her husband's house, has persisted in going out, has acted the fool, has wasted her house, has belittled her husband, he shall prosecute her. If her husband has said, "I divorce her," she shall go her way; he shall give her nothing as her price of divorce. If her husband has said, "I will not divorce her," he may take another woman to wife; the wife shall live as a slave in her husband's house.

142. If a woman has hated her husband, and has said, "You shall not possess me," her past shall be inquired into, as to what she lacks. If she has been discreet, and has no vice, and her husband has gone out, and has greatly belittled her, that woman has no blame, she shall take her marriage-portion and go off to her father's house.

* * *

152. From the time that that woman entered into the man's house they together shall be liable for all debts subsequently incurred.

153. If a man's wife, for the sake of another, has caused her husband to be killed, that woman shall be impaled.

* * *

168. If a man has determined to disinherit his son and has declared before the judge, "I cut off my son," the judge shall inquire into the son's past, and, if the son has not committed a grave misdemeanor such as should cut him off from sonship, the father shall [not] disinherit his son.

* * *

186. If a man has taken a young child to be his son, and after he has taken him, the child discover his own parents, he shall return to his father's house.

188, 189. If a craftsman has taken a child to bring up and has taught him his handicraft, he shall not be reclaimed. If he has not taught him his handicraft that foster child shall return to his father's house.

195. If a son has struck his father, his hands shall be cut off.

196. If a man has knocked out the eye of a patrician, his eye shall be knocked out.

197. If he has broken the limb of a patrician, his limb shall be broken.

198. If he has knocked out the eye of a plebeian or has broken the limb of a plebeian, he shall pay one mina of silver.

199. If he has knocked out the eye of a patrician's servant, or broken the limb of a patrician's servant, he shall pay half his value.

200. If a patrician has knocked out the tooth of a man that is his equal, his tooth shall be knocked out.

201. If he has knocked out the tooth of a plebeian, he shall pay one-third of a mina of silver.

206. If a man has struck another in a quarrel, and caused him a permanent injury, that man shall swear, "I struck him without malice," and shall pay the doctor.

215. If a surgeon has operated with the bronze lancet on a patrician for a serious injury, and has cured him, or has removed with a bronze lancet a

cataract for a patrician, and has cured his eye, he shall take ten shekels of silver.

216.   If it be plebeian, he shall take five shekels of silver.

217.   If it be a man's slave, the owner of the slave shall give two shekels of silver to the surgeon.

218.   If a surgeon has operated with the bronze lancet on a patrician for a serious injury, and has caused his death, or has removed a cataract for a patrician, with the bronze lancet, and has made him lose his eye, his hands shall be cut off.

221.   If a surgeon has cured the limb of a patrician, or has doctored a diseased bowel, the patient shall pay five shekels of silver to the surgeon.

224.   If a veterinary surgeon has treated an ox, or an ass, for a severe injury, and cured it, the owner of the ox, or the ass, shall pay the surgeon one-sixth of a shekel of silver, as his fee.

225.   If he has treated an ox, or an ass, for a severe injury, and caused it to die, he shall pay one-quarter of its value to the owner of the ox, or the ass.

229.   If a builder has built a house for a man, and has not made his work sound, and the house he built has fallen, and caused the death of its owner, that builder shall be put to death.

21.
Desert Highway for Ships

The ancient Egyptians were an ingenious people. With each passing year, new evidence of their inventive minds is uncovered. In the following reading, the author describes a type of highway which the Egyptians built over the sands of the desert in order to bypass a river obstacle. They hauled boats and other heavy objects along this highway.*

INQUIRY: Aerial photography led to the discovery of the Egyptian highway described in this article. Where else might aerial photographs be useful in making archaeological discoveries?

In 1963-64 the French Archaeological Mission in Sudanese Nubia began a systematic exploration of the archaeological concession it had received from the Government of the Sudan. Special surveys were made in the lowest-lying areas most immediately threatened by the waters of the Aswan High Dam.

In these operations, aerial photographs of the area taken during 1958-59

*"Desert Highway for Ships" by Jean Vercoutter. Reprinted from UNESCO COURIER (December 1964).

were invaluable. Standing out clearly on one of these photographs was a kind of track running from the area of the west bank of the Nile northwards to the village of Matouka. I remember saying jokingly that this was no doubt the line of a canal which enabled the Egyptians to outflank the dangerous rapids between Mirgissa-Dabenarti and the Rock of Abusir.

At that time I had no idea how close I was to the truth. The astute Egyptians, however, did not build a canal; instead they constructed a roadway on land for their boats, thus anticipating by many centuries the Greek architects who conceived the idea of roads along which ships were dragged across the Isthmus of Corinth.

The Egyptian technique was remarkably simple. They simply spread a layer of Nile mud on the sands, afterwards reinforcing this half-made track with wooden poles rather like railroad sleepers. The imprint of those poles is still clearly visible although termites have long since devoured every particle of the wood itself.

Illustrations on Middle Kingdom tombs have shown us that the Egyptians used these viscous substances to move colossi far heavier than the boats that plied the Nile. The colossi were moved on sledges pulled by teams of men. The overseer is shown walking ahead pouring water on the ground, and his action reveals the nature of the ground: when silt from the Nile is moistened it becomes as slippery as ice.

An architect friend of mine carried out an experiment which proved this. He laid down a track of silt in the manner of the ancient Egyptians and placed on it a huge block of stone that had fallen from the temple of Karnak. After he had wet the silt, his problem was no longer how to drag the stone along the ground, but how to hold it back and keep it moving in the right direction.

The technique of using wooden posts, as revealed at Mirgissa, is confirmed as a practice of the Middle Kingdom period by a discovery at Lahun. Here the Egyptians had used them to reinforce a track leading from a quarry, down which they slid huge blocks of stone for the pyramid raised by Seostris III.

Thus we have confirmation that the two methods used by the Egyptians at Mirgissa—wet mud and posts reinforcing the road—were already known in Egypt during the Middle Kingdom.

I am quite convinced that we discovered at Mirgissa a slipway that enabled the Egyptians to travel up and down the Nile throughout the year. The passage of the rapids on the Second Cataract is difficult, though possible, when the river is in flood. But during the low-water season the operation is quite impossible.

To maintain a link with Egypt by river when the Nile was at its lowest level, the ancient garrisons in Nubia had two alternatives: either to set out on a long march across the desert until they reached the next navigable stretch of the Nile or to drag their boats bodily overland around the dangerous rocks that barred their way.

The slipway discovered in 1964 is remarkably well preserved. Hidden by only a few centimetres of sand, it still runs straight and level across the land. Even the footprints of the last sailors to pull their boats along it are clearly visible on the dried mud, as also are the marks made by the timbers of the boats.

Already more than one kilometre of the slipway has been uncovered and our next task will be to locate the exact points where this remarkable and original highway begins and ends.

22.
Medicine in the Ancient Middle East

Middle Easterners made notable achievements in the field of medicine many thousands of years ago. In the Code of Hammurabi, for example, surgery is mentioned. The following two selections show something of medical knowledge in the ancient Middle East.*

INQUIRY: The author states that the Egyptian records containing the more rational observations were made in the earlier period. What conclusions can you draw from this statement? Do you think this means that the Egyptians did not learn from experience over a period of time? Why do you think the magical rites were considered more important than the drugs that were used?

MEDICINE IN ANCIENT EGYPT

Roots of the profession of medicine are buried far back before the dawn of history.

* * *

Egypt first became an organized nation about 3000 B.C. Medical interest centers upon a period in the Third Dynasty (2980-2900 B.C.) when Egypt had an ambitious Pharaoh named Zoser; and Zoser, in turn, had for his chief counselor and minister a brilliant noble named Imhotep (whose name means "he who cometh in peace"). Imhotep is said to have constructed the famous step pyramid of Sakkarah, near Memphis, for Pharaoh Zoser. A versatile man, Imhotep seems to have been a priest, a magician, and a poet. But in the Egyptian writings of the Greco-Roman period (third century, B.C.) Imhotep is represented as a physician, and is assigned the role of god of medicine in Egypt. The Greeks identified him with their Asklepios, to whom was attributed a similar regard. In this later period, temples were erected to Imhotep in which patients looked for and supposedly found relief in their sleep.

There is a close association in Egyptian medicine between religion and magic. Egyptian physicians used many drugs, but thought their effects

*George A. Bender, MEDICINE IN ANCIENT EGYPT (Detroit, Parke, Davis & Company, 1957). Courtesy of the author and Parke-Davis & Company; Sir Leonard Woolley, "The Commonwealth of Medicine." Reprinted from the UNESCO COURIER (June 1963).

primarily magical. The papyri (so called because they were written on sheets prepared from the papyrus plant) dealing exclusively with medicine abound with magic formulas and prayers. "In some cases in which human help seemed to be impossible," observes Hermann Ranke, "a last attempt was made to get help from a supernatural source . . ." a practice not incompatible with that of the religious-minded physician of today who through prayer seeks aid and guidance. The gods of the Egyptians were no less real to them than is our deity to us.

Medicine as practiced by the ancient Egyptians was not primitive, however. Just as they had transcended primitive levels in statecraft, agriculture, technology, and especially architecture and art, so did the Egyptians also reach higher levels in medicine. Some medical papyri are predominantly religious, but others are predominantly empirico-rational. Strangely enough, those recording the more rational observations stem from the earliest periods (1600-1500 B.C.). Among these are the Edwin Smith papyrus and the Ebers papyrus. The first was intended primarily for the use of a surgeon; the latter is a collection of recipes for the physician. Each of these documents, though ancient in its own right, appears by language and explanations to reflect traditions much older. . . .

Dealing primarily with wounds, the Edwin Smith papyrus is admired for the diagnostic acumen exhibited in the case histories detailed, where symptoms such as feeble pulse (2500 years before reference to the pulse appears in Greek medical treatises), palsy, and deafness are all recorded and referred to as due to one common cause—a head wound. In addition to many surgical conditions, a great number of recognizable internal afflictions are reported in the papyri, such as worms, eye diseases, diabetes, rheumatism and schistosomiasis. The ancient existence of some of these conditions is confirmed by palaeopathology (the examination of bones and tissues of mummies for evidence of disease); and, unfortunately, those afflictions are still prevalent in Egypt.

The papyri prescribe many rational methods of treatment, such as diet, physiotherapy, and drugs. Many of the drugs named undoubtedly were worthless, but some, such as tannic acid, turpentine, gentian, senna, and lead and copper salts, are still used in medical practice. Castor oil, used externally and internally, was a great favorite with the doctors of Egypt. The style used in prescription writing today is much the same as when these papyri were written.

The cases of the Edwin Smith papyrus are not only systematically constructed, each within itself, but their arrangement throughout is a systematic one. First comes a superscription, which briefly gives the name of the illness. This is followed by a careful description, which always begins with the words "If you examine a man who . . ." has this or that illness. Then comes a diagnosis that always begins with the words, "You should say" he suffered from this or that ailment. This diagnosis always ends with the words "An ailment which . . ." and then one of three possibilities follows. The surgeon may say: "An ailment which I shall treat," or, "An ailment which I shall combat," or, "An ailment which I will not treat." (The latter discrimination was practiced by some physicians in almost all periods and was regarded as ethical up to the eighteenth century). Except in entirely hopeless cases, there followed a method of treatment, beginning with the words, "You must do . . ." this or that. Then the healing substances are given.

* * *

Egyptian physicians were highly respected all over the ancient world for thousands of years. Homer regarded them as the best in his time. Egyptian physicians were called to the courts of Persian emperors and other Eastern potentates; and only in the sixth century B.C. were they replaced by Greek physicians. Beyond the psychotherapeutic values of magic and religion, Egyptian medical men made solid advances in observation and rational treatment. Their contributions are worthy of a place beside other accomplishments of this great ancient civilization. The dominant position occupied by Egyptian medicine for 2,500 years seems fully justified.

THE COMMONWEALTH OF MEDICINE

More perhaps than any other art was medicine in the ancient world internationalized. A famous Egyptian doctor might travel far afield to treat an important patient. Thus Parimachu the Egyptian was summoned to Asia Minor to the sick-bed of the king of Tarkhuntash.

Ramses II, according to a late story, sent his court physician to Hattusas to cure Bentzesh, the sister-in-law of the Hittite king Hattusilis—it is interesting to note that, when the doctor failed to drive out the demon that possessed her, Pharaoh was constrained to send the holy image of the god Khonsu, by whose aid the cure was duly effected.

The same Hattusilis, negotiating for a treaty with Kadashman-Enil II of Babylon, was at pains to explain away the embarrassing fact that a Babylonian physician who was visiting the Hittite country had been forcibly detained there.

Personal visits of the sort were really not uncommon, but what more than anything proves the universality of medicine is the fact that medical books circulated freely from one country to another; Hittite copies of Babylonian medical tablets have been unearthed at Bogazhoy, and it is evident that the pharmacopoeia and the prescriptions based upon it were in some measure the common property of doctors throughout the Middle East.

It is this internationalization of medicine, and the great reputation won by Mesopotamian physicians, that account for the adoption by European peoples (through Greek and later through Arabic) of numerous Mesopotamian plant-names, while, on the other hand, the tablets definitely explain certain plant-names as being foreign and the herbs consequently imported, as, for instance, ricinus from Elam and cardamom from Anatolia.

But while the evidence shows that in the art of healing there was throughout the Middle East a certain amount of free trade in medical service and in medical knowledge, it must still be remembered that by common consent the actual drug was held to be less potent than the magic rites with which it was administered.

The successful physician was he who knew both sides of his profession, and it was because of this duality that there was a limit to the international character of medicine. The gods of the different countries were not the same, and a charm that worked satisfactorily in Babylon might fall upon deaf ears in Memphis. . . .

23.
The Babylonian Astronomers

Among the first serious students of astronomy were the Babylonians, who made significant contributions to the store of knowledge about celestial bodies in the ancient world.*

INQUIRY: Why would it have been necessary to make observations over a long period of time before arriving at a scientific theory concerning the movement of stars and planets?

The Babylonians, possessing a mathematical basis for astronomical calculations much superior to that of the Egyptians, made far greater progress in the astronomical field and started at quite an early date to amass a *corpus* of information which would ultimately supply the material for science. The earliest computations were concerned with (a) the duration of day and night in the different seasons (b) the rising and setting of the moon, and (c) the appearance and disappearance of Venus.

From the time of the Third Dynasty of Ur (c. 2100 B.C.) onwards the omen texts, which combine astrological forecasts with astronomical observations, prove the careful attention paid to astral phenomena. Thus the sixty-third tablet of the great astrological series "Enuma, Anu, Enlil" which was put into shape between 1400 and 900 B.C. contains a list of the heliacal risings and settings of Venus during twenty-one years of the reign of Ammizaduga; the observations must have been made at the time, i.e., in the late seventeenth or early sixteenth century B.C. But what we have here is simply observation which was carefully conducted over a considerable period; it does not involve any scientific theory. . . .

The evidence that we possess justifies us in saying that by 1200 B.C. in Babylonia the foundations of real astronomical research . . . had been well and truly laid. Further it appears likely, though it cannot be definitely affirmed, that already the first tentative steps had been taken in the direction of scientific thinking over the data which careful observation had amassed, and that certain rather crude and elementary results had been achieved which in the course of the following millennium would be developed into the astronomical science inherited by the Greeks.

---

*Sir Leonard Woolley, "The First Astronomers of China and Babylon." Reprinted from the UNESCO COURIER (June 1963).

24:
Cairo: One Thousand Years of History

The Egyptians think of Cairo as the heart of their country. It has been the chief city in Egypt and one of the great cities of the world since its founding in the latter half of the tenth century A.D. From its beginning up to the present, Cairo has been one of the great centers of the Islamic world. Magnificent mosques, brilliant teachers and scholars, comprehensive libraries, and other facilities have drawn many generations of students to Cairo from all parts of the world. The art and the architecture of Cairo bear the deep and undeniable imprint of the Muslim religion. The city also shows evidence of Egypt's pre-Islamic heritage.*

INQUIRY: Did Cairo become a center of learning because it was a capital city or because it was a center of trade? Which would have more influence on its development? What modern capital cities do you know that are not centers of trade?

Strung like pearls on the thread of Islamic history, the names of the great cities of Islam evoke a vision of magical splendour—Cordova, Cairo, Damascus, Aleppo, Baghdad, Bokhara, Samarkand. The list is endless, yet among these cities none stands so pre-eminent as Cairo.

As the capital of Egypt it is as old as Islam itself, and down to the present day it has consistently remained, not merely a bastion of Islam but a treasure house enclosing innumerable masterpieces of Islamic art that cover more than a thousand years.

Its history began when Amr ibn al-As conquered Egypt for Omar, the second of the Mohammedan caliphs, in the years 641 A.D. Amr captured the Roman fortress of Egyptian Babylon which stood at the settlement said to have been founded by emigrants from the ancient town of the same name. Just to the north of this fortress, whose remains still dignify Old Cairo, Amr set up his camp and here he founded the town named Al-Fustat (signifying "the tent").

Later rulers were to add other administrative centres to Fustat—and always to the north—but this was essentially the beginning of Cairo, the capital standing on the east bank of the Nile and replacing ancient Memphis to the west. In the 9th century, for example, Ahmed ibn Tulun, whose great mosque still stands, built Al-Qatai as his capital, north-east of Fustat.

The name Cairo, however, and the beginning of its great splendour date from the Fatimids, a Shiite dynasty claiming descent from Fatima, the daughter of the prophet Muhammad. The first caliph of the Fatimid dynasty in North Africa was Ubaydallah the Mahdi whose reign began in Kairouan, Tunisia, in 910.

Egypt was conquered half a century later, in 969, by Jawhar, vizier and

---

*"Cairo: 1,000 Years of History" by Abdel-Rahman Zaky. Reprinted from UNESCO COURIER (April 1970).

commander in chief of the reigning Fatimid caliph, al-Muizz. The capital of the Fatimid empire was at once established in the new centre that Jawhar had founded and named Al-Qahira (The Victorious), a name which has passed into English as Cairo.

Jawhar had left Kairouan in February 969 with 100,000 men and ample supplies and equipment. By July 9, Fustat had surrendered and the Fatimid army was encamped on the sandy plain to the north of it. That same night a new palace-fortress city was marked out over a square roughly 1,200 yards each way. The south faced Fustat, the west ran beside the ancient canal known as Al-Khalij, the east fronted on the Muqattam Hills, while to the north lay open country and the highway to Asia.

The original wall and the seven gates were of mudbrick. The three magnificent stone gateways and the section of the wall that survive today were part of a grand rebuilding in stone on a slightly different alignment a century later by the great vizier Badr al-Jamali.

The walled Al-Qahira was a royal city, entry to which was forbidden except to those on official business. It was designed to enclose two palaces for the caliph and his family, government offices, quarters for the garrison, the treasury, arsenal, stables and other buildings.

Once the walls were begun, Jawhar's next task was the foundation of a great assembly mosque. On Sunday, April 3, 970, was founded Al-Azhar (the Resplendent), the mosque that is still the glory of Islam. It was finished on June 24, 972, and in 988 it began to be used by scholars and students. It then became what it has ever since remained, one of the chief universities of Islam.

Then, as now, students from every part of the Muslim world gathered within its walls to receive instruction from the lips of great scholars in the Koran, in theology, the Traditions of the Prophet, law, grammar, logic and rhetoric. After the time of Saladin, Al-Azhar became the most eminent centre of orthodox teaching in Islam, a university of unequalled distinction and world-wide reputation.

Within only a few years of its foundation, Cairo had grown to such splendour that in 985, the Arab traveller Maqdisi, could write: "Baghdad was in former times an illustrious city, but it is now crumbling to decay, and its glory has departed. I found neither pleasure nor aught worthy of admiration there. Cairo today is what Baghdad was in its prime, and I know of no more illustrious city in Islam."

For Cairo was no longer a provincial city, the seat of a mere governor appointed by the Abbasid caliphate. It was the capital of a vigorous empire which more than rivalled that of the Abbasids. It had become a Mediterranean power, the equal of all its rivals to east and west.

The naval power and wide connexions of the Fatimids made Egypt a new factor in the power politics of the area. These and the wisdom of Fatimid policies led to Cairo's rise as a centre of trade that flourished on a scale previously unknown.

Writers and travellers have devoted many pages to describing its splendours, climaxed by its two great palaces. Between them lay a square, Bayn al-Qasrayn (Between the Two Palaces), a name which still survives as that of a street flanked by several fine mosques of later date.

The square was used for parades and great ceremonies. To the east lay

Al-Muizz's palace, to the west that built by his son Al-Aziz to overlook the Garden of Kafur (an earlier ruler) that now lay between it and the Khalij canal.

The Egyptian topographer Maqrizi (d. 1441) devotes nearly two hundred pages to a description of the palaces with their four thousand chambers, including the Golden Hall, a gorgeous pavilion in which sat the Caliph on his golden throne surrounded by richly attired attendants, the Emerald Hall with its pillars of marble and the Great Diwan where he sat in state on Mondays and Thursdays at a window beneath a cupola.

Al-Qahira of the Fatimids was indeed a new city. The Fatimids could have echoed the words of the Emperor Augustus, when he spoke of Rome, and boasted that they found their city mudbrick and left it stone. Construction in stone was an innovation at that time, its use having been abandoned since the classical era.

As mentioned previously, Badr al-Jamali rebuilt part of the walls and gateways (1087-1091). They are monuments of magnificent stonework. His own tomb-mosque on the Muqattam is of stone, as was the mosque of Al-Akmar (1125). The minaret of Badr's mosque was also an innovation for Islamic architecture in Egypt.

The next major change in the plan of Cairo came with Salah-ad-Din al-Ayyubi (Saladin), who took over from the Fatimids in 1169 and ruled till 1193. He planned a new wall to join Al-Qahira and Fustat into one great city, thus enclosing an area ten times as great as the Fatimid capital.

Saladin also built what is still the dominant architectural feature of Cairo, the Citadel. It stands on the foothills of the Muqattam, and it was to the Citadel that the centre of government was now transferred. The centre of gravity had moved from the Fatimid city. The old palaces fell into ruin and new buildings arose on their sites. Only a few fragments of their carved woodwork have survived.

Saladin and his successors, who ruled until 1250, brought further changes to Islamic architecture in Egypt. The college-mosque (madrasa) made its appearance, and with it a cruciform plan in both mosque and madrasa. The pepper-pot minaret and the use of stalactite ornament came into use, as did the lavish use of squinch arches and the external ornamentation of the dome.

Under Mameluke rule, which was uninterrupted up to the Ottoman conquest in 1517, commercial prosperity led to further expansion of Cairo, south, west and north. Beyond the northern gates of Al-Qahira there grew up a new suburb. Much survives from Mameluke times—tomb-mosques, college-mosques, schools, inns, public fountains.

Indeed much of the unique beauty of Cairo's architecture is due to the Mamelukes. But of their luxurious palaces we have nothing except some huge walls from Bishtak's palace, a fine gateway from the Yeshbek's mansion next to Sultan Hasan's imposing mosque and the better preserved mansion of the Emir (known as Beyt-el-Cadi). Their sumptuous beauty is something that we can but dimly imagine from the descriptions of travellers and the reare and delicate objects that adorn our museums.

We can still see traces of the exquisite mushrabiyah latticework that embellished the Mameluke palaces. Even today, some markets are shaded by matting or wooden roofs much as they were in those far off times. But the luxurious palaces and mansions, the public baths and gardens, the pleasure kiosks and belvederes, the streets and inns that were the meeting-places of the world, live on only in the pages of the historian Maqrizi.

Under the Mamelukes, Cairo was for two and a half centuries the richest, the fairest and the most populous city of Islam. Its mosques and other buildings testify to the taste and public spirit of its rulers. The variety and subtlety of the architecture is extraordinary.

The 13th, 14th and 15th centuries all have their characteristic master-pieces. From Kalaun, whose period saw the end of the Crusaders, to Qait-Bay and Al-Ghuri, who saw the Ottoman menace about to overwhelm Egypt at the same time that the Portuguese were cutting the vital trade-routes to India and the Far East, one lovely building succeeded another. The façades, the minarets and the interiors grew in delicacy and imagina-tive enterprise.

One particular masterpiece is outstanding because it is quite unlike any other—the college-mosque of Sultan Hasan which was built 1356-1359. Its stones were taken from the Pyramids, and it is perhaps not too fanciful to suppose that something of its uniquely massive and monumental character is due to that inspiration. Its walls rise to a great height and are crowned by a magnificent cornice as splendid in conception as Michelangelo's on the Palazzo Farnese in Rome.

Everywhere the impression is made by size if not by detail. The soaring portal rises the whole height of the building. The interior court is sur-rounded by four noble arches. The whole was once adorned with the finest of craftsmanship in bronze and enamelled glass, some of which can be seen in the Museum of Islamic Art, while its bronze-plated door now beautifies the Muayyad mosque beside the Bab Zuwayla gate.

Arab travellers and writers vied with each other in their accounts of this gracious city. Ibn Battuta, the Marco Polo of Islam, described it in the most glowing terms in 1326. In 1383, Ibn Khaldun the historian, who ended his days in Cairo, called it "the metropolis of the universe, garden of the world, throne of royalty, a city adorned with palaces and mansions, convents, mon-asteries and colleges, and illuminated by the stars of erudition in a paradise so bounteously watered by the Nile that the earth seems here to offer its fruits to men as gifts and salutations."

During this whole period Cairo was the heart of Islam and of Islamic civilization. Baghdad was captured and sacked by the Mongols in 1258 and never recovered its former splendour. Cairo welcomed its refugees. Only Mameluke Egypt in the whole Middle East was able to resist the onslaught of the Mongols. Three times they were driven back and defeated. Egypt's prosperity, indeed, was only the greater because of them. It was the greater, too, because much of its trade passed on to the steadily growing markets of Europe.

The craftsmen of Cairo reached new levels of perfection during this period, and much of their metal, wood and glass work has survived in the mosques themselves and in Cairo's museums. Moreover, the skyline of the city is a symphony of domes and minarets in which architects and craftsmen joined in creating one of the most beautiful cities man has made.

Joseph Gobineau, the 19th century French traveller, wrote: "In Cairo the memory of the Mamelukes dominates everything, so much did they do, so many solid and beautiful monuments did they create. Only they could carve in stone the world of arabesques which adorns with such splendour the buildings of all Asia. Though slaves only yesterday, the Mamelukes, once they laid their sabres down and possessed the authority to rule, seemed no longer capable of anything trivial. Everything that they built is without equal among Muslim architecture in the rest of the world."

With the Ottoman conquest in 1517 a gradual decay set in. Trade with the East steadily diminished. Nevertheless, these centuries are not entirely without importance in the adornment of Cairo. Neither taste nor skill were what they had once been. Yet, in the years up to the beginning of the 19th century, many buildings were added to Cairo that are still a delight to behold.

In 1798, with the appearance of Napoleon, the power politics and new techniques of Europe exploded upon Egypt. Willy-nilly Egypt was dragged into the modern world. The changes have been as tremendous as they have been rapid.

Walking along the Nile or through the streets of the modern city with its skyscrapers and broad avenues, the visitor may not always be aware how old a city Cairo really is until, looking to the west, he sees the ancient pyramids, or to the east the proud citadel of Saladin.

But in the streets of the older city the past is never absent. Cairo, like so many other places in the Nile Valley, is like a book whose pages are of stone inscribed with clear records of man's endless endeavour. Each of them invites the passerby to wonder and to seek to learn the nature of his fellow men in other times and places. In few cities will such an effort be more rewarding than it is in Cairo.

25.
Medieval Arab Medicine

During the medieval period, the Arabic civilization was a center of culture and science. Not the least of its achievements were the great strides made in medical theory and practice. At this period in history the Arabs were probably the most advanced practitioners of medicine in the world.*

INQUIRY: What influence might the rise of Islam have had in the development of Arabic culture? The Roman Empire continued in Byzantium for many centuries after the Western Empire had fallen. Why did the Arabs, rather than the Byzantines, make important scientific advances? Can you argue that the rise and decline of cultural centers occurs in cycles, moving from place to place?

It was one of the striking characteristics of the medieval Arab civilization that it attracted and encompassed people of many races and

---

*Cellestine Ware, "Medieval Arab Medicine: Rationality in an Age of Faith," THE ARAB WORLD, Vol. VIII, No. 2 (February 1967), pp. 10-13.

creeds: Persians, Syrians and Egyptians, Muslims, Christians and Jews. Citizens of the Arab Empire, they identified themselves with the Arab-Islamic civilization, and it was the Arabic language, with its rich resources, flexibility and pithiness, that made them exponents of that civilization.

Between the 8th and 12th centuries, Arabic was as much the universal language of culture, diplomacy and the sciences as Latin was throughout the Middle Ages. To read Aristotle, use medical terms, solve a mathematical problem or write a learned discourse, it was necessary to know Arabic. Hence, references to Arab medicine do not necessarily indicate that all its practitioners were Arabs.

The culture and civilization of the ancient world lay dormant after the fall of the Roman Empire until the Arabs brought the knowledge of the past back to Europe through the lost link of Greek civilization. Western Europe had lost most of its scientific knowledge before the fall of the Roman Empire, and the Byzantines were not greatly interested in this heritage from the past. Only in Arab countries was there deep interest in scientific problems; only in Arab countries were scientists encouraged and supported by rulers. An avid interest in science overrode all religions and racial prejudices. Christian doctors, such as the renowned Jurjis ibn-Bakhtishu (d. ca. 771), attended the caliphs as court physicians, while Jews wrote some of the most important Arab scientific and philosophical treatises.

The process of the revitalization of culture and science started at Damascus, where the early caliphs, the Omayyads, reinstated the court poets, reviving the classical Arabic poetry of the tribal bards and the practice of patronizing scholars and wise men. The Arabic language became the medium of official transactions. By the middle of the eighth century, a vast world of Egyptians, Syrians, Persians, Greeks, Berbers and Spaniards were versed in Arabic. Many of these peoples adopted Arabic names and customs, and a feeling of cultural association with things Arab arose.

* * *

Because of the many creative scholars and intellectuals using it, Arabic eventually became the medium for fresh and original work in science and especially in medicine. This happened because the Arabs had preserved the observations and theories of the Greeks, and of a large part of the heritage of antiquity. Moreover, they had added many facts of their own to the wealth of the past. With their conquest of the Fertile Crescent, the Arabs had become custodians of the great treasure that was the intellectual legacy of Greece. Damascus, Edessa, Alexandria and Antioch were all centers of Hellenism at the time that the Arabs conquered them.

* * *

The basis of Arab medicine was the legacy of the ancient Greeks, and that legacy was unknown to Europe until it became available in Arabic translations, with the commentaries of Arab scholars. The transmission of Greek knowledge was thus the first contribution of the Arabs to European medicine. Between 750 and 900, the Arabs discovered, translated and commented upon, and assimilated the Greek heritage in nearly all branches of the sciences.

* * *

Arab medicine, most remarkably in the Middle Ages, was characterized by the philanthropy that is one of the essential doctrines of Islam. For example, Muslim medical foundations throughout the Arab Empire included lazar houses, where lepers were cared for. Muslim rulers interested themselves in the health and welfare of their subjects. As early as 707, the first great hospital was founded in the Islamic world. It was followed at the turn of the ninth century by the one founded by Caliph Harun al-Rashid in Baghdad, and Cairo got its first hospital in 872.

Such an interest in public hygiene was unknown in the rest of the world at this time. An approximation of a rural health service was organized in tenth-century Baghdad when, on the orders of a *vizir*, a staff of physicians was sent from place to place carrying drugs and administering relief to the sick. Other physicians made daily visits to the jails. Traveling clinics appeared in the 11th century.

The great hospital that the Mamluk Sultan Qalawun opened in Cairo in 1283 is a fine example of the development of public health care in the Arab world. Upon entering the hospital, patients were isolated for study and treatment. Afterward, the hospital separated the patients into wards according to sex and disease. There were separate wards for dysentery, fevers, diseases of eyes and bone diseases.

Up until the time of the Arab reorganization of medical practice, only those people who could pay received medical attention. In fact, since the time of Hippocrates, there had been no readily available medical service for the poor. But Islam teaches that the welfare of the poor is equal in importance to that of the rich. In Arab hospitals, famous doctors, including some Christians and Jews, attended patients regardless of their incomes. These doctors also made house calls, distributing food and medicine.

* * *

Medieval Arab medicine was also characterized by a high degree of organization not present in the Christian world. Following a case of malpractice, a distinguished physician was appointed in 931 by the caliph to examine all practicing physicians and to grant certificates only to those who satisfied standardized requirements.

A third characteristic of Arab medicine in this period was a deep interest in psychology. The study of psychical diseases and of the psychical means of combating them appealed strongly to the Arab imagination. For example, they had carefully studied the effects of music and had even introduced its use for therapeutic purposes in some of their hospitals. Arab psychotherapy is illustrated by anecdotes relating remarkable cures effected by purely psychological means by al-Razi, Ibn Sina and others. Jibril ibn-Bakhtishu (d. ca. 830) is said to have successfully treated a favorite slave of Harun al-Rashid for hysterical paralysis by pretending to disrobe her in public.

* * *

Arab pharmacies became gathering places for physicians, scholars and prominent public figures. In the pharmacies, sitting below the shelves of precious ceramic and majolica medicinal jars, these people exchanged views and data, commented on events and passed information. Doctors checked on the newest drugs and reported on the clinical results of those already in use. Actual cultural centers, the pharmacies were the places from which many new words and expressions entered the Arabic language, to be incorporated later into the European-language groups. Algebra, arsenal, alfalfa, alkali, zero and zenith are examples of such words.

26.
The Scientific Legacy of Iran

The Persians (modern Iranians) have long been known for their contributions to the cultural heritage of the world in the fields of poetry, rug making, bronzeware, silverware, and goldware. They were also the heirs and transmitters of Greek and Indian scientific knowledge. They synthesized this knowledge, added to it, and passed it along to other people in the east and west. The following reading discusses accomplishments of the Persians.*

INQUIRY: How did the geographic location of Iran make it a logical place for the blending of Greek and Indian knowledge? With modern methods of transportation and rapid communication, does the geographic location of a country still play such an important part in its development?

Modern man lives longer, in an environment increasingly understood, thanks in part to the labours of the turbaned scientists of medieval Iran. The munificence of their scientific contribution indeed constitutes a mystery which some writers have tried to unlock by invoking race.

Climate and geography are more rational keys. Iran's climate, torrid in summer and in winter icy, at once stimulated and hardened its sons. Its position as the mountainous turntable linking India, Central Asia, the Middle East and Europe entailed invasions by Greeks and Arabs from the west, by Seljuk Turks and Mongols from the east; its people were thus thrown in vivid contact with varied traditions.

Iran's own periods of attack, when Persian armies moved east or west, played their role in mixing a distinctive blend of humanism, speculation and practicality.

Since the Iranian character typically expressed itself in what was useful as well as beautiful, an appropriate point at which to begin a discussion of Iranian science is medicine, a science which modern man can acclaim without reserve.

Iran's medical tradition was already old when the conquests of Alexander the Great linked the Persian plateau with the Hellenistic world. Persian

---

*"The Scientific Legacy of Iran" by Desmond Stewart. Reprinted from the UNESCO COURIER (October 1971).

myth ascribed the introduction of the healer's art to Jamshid, the Legendary fourth hero and king of Iran.

Much later, the greatest Persian historian of medicine, Ibn abi Usaybl'a believed that so noble a science must, like the Koran, have derived from a revelation of God. With such antecedents, the Iranian physician, usually deriving from a noble family, enjoyed a loftier social position than his confreres in the Greco-Roman world.

At the same time the Iranian openness to outside ideas made such historical kings as Cyrus and Darius proud to have imported Egyptian physicians (particularly those specialized in the eye diseases common in the dusty east) to their imperial courts.

The same tolerant spirit was later instrumental in making Sassanian Iran the originator of medical schools. For in the three centuries between the conversion of Constantine and the rise of Islam the Byzantine persecution of heretics and pagans drove east, first the Nestorian scholar-physicians of Syria and then the last Neo-Platonists of Greece.

All found a hospitable welcome across the border in south-west Iran. One town, Jundishapur near the modern Ahwaz, housed a cosmopolitan university with a scientific bent, which reached its zenith under the 6th century Nushirván, known to the west as Khosroes the Great.

Most of the instruction in its medical school was in Syriac, but its scholars also spoke Sanskrit, Greek and early Persian. Besides translating Greek and Indian authors with an Elizabethan fervour, the university produced original works. One Sassanian product was a thirty-volume encyclopaedia dealing with all then known poisons and their properties.

The Arab invaders of the 7th century respected Jundishapur, but their effect on the Persian language was similar to that of William the Conqueror on Anglo-Saxon. Henceforth for some centuries Arabic was the *lingua franca* of all educated Moslems.

Yet far from restricting Persian genius, the Islamic conquest gave it a 'global village' in which to act. Iranian science particularly flourished once the Abbasids moved the caliphal capital from Damascus, close to the Hellenistic Mediterranean, to the site of Baghdad but a day's journey from the Iranian foothills.

Baghdad was founded in the mid-8th century by Mansur, a belligerent caliph tormented by indigestion. Cured by the chief physician of Jundishapur (he was summoned to the capital when Mansur's own doctors admitted themselves defeated) the Caliph encouraged an immigration of Iranian scholars from Jundishapur, which increased under his descendents.

The Abbasids lasted in Iran from the 8th Century until their final defeat by the Mongols in 1258. They not only married Iranian women but sponsored a cultural compost in which Arabs largely dominated the studies linked to language—theology, poetry and law—while conceding to foreigners, and in particular Persians, what we would think of as the physical or practical sciences, but which they termed "foreign".

Mansur's great-grandson, al-Ma'mun (whose mother and wife were both Persians) founded a "House of Wisdom" comparable in cultural importance to the Mouselon founded by the Ptolemies in Alexandria more than a thousand years before. Appropriately, much of the science of Alexandria was translated into Arabic, often via Cyriac, for Ma'mun's *Dar al-Hikmah* (DAR).

The institution's most famous head was Hunayn ibn Ishaq, born at Hira in Iraq. Hunayn pursued the medical manuscripts of Galen with a lover's passion. He was never satisfied until he had obtained the most accurate text available even if this necessitated exhausting Middle Eastern journeys.

Other scholars translated the geometry of Euclid, the Almagest of Ptolemy as well as the works of Archimedes, the greatest practical scientist of the ancient world. It was not until the late 12th century, three hundred years after Hunayn's death, that these works were restored to Europe through the activities of men such as Gerard of Cremons working in Toledo at the frontiers of Christian and Moslem Spain.

But Iranian physicians who made original contributions both in the diagnosis of diseases (one was whooping cough) and, most important of all, in treatment. The modern hospital is the lineal descendant of the Islamic *maristan*, seen by Crusaders in the Holy Land and visitors to Egypt. It derived from Persia.

The greatest medieval clinician was Razi, born near the modern Teheran in 865. Living seven centuries before the theory of bacteria was first proposed, Razi intuitively discerned the importance of hygiene. When commissioned to choose a site for a new hospital in Baghdad, he hung joints of fresh meat at different points round the sprawling, circular city. Where the meat took longest to decay, there he sited his *maristan*.

Razi was a prolific writer, devoting half of a reputed output of 200 works to medicine. His description of smallpox, clearly differentiating it from other disruptive ailments, enabled later physicians both to diagnose the dread disease and predict its course. His treatment was based on good diet and nursing amidst clean and comfortable surroundings. It has not been radically bettered since.

Razi's most important legacy was his monumental encyclopaedia. In this he recorded both the extensive clinical observations which earned him his honorific title "The Experienced" and the collected knowledge of Greek, Syrian, Arab, Hindu and Persian doctors.

An equally versatile physician was Ibn Sina (980-1037), the Latin version of whose name, Avicenna, testifies to a reputation that leapt the frontiers of faith. It leapt centuries too. His *Canon of Medicine*, a million-word encyclopaedia dealing with the treatment of disease in all its aspects, was the standard teaching text in European universities from its translation into Latin in the 12th century until the medical revolution of the 17th: a record for durability beaten only by Galen.

Razi and Ibn Sina, though living in successive centuries, shared the polymathic approach to learning characteristic of medieval Islam. The hundred or so works of Razi which were not concerned with medicine dealt with alchemy, theology and astronomy; Ibn Sina's non-medical writings treated philosophy (in which he synthesized Aristotle, Neo-Platonism and Islamic theology), astronomy and mathematics. As an interesting innovation, he wrote some of his books in Persian.

Persia was an important transmission point for Hindu numerals in their voyage to the west. They were first publicized to the Islamic world in the first half of the 9th century by al-Khwarizmi, whose name shows that he comes from a city just south of the Aral Sea. Astronomer and geographer, he also served as court mathematician to al-Ma'mun, the founder of the House of Wisdom. . . .

Yet there was again a surprising time lag in the European acceptance of Hindu numerals. Not until 1202 did Fibonacci (an Italian with North African contacts) publish his oddly named "Book of the Abacus"; this for the first time explained the numeral system which would, slowly, put paid to the abacus.

Because the Hindu numerals, as modified by Moslems, had by this time been used by the Arabs of North Africa for some centuries, Europeans designated them as Arabic; others at the time called them "Jewish", since the Jews were far in advance of their Christian contemporaries in knowledge of Islamic science.

Along with Hindu numerals, the Hindu decimal system and the concept of zero were transmitted through Iranian mathematicians such as al-Khwarizmi. The Arabic word for an empty object, *sifr*, was translated as *zephyrum* in Latin. Besides using its Italian derivative *zero*, English keeps the original *sifr* as "cipher".

The use of Hindu numerals and the zero made it possible for al-Khwarizmi to compose the first easily intelligible text-book on Algebra. The word probably derives from al-Khwarizmi's *Ketab al-Jabra wa'l-Muqabala*, which can be roughly paraphrased as "the art of bringing together unknowns to make a known quantity."

Al-Khwarizmi took three centuries to reach the west. In 1126 Adelard of Bath, an Englishman who had travelled as far as the Middle East, translated his astronomical tables, which included tables of sines, into Latin. Adelard thus introduced trigonometry to Europe. Algebra was introduced through two versions published in the same year, 1145. The first was made by John of Chester (who had lived in Spain), the second by Plato of Tivoli from the Hebrew translation of his friend, Abraham bar Hiyya.

Sometimes an Iranian scientist would be his own transmitter. An outstanding example was ai-Buruni, roughly a contemporary of Ibn Sina's and born, like the inventor of algebra, in Khwarizm. As well as being a mathematician, astronomer, encyclopaedist and rational philosopher (he argued that the exclamation "Allah knows best!" was no excuse for ignorance), al-Buruni was also a geographer who travelled widely.

He translated works of Sanskrit science into Arabic and at the same time transmitted Moslem knowledge to Hindus. Since he had himself accurately determined latitudes and longitudes and discussed the rotation of the earth on its axis, he had much to transmit.

One of the last great Iranian mathematicians died just a few years before Adelard of Bath published his translation of al-Khwarizmi. Omar Khayyam (whose quatrains, woven into a connected poem, *The Rubaiyat*, would burst into the western consciousness with Edward Fitzgerald's 19th century translation) was renowned in his own time (mid 11th to early 12th century) as a mathematician.

"His Algebra," George Sarton, the historian of science, has written, "contains geometric and algebraic solutions of the second degree; an admirable classification of equations, including the cubic; a systematic attempt to solve them all, and partial geometric solutions of most of them." His calendar was probably more accurate than the Gregorian.

The Mongol invasions shook the foundations of Islamic culture. But it is worth remembering one positive result of their rule over Iran. Islamic theologians, like their Christian equivalents, had condemned the practice of dissecting corpses, and so made difficult the serious study of anatomy.

In the 9th century, it is true, Yuhanna ibn Masawayh had kept monkeys for the purpose of dissection. But systematic study only became possible under the relative freedom of Mongol rule. The result was the 1396 *Illustrated Anatomy* of Mansur bin Faqih Ilysas. Its illustrations (also abhorrent to the theologically strict) were another result of Mongol tolerance.

After the Mongol invasion, the study of mathematics and astrology continued to flourish, as shown by the construction of observatories at Maragheh and Samarkand.

Limits of space have restricted this discussion to peaks, at the expense of the lesser heights and valleys without which no mountain range exists. Not only have such branches of science as optics been passed over but important names have been omitted. Nor has the question whether some of the scientists were wholly Iranian been discussed.

This suggests indeed a final tribute. To these Iranian physicians, chemists and astronomers the question of their national origin would have seemed irrelevant in a discussion of their work.

Ignorant of racism, though aware of their particularity, they stood as conscious heirs of Greek and Hindu forerunners. They saw their contributions as part of an interwoven human endeavour which had its source in God, the origin of knowledge, and its purpose as the service of his creation, mankind.

27.
Ibn Khaldun: Historian

The fourteenth-century Muslim scholar and eminent historian, Ibn Khaldun, was far ahead of his time in his attempt to treat history as the proper object of a special science. The following selection, describing significant events in his life, helps to explain his historical perspective.*

INQUIRY: The author states: "only the study of man in all his innumerable activities can reveal the true significance of so-called historical events." If this is true, is there any subject that you study which is not related to history? How many arguments can you find for and against this theory?

When he was seventeen Khaldun lost both his parents and many of his teachers in the Black Death. Three years later he was given an important appointment at the court of the Hafsid rulers of Tunis, but he pre-

*Barbara Bray, "Ibn Khaldun: Man of History." Reprinted from the UNESCO COURIER (June 1966).

ferred to leave this and travel gradually westward across North Africa, pursuing his studies, and passing the years from 1354 to 1363 at the Merinid court in Fez. The development of a Moslem scholar was regarded as a life-long process, and the list Khaldun scrupulously gives of the men at whose feet he sat is a formidable one. But in giving the list he was also presenting his academic credentials, and these show that his interests were wide, not to say encyclopedic, rather than specialized. This is an important factor in relation to his life-work.

North Africa was at this time divided into three warring kingdoms, each of whose ruling dynasties was torn by internal dissension. It was here, taking an active part in politics, that Khaldun got most of his material for his theories about the rise and fall of nations. In such an atmosphere it was hard for someone like him to keep out of hot water. At one period he found himself on the wrong side and spent nearly two years in prison, and later he found it prudent to cross over into Spain, to Granada. But in 1365 he was back in North Africa, in Bougie, as Prime Minister.

The nine years from 1365 onwards were the most precarious in all Khaldun's hazardous career. It was no easy matter to be always on the right side in the complicated and fluid chaos that North Africa had become. . . . Khaldun's services as judge, civil servant and politican were always in demand, and all his attempts to escape to scholarly peace and quiet were foiled by suspicious rivals and demanding princes. Finally, however, he managed to get permission from the ruler of Tunis to install himself and his family in a secluded pavilion at Ibn Salamah in the province of Oran. Here he spent over three years in comfort and solitude, and started to write his great history of the world.

"I completed the Introduction in the remarkable manner to which I was inspired by that retreat, with words and ideas pouring into my head like cream into a churn," he recorded.

It took him three more years, and the opportunity to consult the libraries in Tunis, before he completed his enormous work, and even after that he was always correcting it and bringing it up to date.

The first volume consists of the *Muqaddimah* or *Prolegomena*, which is probably Khaldun's greatest claim to lasting fame, containing as it does the first real theory of history. Volumes II to VII deal with the events of the pre-Islamic world and Arab and Eastern Moslem history. But Volumes VIII and IX deal with the history of the Moslem West. Much of the material is based on first-hand knowledge, and it remains our most important source for Northwest African and Berber history.

* * *

As far as we know Khaldun was the first historian ever to regard history not as a chronicle of more or less fortuitous events, but as a continuous, collective and organic movement governed by hidden but discernible laws. Moreover, he identified the science of history with the science of civilization as a whole, and realized that only a study of man in all his innumerable activities can reveal the true significance of so-called historical events, so that the study of those events may act as a practical guide to the statesman.

So Khaldun, considering everything as a function of man and his social organization, takes all knowledge as his province, and re-evaluates every aspect of the highly developed civilization in which he lived.

The element of intellectual orthodoxy from which he could hardly be expected to escape only serves to emphasize the real originality and breadth of his mind. Picturesque and touching as it is, then, it is no wonder that Professor Arnold Toynbee, one of the most celebrated historians of our own day, cites this fourteenth-century Arab as the inspiration of his own monumental work, and salutes Ibn Khaldun as the founder of the science of history.

28.
Gilgamesh

Gilgamesh is a remarkable epic which was begun by the ancient Sumerians. Succeeding generations of Babylonians contributed to its composition. Scholars believe that by B.C. 2000 the *Gilgamesh* epic had substantially the same content and form it possesses today. According to tradition, Gilgamesh was the son of a goddess and a mortal man and was endowed with more than ordinary strength. He performed many super-human feats and won many victories, but always there was frustration at his limitations. His victories were never really complete, and he never escaped the inevitability of death. He shared with all humans the imperfections of humanity. Because the epic of Gilgamesh is essentially a story of human life, it is as fresh and valid today as it was in the ancient Middle East. The following reading is a description of the history of the *Gilgamesh* and an excerpt from the epic itself.*

INQUIRY: Why do you think the composers of the epic made Gilgamesh half-god and half-mortal? What qualities does this give to his character? Do modern authors use this technique by painting their characters "larger than life" or giving them extraordinary qualities of character? Are stories about very ordinary people usually exciting?

In the nineteenth century a number of clay tablets on which the *Gilgamesh* was written were discovered in the temple library and palace ruins in Nineveh, once the capital of the ancient Assyrian empire, by two Englishmen, Austen H. Layard and George Smith, both of the British Museum, and the Turkish archaeologist Hormuzd Rassam. In 1872 George Smith delivered a paper before the Society of Biblical Archaeology which included his partial translation of the cuneiform texts along with an analysis of several episodes of the *Gilgamesh* epic, especially the narrative of the flood. The reaction to this "new" material, with its far-reaching implications for Biblical history in particular, was one of great enthusiasm and curiosity, and spurred others on to further explorations in the ruins of Mesopotamia's ancient cities and to an expanded study of cuneiform inscriptions in general.

This spreading interest and scholarly research led to the discovery of other tablets and fragments concerning Gilgamesh and his adventures, and, eventually, to a continuing appearance of annotated editions and translations in European languages which, if not yet definitive, have been based on steadily accumulated knowledge.

The epic, in at least a number of its stories, was Sumerian in origin and was later added to and unified as a national epic by the Semitic Babylonians, heirs in the Tigris and Euphrates valley to Sumerian culture and civilization. The tablets from Nineveh, which constitute the largest extant portion of the epic, date from the seventh century B.C. and were probably collected at that time from much older Sumerian texts and translated into the contemporary Akkadian Semitic language at the request of King Assur-banipal for his palace library. From the existence of tablets found elsewhere in Mesopotamia and in parts of Anatolia in the older Sumerian language and in Hurrian and Hittite translations, each depicting portions of the *Gilgamesh* story, scholars have been able to date the epic at about 2000 B.C. However, the most recent scholarship believes that all extant portions are copies of still older originals deriving from a much earlier time, and moves the epic's creation back as far as the third millennium B.C. It is virtually impossible to determine when the material was first written down, let alone when it originated orally or how long it existed in an oral tradition. Rather it can be assumed, from the materials handed down from succeeding ancient peoples and languages, that it was not composed all of a piece and at one time but was added to gradually and varied by many tellers.

The *Gilgamesh* is unquestionably older than either the Bible or the Homeric epics; it predates the latter by at least a millennium and a half. The discovery of a fragment of the epic in Palestine suggests the existence of a version known to early Biblical authors. Though we cannot know how widespread knowledge of the *Gilgamesh* epic was in the ancient Near East, we can say with surety that it is one of man's oldest and most enduring stories.

As to Gilgamesh's historical identify, the Sumerian king list establishes a Gilgamesh as fifth in line of the First Dynasty of kingship of Uruk following the great flood recorded in the epic, placing him approximately in the latter half of the third millennium. He was supposed to have reigned a hundred and twenty-six years. He was known as the builder of the wall of Uruk, and his mother was said to be the goddess Ninsun, wife of a god named Lugalbanda, who however was not his father. His real father was, according to the king list, a high priest of Kullab, a district of Uruk, from whom he derived his mortality. These few details are drawn from the epic itself and from a number of Sumerian inscriptions listing kings, rulers, and princes. Gilgamesh's name was associated with many stories and fabulous adventures as well as with the experience of grief.

Probably there was a Gilgamesh and he was endowed by tradition with a superhuman mind and spirit. Perhaps if we were to doubt the reality of Gilgamesh because of the folkloric hyperbole about him and his emotions as drawn in the epic, we would have to doubt whatever it is in ourselves that identifies with him—or, for that matter, with the Biblical Job or the Shakespearean King Lear. Looked at in this light, the *Gilgamesh* has survived in our world because a constellation of our emotions is reflected in it. We could almost say that anything so profoundly human as the image of Gilgamesh was bound to reappear, yet we are still surprised to learn that one of the very oldest stories of man is so inherently contemporary.

It is the epic's emotional power which assures its place in world literature. The *Gilgamesh* is a kind of touchstone to other, more "modern" works. It reminds us of many stories of the Bible and episodes in Homer that are part of our cultural consciousness: of the universality of the friendship theme and of the experience of heartbreak over loss, of Achilles' reaction to the death of his friend Patroklos in the *Iliad*, or even the depth of Lear's grief at his daughter Cordelia's death.

Certain structural formulas in the *Gilgamesh*, of recurring themes and architecturally sequential episodes (which in this instance scholars have had to reconstruct tentatively), places it in the company of the *Odyssey* and the *Iliad*. Though non-oral epics like Virgil's *Aeneid* and Dante's *Divine Comedy* have an intellectual coherence to us which it lacks, its intense and sophisticated grouping of stories around the theme of death and the human challenge to death gives it an elemental coherence which cements and heightens its otherwise rambling structure, and places it in their magnificent company.

What such "classics" do for us by the very rarity of their occurrence is to give us what W. H. Auden once called "a high holiday." They show us, by their concentration on a great soul's struggles to reach a passionately desired goal, our essential human drama raised beyond our everyday recurring life. They show rather than preach how acceptance of limitations in the face of metaphysical facts actually occurs. They begin in a world where impending doom is felt as a living force and gain their momentum as the individual feels power to challenge that force and finally to obtain the spiritual courage to accept the danger of being crushed by its superior power and mystery. In the *Gilgamesh*, particularly, life is very serious and "the world is redundant with life," as Thorkild Jacobsen says in *Before Philosophy*. This seriousness is expressed in the total oneness of people, animals, plants, dreams, and what to us would seem dead things, stones and gates. Professor Jacobsen has described the inner action of the *Gilgamesh* as "a revolt against death." This revolt, in a universe once thought to be ordered and good, grows from a belief that death is evil and a crime against humanity's growing consciousness of human rights. Hence, it is an outcry on behalf of life and its injured kindredness.

The survival of this great poem in the world must relate partly to the survival of the same vision in a few people in our world, people who may not consciously believe in personified gods nor have culturally handed-down names to give them, but who through pain of loss may have made this "revolt," or through compassion may understand how intimately related they really are to all the creatures and things of the universe. In an age in which we consume and are consumed by a superfluity of one-dimensional images, this poem calls us to be profound. And in a war age in which all kindredness is overlooked and life and substance are destroyed indiscriminately, this very old story reminds us what human history, our destiny, and we ourselves really are.

At the end of the epic a serpent finds the power to renew its life, which a man had sought and finally lost. In a very large sense, the reader must decide what that ending means for himself. It is an inward problem. One can view the loss tragically, as perhaps the Sumerians and Babylonians did, and despair in this as the ultimate fate of man. Or one can believe and hope that for the human being the experience of wisdom is more important than possession of even the highest things.

There are extant tablets which can be viewed as sequels to this ending. One depicts the death and regal funeral of an old and honored Gilgamesh. Another contains a Semitic version of part of a Sumerian story relating additional experiences of Gilgamesh and Enkidu.[1] This tablet tells of a sacred tree which Gilgamesh has lost to the Underworld. Enkidu, the one who brings back lost things, offers to go down into the Underworld and retrieve it for his friend. The story includes a long lamentation by Gilgamesh over the loss of the tree and an illusion of Enkidu's physical return after death has devoured him in the Underworld. From this latter illusion the tablet has been called "Enkidu's Resurrection."

The following lines are based on the last portion of Gilgamesh and Enkidu's illusory reunion and, as an interpretation only, represent an afterglimpse into Gilgamesh's state of grief.

One night in his loneliness
Gilgamesh pleaded with Ea
To open the door of death
To let the spirit of Enkidu
Return to him a moment.

For a moment, by Ea's grace,
The two friends met
And almost touched. Gilgamesh
Could not hold back his tears
And begged him to come near.

You have wept enough for me,
Enkidu said.
A friend is not allowed to add to grief.
I have grown weak, devoured
In my flesh. You must not try to touch me.

I need to see you are the same,
Cried Gilgamesh.

---

[1]See Alexander Heidel, *The Gilgamesh Epic and Old Testament Parallels*, 2d ed. (Chicago, 1949) and Samuel N. Kramer, *Sumerian Mythology* (Philadelphia, 1944).

I am afraid that you will hate
The friendship we have known
Because it did not last forever.

Gilgamesh, not listening, reached out
To the image of his friend
Trying to see what Ea veiled.

If you are my friend, Enkidu said,
You must not touch me. Treat me
As Utnapishtim treated you.

He gave me a plant
He knew that I would lose!
He gave you the wisdom of your soul.

Gilgamesh stood still
In the darkness, conscious
Of the silence once again
And of the shadows which had held for years
The absence of his friend,
As if just drawn
From recollection
Back to life.

The noises in his city
And laughter from outside
Had reached his ears, or was
It just another dream
Or Ea's further tricks of grace?

No matter which, he went outside
To see himself
Just what had drawn them
Into celebration.

29.
Middle East Tales

Like people everywhere, the people of the Middle East have always delighted in well-told tales. Sometimes these folk tales have morals. The following two stories catch the spirit of a typical Middle Eastern story.*

INQUIRY: Are these Middle Eastern tales moralistic in tone or do they seem to be intended chiefly as humor? Are there any American folk stories you know that are similar in any way to these stories?

JAMIL AND THE BEGGARS

. . . a young man from Damascus named Jamil . . . was walking along the street when he saw three blind beggars drawing into a side alley, holding hands and pulling each other out of the street. He followed them to see what they were doing. Each of them had the day's takings of little coins, and they were pooling the money into one bag, and then passing it from hand to hand, so that each one could heft it and estimate their common gain. Jamil quietly thrust his hand into the group, the bag was placed in it, and he stole silently away with it.

Well, Jamil and his wife thought that it was a great joke, which others might enjoy. So that night they gave a dinner party and invited a number of guests, including the three blind beggars, for it was thought a very charitable thing to include beggars at a dinner. Jamil told the story to all the guests, and there was a general laugh at the expense of the beggars. When the party was over, they found that it was raining, so Jamil invited the beggars to spend the night and gave them a separate room to themselves. He said that he would give them back their bag of coins in the morning.

Jamil's wife was going around the house, doing the last minute things after a party, and she heard the beggars arguing in their room. So she went to the door and listened. They were discussing how much they would claim that they had in the bag, for of course Jamil would be shamed if he did not return everything. One proposed that they would say three hundred pieces; another said five hundred; and the third insisted that they would claim seven hundred from a day's taking by three men.

Well, Jamil's wife was furious. She went to her husband, and she cried out: "I hope they all die, those miserable beggars!" Jamil tried to hush her up, because that is a terrible wish to make about guests in one's house, but she repeated it again and then a third time, a curse against people taken into her own home. Finally he quieted her, and they went to bed.

The next morning they went to call the beggars, and there was no answer. When they opened the door, there were the three beggars stretched out stiff and cold. The wife's curse had been all too effective. Well, Jamil and his wife were in a terrible fix: people would think that they murdered these three poor old men for their little bag of money. But Jamil thought a while, and then he said: "Never mind, I'll fix it up."

So he persuaded his old blind father to go across town and visit his

*John A. Wilson, "Would You Believe . . ." CHICAGO TODAY, Vol. 4, No. 1 (Winter 1967), pp. 32-33; "The Tales of Hoca," TURKISH DIGEST, Vol. 3, No. 1 (January 15, 1967), p. 13.

daughter, who lived on the other side of Damascus. Then he went to the mosque and found there the old beggars who bury the dead. He said to them: "My poor old blind father has died. Will you bury him?" They said they would, but he said: "It's rather a delicate situation. You see, my father and my wife always quarreled, and he swore that after his death he would come back and annoy her. Will you bury him so that he won't come back?" They assured Jamil that they would, but he persisted: "If he should carry out his threat and come back, will you bury him again?" The beggars agreed that they would bury him again. The beggars agreed that they would bury the old man as many times as he returned.

Well then, they went to Jamil's house, found the corpse, took it across town to the cemetery, and buried it. When they came back for their pay, Jamil met them with a long face: "He's done it! He's carried out his threat and has come back!" Sure enough, when they went into the house, they found a corpse, so they took it out and buried it. When they came back Jamil was still distressed: "I'm sorry, but the old man has come back again. I'll pay you men a little extra, but, please, this time bury him deeper." So they took a body out the third time and buried it.

When the beggars came back from the third funeral they said, "This time he hasn't come back, has he?" And Jamil agreed that he had not returned at all this time. "No," said the beggars, "we were sure that he wouldn't come back this time. While we were coming back from burying him the third time, just beside the Turkish bath, we met an old blind man coming this way. So we stopped him and asked him if he were your father, and he said that he was. This was right where they have the big furnace to heat the water for the bath. So we picked him up and pushed him into the furnace!"

THE TALES OF HOCA

Timur Leng took Hoca into the field where his archers were practising.

"I am very good at archery," boasted Hoca, and suddenly found himself faced with the task of proving it, for Timur commanded him to take his bow and loose some arrows at the target.

Then Hoca took the bow and shot an arrow.

It flew past the target several feet wide.

"That is how the cadi shoots," he said.

His second shot also went wide.

"That is how the mayor shoots," he said.

His third shot, by a fluke, scored a bull's-eye.

"And that is how Nasreddin Hoca shoots!" he said proudly.

30.
Persian Tales

The Middle East has been an original source for many folk tales, some of which have come to be known throughout the world. In the following tale, the wife is admonished never to trust completely the friendly face of a stranger, but to put her trust in a wise husband.*

INQUIRY: Why does the storyteller give the details of the blizzard and the buying of the dog, cat and pigeon before Malek finds the ring? How did Malek know that the other prince kept the ring in his mouth?

KING SOLOMON'S RING

There once lived an old man who had a son called Malek Ebrahim. When he felt the time was drawing near for him to die, he called his son and gave him the three hundred tomans that he had put by, and said that this was all he could save during his lifetime. "Take these three hundred tomans my son," said the old man, "and start a new life for yourself. See that you do not waste the money, for if you do, you will have no one to help you out. Go to the man who sells advice and buy some useful ideas from him."

Malek Ebrahim took the money from his father and went to the advice-giver and gave him one hundred tomans and asked for advice. The wise old man in return advised Malek not to travel abroad when the weather was bad. This he said and said no more.

When Malek handed out another hundred tomans and asked for some more advice, the old man opened his mouth a second time and said: "Whenever you see a pigeon or a cat or a hound for sale, buy it and look after it with the greatest of care."

Malek Ebrahim, however, felt that he was in need of further advice so he took out the remaining hundred tomans and put the money into the hands of the old man and asked for more advice. The old man looked gravely at the young boy before him and said: "Do not pass on the advice that I have given you to anybody else nor ever allow any strange women into your family."

Malek had enough advice by now. Moreover, he had no money left to buy more so having packed up his things he left in search of his fortune. While traveling with a group of companions, the sky one day became overcast and it looked as though a storm were brewing. Malek immediately called to mind the old man's advice that he should not stir abroad when the weather was bad. So he stayed indoors and watched the pouring rain and listened to the howling winds refusing to continue his journey. But his companions merely laughed at him and leaving him behind proceeded on their way. Soon, however, they were caught in a terrible blizzard, and not being able to find their way back, froze to death in the wilderness.

When Malek passed by that way a few days later he found the bodies of his companions and buried them and while doing so some money dropped out of the dead men's pockets. This he kept for himself. As he went along on his way he came to a place where a dog, a cat and a pigeon were offered

---

*"Persian Tales," *Iran Today*, 1963. Reprinted by permission.

for sale. Malek at once remembered the second piece of advice the wise old man had given him saying that he should buy animals like these if he found they were being sold. So he bought the animals with the money he had collected from the dead men's pockets.

Soon, however, these pets of his began to cry out for food but Malek found he had no more money left with which he could buy food for them. Weary and hungry he fell asleep.

He hadn't slept long when he had a strange dream. He thought he saw a ring lying beside him a ring with magical powers. This was the ring which King Solomon himself was said to have worn and now whoever was lucky enough to find it and put it on his little finger and turn it round three times he could wish for anything that his heart desired and his wish would be granted

Malek awoke and the dream being fresh in his mind he looked around for the magic ring and there indeed he found a ring lying right beside him. He picked it up and slipped it round his little finger and turned it round three times and wished he could have some steaming hot, delicious and filling food for himself and his pets. Presto, his wish was granted and before him spread a white cloth on the grass and on it dishes of hot food appeared from nowhere. Malek set apart the pets' food for them then he himself fell to eating and soon had his fill.

Malek then turned the ring round again three times and asked for a palace made of bricks of gold and silver. Immediately a palace arose before his wondering eyes, a palace such as no one had ever before set eyes upon. Then having asked for the best furnishings for this palace he housed his pets in a comfortable corner of the great gardens, then he himself settled down to live there.

One day as he was riding through the forest surrounding his palace he came upon another beautiful house. As he looked admiringly at the dwelling a beautiful damsel came out to water the plants. She was more beautiful than the sun and stars and no sooner had Malek Ebrahim set eyes on her than he fell head over heels in love with her.

Having inquired who she was he found out that she was the King's daughter living in her Summer Palace. So he sent a messenger to her father, the King, to ask for her hand in marriage. But the King would hear none of it for he did not know the young man's parentage. But the King's minister told him that if he could have a palace made of gold and silver bricks and fifty camels laden with jewels and fine things as presents for the bride, the King might reconsider his decision.

For Malek Ebrahim of course this was not difficult to provide. When the fifty camels laden with jewelry and fine things reached the gateway of the Royal Palace where the King lived, the King could no longer bring himself to refuse his daughter's hand in marriage to this fine suitor. So a grand wedding was celebrated and the bride and bridegroom went to live in the Palace made of gold and silver.

But one day another prince—a mean, covetous man—rode by the Palace where they lived and having been astonished at the sight of such luxurious Palace, all made of gold and silver he wondered whom it could belong to. The prince sent a cunning old woman to find out. This old crone made her way into the Palace right up to the princess' chambers. She was so sweet to the young bride and so helpful that the princess began to trust the old woman entirely.

One day the old woman asked the princess how it had been possible for the young prince, her husband, to have built a palace as wonderful as this. The princess, of course, didn't know so she asked her husband to tell her how he had come to have this palace built. But the young man remembered the advice-giver's words and would not let his wife into the secret. The young woman however started weeping and said he did not love or trust her or else he would share his secret with her who was, after all, his wife.

Malek Ebrahim not being able to bear the sight of his wife in tears told her about King Solomon's ring and the wonders it had wrought. After her husband left her the princess went to the old woman and thinking she was a real friend let her into the secret.

The old woman then begged of the princess to get hold of the ring and pass it on to her so that she could ask for some of the things she wanted very badly herself. The princess did as she was told and having taken off the ring from her husband's finger as he lay asleep she passed it on to the old woman.

No sooner had the old woman worn the magic ring round her finger and turned it round three times than there was no sign left of the palace or its attendants.

When Malek Ebrahim awoke from sleep he found himself lying on the grass with his three pets by his side. Immediately he realized what had happened. Some one must have got hold of the magic ring he thought and true enough it was no longer on his finger.

He sat up and thought hard for a while then he wrote a note to his wife and having tucked it among the feathers of the pigeon set it off flying towards the palace of the prince who had stolen the ring from him. The pigeon alighted on the balcony of the palace and went up to the princess who on stroking his wings discovered the note that her husband had sent her. She quickly read the note and acted according to the directions given by him. She was to tickle the other prince's nose with a feather as he lay asleep then he would sneeze out the ring which he kept in his mouth for safety.

This the princess did and as the ring flew out she quickly picked it up and put it on her finger and having turned it round three times wished for her own palace and to be back with her husband and his household. And so it came to pass.

When she was back in her own palace with her husband he told her why this misfortune had befallen them. It was because they had let in a strange woman into their household. Then he advised her never again to trust people who wandered in. She should always take the advice of her own husband he said and not listen to the requests of other people no matter how friendly they may appear to be. This advice the princess took seriously and never again did she do anything without first letting her husband know of it. So never again could anyone trick them out of the possession of the ring and so, they lived ever after in their golden palace.

31.
Homage to the Artist

Admiration and respect for the artist have been a dominant attitude in the Middle East. Mustafa Kemal Atatürk, founder of modern Turkey, proclaimed this feeling in the following words.*

INQUIRY: Compare Atatürk's attitude toward artists with attitudes in your own society. Why is it difficult to judge whether or not an artist has ability?

"You can be a member of the Parliament, you can be a Minister. . . . You can even be the President but you cannot easily become an artist. Therefore give these young artists their due credit."

*TURKISH DIGEST, Vol. 3, No. 11 (November 15, 1967), p. 4.

32.
Persian Miniature Paintings

Mani (216-276 A.D.) founder of the Manichaean religion is said to have introduced miniature painting into Persia. He learned the art in China. The Persians adapted this art to their own special genius and environment and made it into something distinctly Persian. This is another instance of cultural diffusion resulting in the development of new techniques, new styles, and greater heights of accomplishments.*

INQUIRY: How do paintings from past times give us information about the life of people in those times? What forms of art do we have today that might be of interest to historians five hundred years in the future?

Persian miniature painting is a form of art that is widely sought after by museums, art galleries and private collectors with an eye for the beautiful, the exquisite, the exotic and the unusual.

This form of painting was introduced into Iran, according to many historians, by Mani, the Persian sage, sometimes called the last of the

*"Persian Miniature Paintings," *Iran Today*, 1963. Reprinted by permission.

Gnostics, who founded in the third century A.D. a religion which for a while seemed a serious rival to Christianity.

From the 4th century to the 12th century it spread widely and with great rapidity in the west as far as France and in the east to the China coast, where Marco Polo found Manichaean communities at the end of the 13th century.

Mani was born of Persian parents about 216 A.D. in Babylonia and piously reared in a local . . . sect. In his 12th year he underwent a religious experience and 12 years later he experienced another as a result of which he went forth to preach a new religion—a mixture of Zoroastrianism and Christianity.

Mani had spent some time in China where he had mastered the Chinese art of miniature painting and manuscript illumination. He illuminated his own manuscripts. His paintings were so exquisitely beautiful, so brilliantly executed and so life-like that many took them as a manifestation of divine guidance. That, it seems, was the beginning of miniature painting in Iran.

Chinese influence was strongly felt in Persian paintings and hence in other decorative arts, especially through the introduction of the lotus, the dragon, the phoenix and cloud symbols.

Toward the middle of the 14th century there was an upsurge in miniature painting in Iran. Already it had developed into a distinctive Persian art with an ultimate amalgamation of Persian, Mesopotamian and Chinese elements, the strong Persian motives gradually pushing the other two into insignificance.

Persian miniature painting found perfect expression in the volumes turned out for the Timurids by the court ateliers in Shiraz and Herat. The art culminated at the end of the 15th century in the person of Behzad, the best known Persian miniature painter.

The miniatures usually illustrate epic or romantic poems. Iranian miniaturists use bright opaque colors in small units which cover the whole picture area and often part of the margin.

On account of the perspective the scenes appear to be observed from a high point, and with the horizon toward the extreme upper edge of the picture. The figures are diminutive, puppet-like and without three-dimensional quality. Manuscripts usually have elaborately decorated frontispieces in which gold and blue (derived from lapis lazuli) are the main colors.

The art of painting—as well as other decorative arts—thrived during the Safavid period (1502-1736). The greatest King of that illustrious dynasty was Shah Abbas I (1586-1628) who used an ambitious scheme of city planning in his capital, Isfahan, which through his efforts became one of the truly beautiful cities of his day.

Miniature painting kept on a high level until the end of the reign of Shah Abbas the Great. Realistic scenes and detached paintings with one or two figures became the fashion. The rich coloristic style started deteriorating from the middle of the 16th century and even the best artists started working in a style in which only the main figure is coloristically treated. Many of them worked in a pure linear style of calligraphic quality.

Reflecting the political situation, all arts, including miniature painting, suffered a continuous decline from about 1700 on. Nowadays Iranian artists, led by the Government through its Fine Arts Department, try to emulate the glories of past ages by reviving their arts, especially those of the 16th and 17th centuries.

This movement was started some thirty years ago by Reza Shah the Great, generally known as the founder of modern Iran.

The best-known Iranian miniaturist and the undisputed master of this fine Iranian art is Hosein Behzad who is known not only in his own country but by art lovers all over the world.

society

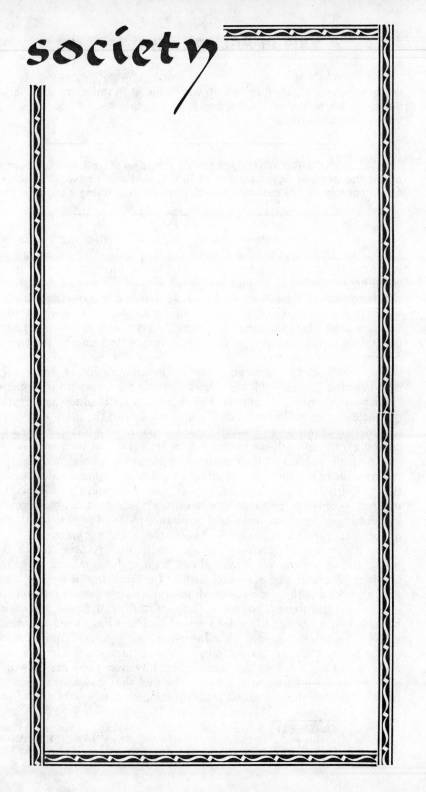

33.
A Villa in Ancient Egypt

The rich lived the good life in ancient Egypt. This is evident in the grandeur of their villas, which were placed in the midst of lovely gardens. In the following article, the reader is taken on a tour of a typical ancient Egyptian villa.*

INQUIRY: What does the description of an Egyptian house tell about the ancient Egyptian way of life? Could you arrive at conclusions about contemporary customs and culture by describing a modern house?

. . . We shall inspect the villa of a well-to-do citizen of the Eighteenth Dynasty, the kind of villa which would incorporate many of the features of royal palaces on the one hand, and most of those of humbler dwellings on the other. From the point of view of design and construction it will be typical of the houses of the whole dynastic epoch—for in a country where the conservative habit of mind was innate, where technical innovation was rare, and where the range of raw materials remained constant from one generation to the next, one would not often expect to stumble on a mansion of revolutionary aspect.

Our villa could be situated either in the countryside—among, say, the bird-haunted marshes of the Delta—or in the prosperous upper-class suburbs of Thebes or Memphis. The rule in the cities of ancient Egypt was the same as that in the cities of the modern world: the poor were huddled together in cramped and overcrowded conditions, while the wealthy occupied choice and self-contained houses that stand in their own well-kept gardens, surrounded by leafy palms and protected by high walls.

The walls of the surrounding villas are plain and square, but we note that the wall of the one which we are now to visit has a prettily scalloped top to it. There is only one entrance into the compound: stout double doors set in a charming gateway shaped like a miniature pylon. The wooden doors are opened for us as we approach by two of the estate workmen.

We are immediately struck by the 'contemporary' appearance of the house and its setting. We catch sight of it through an arching pergola with climbing plants trained across its latticed timbers. On our right is a square pool sprinkled with fat pink water-lilies, on whose waxen fronds butterflies are sunning themselves; and on our left are neatly dug flower and vegetable beds. If it was not for the palm trees, the garden has the appearance of a well-tended country garden on a July afternoon in the south of England.

The house itself has the straight lines and 'functional' air of a modern building. In deference to local conditions, however, there are no windows, only grilles set high up in the walls. The fact that it is a wide, one-storey building with a slightly raised centre section that serves as a roof garden

---

*Reprinted by permission of B. T. Batsford, Ltd., London British Commonwealth, and of G. P. Putnam's Sons from EVERYDAY LIFE IN ANCIENT EGYPT by Jon Manchip White. Text copyright © 1963 by Jon Manchip White.

heightens the impression that it is the kind of villa that Mies van der Rohe, Gropius or Maxwell Fry might have devised for a wealthy client. It is a large, dignified house, completely square in plan, with a frontage of approximately 100 feet. We calculate that it could easily contain 25-30 rooms.

When we come nearer, we can see that it stands on a kind of solid brick platform; the front door is four to five feet above ground level, and is reached by means of a gently inclined ramp. The ramp leads us to a small projecting vestibule, through which we see the inside of the house. On entering, we find ourselves in a spacious oblong hall, embellished with a double row of columns. This is the hall in which guests and visitors gather before moving into the inner apartment. The columns are of wood, and stand on round stone bases. Wood is a scarce commodity in Egypt, a land in which trees are scanty, and to which cedars of Lebanon were floated down from Byblos in the time of the Second Dynasty, and probably even earlier. Much of the wood which we shall see in the villa, whether used for the columns or elsewhere, is actually a veneer or facing covering the prosaic mud-brick beneath. Wood and stone were very scarce materials, rendered even more so by the cost and difficulty of transport. It is therefore not surprising that, when an Egyptian moved house, or built himself another one, he packed up his wooden columns, wooden panels and bits of stone, and took them with him with the rest of his furniture.

We pass from the pillared hall into the central portion of the house. Here we find ourselves in a lofty, regular apartment, at least 30 feet square, which obviously serves as the main drawing-room and dining-room combined. It has painted wooden pillars, four in number, taller than the pillars in the hall: which explains why, viewed from the garden, the central part of the house stands higher than the rest of it. Between the pillars, on a raised hearth, is the small brazier which holds the fire that will be needed in the wintertime; and facing the hearth, occupying almost the whole of one wall and projecting nearly as far into the room as one of the pairs of pillars, is a low raised platform. Here the owner of the house, his family and his guests will recline on rugs and cushions to talk, take their ease and eat their meals. Near at hand a second smaller platform is furnished with an array of handsomely-decorated water-jars and pots of unguent. It is the custom for people to pour a little water over their hands before they eat, or to anoint themselves before worshipping at the small concealed shrine that is probably somewhere near at hand. The shrine will be hidden in an alcove, or a room opening off the living-room, or even in the living-room itself—perhaps behind the closed doors of what looks like a decorated cupboard on the far wall.

In this central living-room, as in the hypostyle halls of the temples, the windows are small and situated high up in the wall. In a country where the sunlight is as merciless as it is in Egypt there is no call for the picture-windows which are popular in countries like our own, where the light is weak. It is also no accident that the much-used living-room is situated in the middle of the house, enclosed on all sides by a mass of smaller rooms. It thus receives the benefit of retaining the heat in the winter and repelling it in summer.

In the third and rearmost portion of the house, behind the living-room, is the private suite of the master of the house and his family. If we peep into the various rooms, we will see the main bedroom; the robing-room; the bathroom with its neatly devised pipes and plumbing, its modern-looking lavatory seat, and the stone slab on which one lies to be washed and massaged; and the office in which the master transacts the business of the estate. Well away from the family bedrooms and the office are located the well-stocked larders and the rooms allotted to the house-servants. The kitchen, with its over-pervasive odours, is sensibly situated in a separate building away from the house. Most of the servants do not live in the house itself, but in huts in the compound near the stables and workshops in which they do their work or the sheds in which they store their tools. Here too the head steward and favoured retainers will have neat little houses of their own.

We also note, in this rear portion of the house, the back door with its own ramp, and the interior ramp that leads upward to the roof, where the family can retire to sun themselves. Some villas have attractive upper loggias or balconies that make them pleasant spots to sit and look over the wall and across the surrounding countryside. Some houses possess two or even three storeys, although the upper rooms generally possess low ceilings and are somewhat poky. And not all villas, by the way, possess ramps, but have proper staircases, The Egyptians were not, however, much given to staircases, although there was a handsome example in the South Temple at Deir el-Ballas.

We might comment, as we leave the house, that it was not as lavishly decorated as we might have expected. This was an unusually spacious house, belonging to a highly-regarded member of the community, yet it possessed none of the lively frescoes which are so much in evidence in the temples and palaces. The talents of the best artists, of course, have been commandeered for the buildings of royalty, and are not usually available for the dwellings of lesser citizens. The main decoration in our villa has consisted of patterned friezes near the top of the rooms; dados of beautifully wrought faience tiles or of wood panelling; and painted ceilings in the principal hall and central living-room. In the main bedroom was a gay 12-foot-long mural depicting geese and ducks in flight, painted on plaster and mounted in a wooden frame on the wall behind the bed. Otherwise the walls were covered with a flat wash in a tasteful pastel shade. Here again we are reminded that the thoughts and energies of the individual Egyptian, particularly an Egyptian of high rank, are focused on the palaces and temples in which they perform their daily duties.

Outside, we just have time for a stroll around the garden. Tucked away in one corner is a charming little building, resembling a summerhouse, that immediately catches our eye. It has a portico with twin pillars, behind which is a door. The building is a shrine, although the devotees also like to loll in the shade of the two old tamarisk trees that flank it when, on limpid summer evenings, they come to pour over the image a leisurely libation of milk or honey.

The garden, arranged around its central pool, is mature and immaculate, the product of an age-long tradition of horticulture. There are willows, sycamores, pomegranates, figs, persea trees and two varieties of palm trees, all disposed with the eye to effect of a skilled gardener. Choice specimen trees and bushes have been planted in pots of painted earthenware. There is a row of beehives and, behind the house, a congregation of tall conical structures with square holes near the top and bottom which are the granaries in which the wheat and barley are stored under the watchful supervision of the overseer.

The gleaming villa, dreaming in the sun, with its range of trim white-washed outbuildings and its lovingly tended garden, makes a perfect picture of peace and wellbeing. It is little wonder that the people who lived and laboured in such surroundings should have represented so mild and tolerant a civilisation.

34.
Food and Drink in Old Egypt

The ancient Egyptians ate well when they could afford it. They had many varieties of food—meats, vegetables, fruits—and they savored them all. They had poultry farms where they force-fed their fowl and they had carefully recorded vintage wines which they aged in special jars. They also imported wines and other edibles. Most Egyptians, especially the poor, drank beer, and they consumed enormous quantities of fish. They had many varieties of bread and cake made from wheat and barley.*

INQUIRY: How does a knowledge of what people eat and drink reveal information about their style of life? Could you draw conclusions about the agriculture, climate, and economy of another country if you knew the diet of its people?

. . . The ancient Egyptians were notable trenchermen, and where the good things of the table were concerned, no less than with their other creature comforts, their standard of living was probably higher than it is now.

The ornamental trees around the villa bore several excellent varieties of figs and dates; and from the beginning of the New Kingdom apples and pomegranates were also cultivated. Coconuts were a luxury, while the more luscious fruits such as oranges and lemons, pears and peaches, cherries and bananas, were not grown at all during pharaonic times. . . . It [fruit] was generously supplemented by the universal presence of the grape. In every garden a profusion of vines would be curled up poles, twined round pergolas, or trained against the wall of the house or compound. . . .

The selection of vegetables was much wider than that of fruits. There was a plentiful supply of onions, leeks, beans, garlic, lentils, chick peas, radishes, spinach, turnips, carrots and lettuces. The most suitable of these were sun-dried and stored for the winter. Cucumbers and several sorts of melons,

---

*Reprinted by permission of B. T. Batsford, Ltd., London British Commonwealth, and of G. P. Putnam's Sons from EVERYDAY LIFE IN ANCIENT EGYPT by Jon Manchip White. Text copyright © 1963 by Jon Manchip White.

pumpkins and gourds were also grown in large quantities. Many of these vegetables, particularly the fleshy and ever-popular lettuce, were probably served with oil, vinegar and salt, and there is no doubt that the art of dressing a salad is an ancient one. Edible oils were derived principally from the *bak* tree, at least until the late advent of the olive, while castor oil was extracted for medicinal purposes and for lighting lamps.

Meat was consumed in vast quantities. The staple meat was beef, and herds of oxen, derived from the long-horned wild ox, were specially fattened for slaughter. As in our own day, the fillet was regarded as the choicest cut. Smaller quantities of lamb and goat, the former derived from the reddish-coated Mouflon, were also eaten; and there was a limited demand for the more exotic meats that occasionally reached the larder as a result of the exertions of the huntsmen. These included the oryx, the gazelle and the ibex. Next to beef, by far the most common meats were those of birds. The wild-fowling industry was large and highly organised, particularly in the marshes of the Delta. Ducks, wild geese, pigeons, quails and cranes were trapped in enormous numbers, and flocks of domestic geese and ducks were hand-reared for the table. The taste for fish was more equivocal. Either fresh-run, or dried and salted, they were eaten in shoals by the poorer classes, for whom it was in the nature of a steady diet; and there were permanent fishing fleets at work in the Delta and the Fayûm. But in primitive communities fish are often the subject of complicated tabus, and even in dynastic times certain kinds of fish seem to have been prohibited in some of the nomes or provinces. The fact that the fish was sacred to the malignant god Seth may have induced people to treat it with caution. That tabus of this kind operated is indicated by the fact that the flesh of the pig was eschewed as totally unclean.

In the matter of drink the ancient Egyptian had a wide choice. We have already mentioned the cultivation of the grape, from which many varieties of wine were made. The Egyptians certainly liked their wines sweet, and on occasion spiced it with honey and the juice of dates or pomegranates. Wine jars with individual clay sealings occur as early as the First Dynasty. In Old Kingdom times the wines were predominantly red, but from the Middle Kingdom onwards white wine became increasingly popular. Certain vineyards acquired an enviable reputation, the wine of Buto in the Delta being particularly coveted. The inscriptions on one series of jars reads 'excellent wine of the king's growth'. Cellars of wine were systematically laid down, with the vintages carefully recorded, and the tall, tapering amphorae were racked and re-racked to improve the quality. To provide variety for their practised palates, the Egyptians also imported wine from Syria and Palestine, and later from Greece.

It is probable, of course, that wine-drinking was mainly confined to the upper classes, for the chief national drink was beer. This was manufactured by lightly baking thick loaves of wheat and barley, then allowing them to ferment in vats of water. Milk was highly prized, and so were its derivatives, butter and cheese. Eggs, on the other hand, were plentiful in view of the hundreds of thousands of birds which were caught or bred (although our own domestic hen was not known).

Wheat and barley provided the baker with the raw materials for the countless varieties of bread and cake in which he specialised. The wheat was not the widely distributed bread wheat . . . but the more restricted variety known as emmer . . .; and the Egyptian baker worked wonders with it. With a loaf of fragrantly-smelling bread, fresh from the mould, a jug of beer and an onion, the Egyptian peasant in his reed hut could munch away with as much contentment as the nobleman enjoying an elaborate repast in his pillared hall.

Like the peasant reclining on his mat of rushes, the nobleman seated on his carved chair ate his food with his fingers. On chairs nearby sat his principal male guests, while the less important diners, the women and lesser members of the family, occupied cushions on the floor. Even pharaoh, with the little tables in front of him laden with beautifully wrought jars and vessels, would gnaw at a beef-bone while his queen picked daintily on the wing of a plover. Between courses the servants brought forward basin and ewer for the diners to rinse their hands. By our own standards, to eat with one's fingers seems uncouth and unsophisticated; but one ought perhaps to remind oneself that knives, forks and napkin-rings may not, after all, be a very profound index of a civilised condition.

* * *

35.
Dress, Make Up, and Furniture in Old Egypt

Much can be learned about the cultural life of a people by reading about such everyday matters as how they dress, what furniture they use, and how they adorn their bodies. There are, of course, many differences between the ancient Egyptians and modern peoples, but there are also many fundamental similarities.*

INQUIRY: What modern garments are used only by people in certain professions and for ceremonial or special occasions? Do modern cosmetics seem to have the same purpose as those used by ancient Egyptians? Would modern magazine advertisements give a more detailed or less detailed view of our lives to future historians than Egyptian paintings give to us? How accurate would that picture be?

THE HOME

Dress

From the frescoes in the palaces and temples, and from the murals and furnishings in the tombs, we can see that the typical Egyptian

---

*Reprinted by permission of B. T. Batsford, Ltd., London British Commonwealth, and of G. P. Putnam's Sons from EVERYDAY LIFE IN ANCIENT EGYPT by Jon Manchip White. Text copyright © 1963 by Jon Manchip White.

tended to be slender, broad-shouldered, long in the hands and feet, and with muscular arms and legs. He was usually square-chinned and wide-lipped, with a broad forehead, large eyes, and a nose that was often somewhat short and hooked. Whether he was partly Asian by descent and lived in Lower Egypt, or partly African and lived in Upper Egypt, in both cases he appears to have been brown-haired and light-skinned. From time to time the frescoes and monuments depict the invaders who ruled Egypt at various periods, and we can discern that they possessed widely different physical characteristics: the negroid features of the pharaohs who hailed from Nubia or the Nubian border; the bedouin appearance of the Libyan kings; the semitic features of the nomadic Hyksôs or 'Shepherd Kings.' The Egyptians, like most shut-away people . . . were always fascinated and diverted by foreigners, and any trader or traveller who went down into Egypt was sure to have his portrait painted in meticulous and often malicious detail. Foreigners, like dwarfs, animals and acrobats, provided the painter with a welcome change from the routine repertoire of native subjects.

The Egyptian artists also recorded the entire range of Egyptian fashions in dress, from the *haute couture* of the court to the loincloths of the peasants. Prominent as the focal point of every important mural, or the centrepiece of every group of statues, would be the figure of the king. In the plain-living and high-thinking days of the Old Kingdom, the king is depicted with his body bare to the waist: a king who is ready for work, despising effeminate frills. Even in the self-indulgent days of the New Kingdom and Late Dynastic Period, the royal limbs are wrapped in the simple role which was the common apparel. What really marks him off from the subjects who surround him is, as you will see from the paintings, the distinctive crown that he wears. If you look through a picture book of Egyptian art, you will see that in actual fact the pharaoh is endowed with a wide variety of crowns, and you may be able to count as many as 20 in all. One of those most frequently portrayed is the White Crown of Upper Egypt—a tall, graceful, conical hat of stiff white linen. The White Crown is also the crown invariably worn by the god Osiris, the King of the Dead, who owed his status as a national god chiefly to the hold which his cult had come to exercise over the minds of the citizens of Upper Egypt. In addition to the White Crown, the king also possessed a Red Crown, which was the national diadem of Lower Egypt. This was a round flat-topped cap with a tall upright projection rising from the back and ornamented in front with a curving strip of metal ribbon.

On ceremonial occasions the king wore the Red or White Crown, according to whether his dynasty hailed from Lower or Upper Egypt; and sometimes the two individual crowns were combined together into the rather ungainly Double Crown, symbolising the union of the two kingdoms. At other times the king's headdress was garnished with two stiff feathers, to signify his relationship with the falcon-god Horus, with the goddess of Truth, Maat, and also with a potent primitive chieftain called Anzti whose form and functions had been taken over by Osiris. And for very important festivals, when the king wished to place special emphasis on his kinship with Osiris or with the ram-headed god Khnum, who had fashioned the world upon a potter's wheel, he would wear an extraordinary and intricate headdress known as the *atef*-crown. . . . It consisted of the

White Crown flanked by sweeping feathers, ram's horns and sacred snakes, the whole besprinkled with discs representing the sun. It is hardly surprising that in the New Kingdom this bewildering collection of royal headgear fell largely into abeyance, and gave way to the practical and attractive *khepresh* or Blue Crown. The Blue Crown, made of moulded leather studded with gold sequins, was encircled by the uraeus or sacred cobra. The cobra was the emblem of the goddess Buto, patroness of Lower Egypt, who in turn was associated with the vulture-goddess Nekhebet, patroness of Upper Egypt. Thus the cobra, with its encircling wings and disc of the sun, represented the indissoluble union of pharaoh and his two kingdoms.

Among the other regalia which are depicted by the artist, one ought to mention the false beard. Unlike their neighbours to the north-east, the Egyptians do not appear to have possessed the hairiness of Esau and his brothers; they were not remarkable for body hair and prided themselves on being clean-shaven, using well-made razors which they kept in neat leather cases. Thus the plaited beard, which could be attached to the sidepieces of royal wig or crown, was actually an artificial one. Its purpose is obscure. It may have been meant to remind pharaoh and his people of what they believed to be their racial origins in the interior of Africa, where the Nile flowed out of the land of Punt whose inhabitants were heavily bearded. But there is no mystery about those other symbols of royal power: the crook and the flail. These warned the king's subjects that, although from earliest nomadic days he had been an ever-watchful shepherd who had guided and guarded them, he could also if need be goad them forward by means of a less tender instrument.

The head-covering which we most often associate with pharaoh is, perhaps, the *nems*. This was the simple striped cloth placed round the wig, brought across the forehead and behind the ears, and tied at the base of the neck, leaving two lappets to fall forward over the shoulders on to the chest. Wigs were in fact a very prominent article of upper-class apparel. In that hot climate, men generally wore their hair cropped short, or even shaved close, although on important occasions they would don elaborately curled, combed and pomaded wigs. In any event, they took a pride in seeing that their hair was carefully groomed and combed, in marked contrast to the hair of the unkempt and barbarous foreigner. Generally women too embellished their already complicated coiffures with wigs of ample dimensions, adorning them still further with hair-bands of beads or metal, or tasselled ribbons and tiaras. The wigs of both sexes are frequently seen with a white conical object perched on top of them. We are not altogether sure what this was, but it may have been a cone of solidified wax, impregnated with perfume. As the banquet or gala evening progressed, the cone would melt, and the face and neck of the wearer was laved with a delicious scent.

In a country where the majority of the inhabitants wore loincloths, or simply walked about naked, the basic garment of the upper classes was the robe of white linen. Men wore it over their loincloth and women over their petticoat or shift. The peasants did not even possess a robe for high days and festivals, and wore the loincloth winter as well as summer. Mostly they went naked, like their wives, sisters and daughters who worked in the great houses. The Egyptian attitude towards nudity was unselfconscious.

Princes ran around naked like the children of the poor, and noblemen would wear the simple loincloth in the privacy of their houses or when pottering around their estates.

For ceremonial purposes, the most coveted garb was a robe of "fine linen of Upper Egypt." The robes of a rich man or woman would be tailored with the deceptive simplicity which a length of plain material can assume in the hands of a Paris dressmaker, and the Egyptians were experts in the arts of pleating, crimping, gauffering, and making accordion pleats. A man's robe was supported by means of shoulder-straps, or worn loose and tied at the waist with a wide strip of linen. The belt was knotted in such a way as to give the effect of a kind of triangular apron or kilt. Sometimes women would prefer, instead of a sari-like robe, a tight-fitting linen tunic resembling a modern summer frock.

Although the robe itself was artless and functional in style, it was enhanced by a colorful array of necklaces and bracelets. The Egyptians, rich or poor, men as well as women, were passionately addicted to jewellery. They were also a remarkably superstitious race, and the jewels that swayed and clinked on their necks and wrists served a magical as well as an aesthetic purpose. Pretty rings and brooches were not only nice to look at, but if they were modelled in the form of the life-giving *ankh* or the eye of Horus they could also prevent sickness and ward off the evil eye.

Egyptian jewellers were marvellously skilled. Their best work has never been surpassed, and their masterpieces bear comparison with those of a Cellini or a Fabergé. The goldsmiths of the Twelfth Dynasty, for example, achieved an extraordinary standard of excellence, and their pieces are marked by a delicacy and refinement which is sometimes lacking in the jewels that reflected the later, heavier taste of the Empire. We are fortunate in possessing a number of wonderful specimens of their handiwork. From the tomb of the Princess Khnumet, the daughter of Amenemhat II, who was buried beside her father's pyramid at Dahshur, was recovered a pair of delicate crowns, one of them a fairy-light circlet of gold, frothing with little cornelians and inlaid with turquoise. Also from Dahshur came the jewellery, contained originally in two ivory-inlaid caskets, which had belonged to Queen Merenit and Princess Sut-Hathor, who were buried near the pyramid of Sesostris III. The caskets contained no less than five magnificient pectorals or breast-ornaments, which had been presented to these favoured ladies by the pharaohs Sesostris II, Sesostris III and Amenemhat III, whose royal ciphers they bear. Another Egyptian princess, Sat-Hathor-Yunet, who was buried near her father's pyramid at Lahûn, was the child of the first of these kings. A pair of pectorals found in her grave bear the names of her father and of Amenemhat III; and in addition to the pectorals the grave yielded her charming little crown, ornamented with the uraeus, the two feathers, and dainty rosettes in the form of lotus-flowers.

Another common article of adornment which one sees in the tomb paintings is the bead collar. This was worn in the earliest times, and consisted of rows of tubular beads divided by bands of circular ones. The collar was normally at least three inches deep, but on occasion it became so broad that it covered the upper shoulders as if with a short cape. Many varied effects could be procured in the colour, arrangement, and stringing of the beads. The clasps were often elaborate, and the hawk-head of the

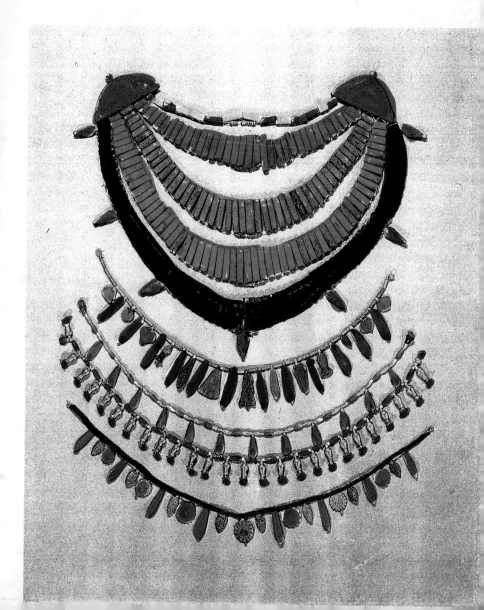

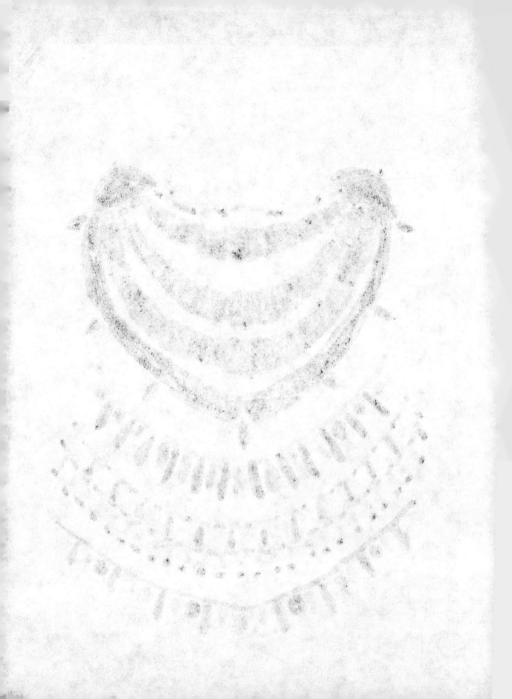

god Horus was a popular motif for the terminals. Jewelled bracelets were worn by both sexes, and on occasion the king sported a jewelled belt adorned with his personal cartouche or cipher. Women were fond of wearing bracelets around their upper arms, as well as round the wrists and ankles. Rings, of course, were universally favoured, while earrings were fastened to the perforated lobe of the ear by means of a plug, and were sometimes so large and heavy that the whole ear was pulled out of shape. It might be mentioned, in passing, that the precious and semi-precious stones which the Egyptians employed were, in alphabetical order: agate, amethyst, beryl, calcite, cornelian, chalcedony, coral, felspar, garnet, haematite, jade, jadeite, jasper, lapis lazuli, malachite, olivine, onyx, pearl, peridot, rock-crystal, sard, sardonyx and turquoise. Diamonds, opals, rubies and sapphires were unknown.

To complete their *ensemble*, Egyptians would wear sandals of leather or woven papyrus. The sandals were usually of traditional design, with one transverse and one longitudinal thong; but occasionally the longer thong would be curved back from the toes to fasten again at the instep, like pointed shoes in mediaeval Europe. The Egyptians were not a shoe conscious people, and except on polite and formal occasions even noblemen would go barefoot. On the famous slate palette depicting the first pharaoh, Narmer, the king is shown barefoot, while behind him his servant carries his sandals. It is doubtful whether a peasant ever owned a pair of sandals in his life. However, the Egyptians had to pay for this small freedom in the penalty of many painful kinds of foot ailment, as we know from the sections that discuss these particular afflictions in the great Hearst and Ebers Papyri.

The Egyptian woman in her full glory was an awe-inspiring spectacle: the triumph of art over nature. Nature indeed had dowered her with a rare beauty: but she still found it advantageous to add innumerable little touches. In ancient Egypt the cosmetics industry was as busy as in modern Europe or America. To begin her toilet, the Egyptian lady washed her body with that thoroughness which was a fetish in Egypt. For this purpose she used a special cleansing paste, and water that was purified by the addition of salts of natron. Then, after primping and frizzing her hair to her satisfaction, she picked up her round bronze mirror with the ebony handle and started to make up her face. This could be a lengthy business. In the British Museum you can see the wooden toilet-case of Tutu, the wife of the scribe Ani, which is typical of many another feminine "box of tricks." Its four compartments holds jars and phials containing salves and unguents; a little palette for mixing cosmetics and eyepaint; a piece of pumice stone for removing superfluous eyebrows or hair; an elbow cushion to sustain the weary arm during the course of the toilette; and an exquisite pair of pink boudoir slippers made of softest antelope leather.

When preparing to put on her "war-paint" for the evening, Tutu would first of all pay attention to the appearance of her eyes. The "doe-eyed" look or the almond-shaped eye was fashionable in Egypt. She would pluck out a few errant eyebrow hairs with her silver tweezers, then wet the tip of her finger or the end of a little brush and dip it in the bottle containing kohl. She would draw a thick ring round each eye, and apply more kohl to her eyelids. Until the close of the New Kingdom, kohl was manufactured from malachite, the green ore of copper; later galena, the grey ore of lead, was also widely used. When Tutu felt that her eyes were sufficiently mysterious and compelling, she would pour a little powdered red ochre on to her palette and rub it judiciously on to her lips and cheeks. Then she would tint her nails with henna, a dye which was in common use, as it still is today, for heightening the colour and lustre of the hair. She would also use a little henna to redden her palms and the soles of her feet. Finally she would dip a tiny spoon into an alabaster jar and anoint her skin with perfume. A large collection of subtly blended and matured perfumes was available to her. Lacking the isolates and synthetics which modern perfumiers employ as fixatives, the perfumes of Egypt were in reality scented oils. Ingredients included bitter almonds, cardamons, cinnamon, galbanum, frankincense, myrrh, sweet rush, castor oil and wine. There were many lotions for removing wrinkles and blemishes. These included preparations containing asses' milk, alabastron, natron and honey. A popular "mud-pack" treatment was based on powdered alum.

A special word ought to be said about the peculiar beauty of Egyptian toilet articles. The small personal chattels of the Egyptian man or woman were often of the most exquisite workmanship. The stone or alabaster jars and bowls which held the water for their ablutions were heirlooms, and were generally fashioned by the finest craftsmen. So were the miniature bottles, often of glass or gaily-patterned frit or faience, moulded in the entertaining shape of fishes or birds, which contained the powders and unguents. When one becomes jaded by the bulk of the pyramids and pylons, the petrified glades of the hypostyle halls, or the seemingly endless vistas of frescoes and friezes, it is always pleasant to turn to the little personal objects which the Egyptians carried about with them, or which littered their cupboards and dressing-tables. These would include their walking-sticks and riding-whips, their bows and boomerangs, their pins and combs and buttons. It is these tiny trifles, perhaps even more than the mighty monuments, that allow us to sense the true quality of their civilisation. Here there is none of that urge to impress that often induces a sensation of monotony; here the Egyptians reveal only their charm, their taste, their practicality, and their sense of humour. If one were a very wealthy man and were visited by the itch to collect, one could hardly do better than to collect, Egyptian salve-holders and perfume spoons. This small class of objects is a source of constant pleasure. If posterity only knew about the Egyptians from their surviving monuments, there would be some excuse for believing them to have been stiff and pompous. But the sight of these little intimate objects immediately redeems and humanises them.

Furniture

The tombs of Egypt have not only revealed to us how their owners looked and acted, but have also bequeathed to us the actual movables and furniture that once graced their houses. In 1925, for example, a discovery was made near the Great Pyramid which showed that 45 centuries ago the furniture makers of Egypt were masters of their craft. In a tomb-chamber beside the pyramid causeway, the famous Egyptologist Reisner had the good fortune to unearth the funeral cache of Snofru's wife, mother of the even greater pharaoh Cheops. For some mysterious reason the body of the queen, who was called Hetephras or Hetep-heres, was not present in the narrow tomb; but Reisner recovered the elegant suite of furniture which she had used when she was alive. By careful and skilful handling he was able to restore the dry and powdery timbers to the appearance which they had originally possessed. First he disentangled and re-erected the supports and uprights of the royal canopy, which the undertakers had dismantled; then he reassembled the queen's carrying chair; finally he put together her bedstead and head-rest, her two chairs, and the other items of furniture. The bed-canopy, a present from her husband, was cased in gold. From it hung mats or curtains to provide her with privacy, and perhaps to keep out noxious insects. This was a unique find: but the pattern of the smaller pieces demonstrated that the basic design of Egyptian furniture had been formed in the Old Kingdom and were not greatly altered thereafter—another instance of the Egyptians' innate conservatism. Of course, since the shape of the human frame remains constant, the number of variations which the furniture-maker can introduce is necessarily limited; yet there are fewer points of difference between the chairs and beds found in the tomb of Hetephras and the tomb of Tutankhamon, buried more than a thousand years later, than between modern English furniture and the designs of Chippendale or Hepplewhite.

* * *

36.
Songs of the Common People

Peasants in the Middle East today still sing work songs as they did in ancient times. The texts of the following songs were uncovered from an agricultural scene in an Eighteenth Dynasty (16th-14th centuries B.C.) tomb at el Kab.*

INQUIRY: What does this work song reveal about the ancient social organization of Egypt?

WORKERS IN THE FIELD

The Plowmen sing:
A good day—it is cool.
The cattle are pulling,
And the sky does according to our desire—
Let us work for the noble!

---

*ANCIENT NEAR EASTERN TEXTS RELATING TO OLD TESTAMENT, edited by James B. Pritchard 3rd. rev. edn, with Supplement (copyright © 1969 by Princeton University Press): "Songs of the Common People," in "Egyptian Secular Songs and Poems," transl. by John A. Wilson, p. 469. "Reprinted by permission of Princeton University Press."

The Reapers reply:
   The answering refrain which they say:
   This good day is come forth in the land;
   The north wind is come forth,
   And the sky does according to our desire—
   Let us work as our hearts may be bound!

The Thresher sings as he drives his cattle around and around to thresh out the grain:
   Thresh ye for yourselves, thresh ye for yourselves, O cattle!
   Thresh ye for yourselves, thresh ye for yourselves!
   Straw to eat, and barley for your masters—
   Let not your hearts be weary, for it is cool.

37.
Letter of Complaint

A few thousand years removed perhaps, but this letter from a Mesopotamian schoolboy would sound familiar to the parents of any child away at school today.*

INQUIRY: How do original sources, such as letters, give a picture of life in other times? Would it be possible to base the study of history solely on original sources? What would be the disadvantages of such an approach?

DAILY LIFE

   Tell the Lady Zinû: Iddin-Sin sends the following message:
   May the gods Samaš, Marduk, and Ilabrat keep you forever in good health for my sake.
   From year to year, the clothes of the (young) gentlemen here become better, but you let my clothes get worse from year to year. Indeed, you persisted (?) in making my clothes poorer and more scanty. At a time when in our house wool is used up like bread, you have made me poor clothes. The son of Adad-iddinam, whose father is only an assistant of my father, (has) two new sets of clothes [break] while you fuss even about a single set of clothes for me. In spite of the fact that you bore me and his mother only adopted him, his mother loves him, while you, you do not love me!

                                                              TCL 18 111

---

*Reprinted from LETTERS FROM MESOPOTAMIA by A. Leo Oppenheim by permission of The University of Chicago Press. © 1967 by The University of Chicago. All rights reserved.

38.
A Schoolboy in Sumer

The demand among the Sumerians and Babylonians for a literate element of the population to carry on the work of scribes in court, commerce, and government resulted in the establishment of numerous scribal schools. It appears that only boys had the privilege of attending these schools. The following selection reveals that the schoolboy of Sumer may have had some things in common with his modern-day counterpart.*

INQUIRY: How does this reading reveal similarities between Sumerian schools and modern schools? What evidence does it give to show differences?

The full school course was a long one, lasting for many years, "from the time of childhood to maturity," but after about two years a lad might qualify as a *dubsar tur*, a junior scribe, and would be entrusted with the task of helping in the education of one of the smaller boys, setting his exercises, instructing him in the way in which they should be done, correcting them (prior to final correction by the headmaster) and flogging him when he deserved punishment.

Discipline was strict. Boys might be "kept in" over long periods; probably already they were given impositions, though it is only in the Neo-Babylonian time that we find actual examples of pupils having to write "fifty lines" or "a hundred lines" by way of punishment: but for the most part correction was by the stick, and the stick was used freely, by masters and by pupil-teachers alike.

This is made very clear in the "Schooldays" essay. "What did you do at school?" "I reckoned [or 'recited'] my tablet, ate my lunch, fashioned my [new] tablet, wrote and finished it; then they assigned me my oral work, and in the afternoon they assigned me my written work. When the school was dismissed, I went home, entered the house, and found my father sitting there. I told my father of my written work, then recited my tablet to him, and my father was delighted."

This must have been a lucky day, but on the morrow the boy was to be less fortunate. "When I awoke early in the morning I faced my mother and said to her: 'Give me my lunch; I want to go to school, My mother gave me two rolls and I set out. In the school the 'man on duty' said to me: 'Why are you late?' Afraid, and with my heart pounding, I entered before my teacher and bowed."

But the teacher was correcting the student's tablet of the day before and was not pleased with it, so gave him a caning. Then the overseer "in charge of the school regulation" flogged him because "you stared about in the street," and again because he was "not properly dressed" and other mem-

---

*Sir Leonard Woolley, "A Schoolboy in Sumer." Reprinted from the UNESCO COURIER (June 1963).

bers of the staff caned him for such misdemeanours as talking, standing up out of turn and walking outside the gate; finally the headmaster told him, "Your handwriting is unsatisfactory." and gave him a further beating.

The luckless youth appeals to his father to mollify the powers above in the orthodox way, so the father invites the headmaster to his home, praises him for all that he has done to educate his son, gives him food and wine, dresses him in a new garment and puts a ring on his finger; the schoolboy waits upon him and in the meanwhile "unfolds to his father all that he has learnt of the art of tablet-writing."

The gratified teacher reacts with enthusiasm: "Of your brothers may you be their leader, of your friends may you be their chief, may you rank the highest of the schoolboys. You have carried out well the school's activities, you have become a man of learning," the schoolboy, claiming now the proud title of "Sumerian. . . ."

39.
Atatürk and the Emancipation of Women

The women of Turkey will always have a special place in their hearts for Mustafa Kemal Atatürk, President of Turkey from 1923 to 1938. He released them from the stifling confinement of the veil and the enveloping wrap. Atatürk opened the way for Turkish women to receive an education, take part in public service, and pursue careers. His reforms gave women pride in themselves as individuals. He liberated them from servitude and gave them equal rights with males. He swept away segregation of the sexes and offered women an abundance of opportunities to lead rewarding and constructive lives.

Of course there was resistance, especially from those who had benefited from the old customs. But Atatürk was a dynamic and strong man, and he wanted a democratic Turkey as soon as possible. To do this he needed the support of the women. They gave him their support, and today they are carrying on his work.*

INQUIRY: What might be the effect on an individual of changes as drastic as those made by Atatürk? Think of changes that could be made in your own society that might be equally shocking to many people. Do you think they could be made without great resistance?

Turkish women of the Ottoman era (14th to 20th centuries), especially those in the cities, spent their lives in the complete seclusion of the harem. Their occupations consisted mainly of doing or supervising the

---

*"Atatürk and the Emancipation of Women" by Afet Afetinan. Reprinted from UNESCO COURIER (December 1963).

housework, looking after the children or embroidering. Their social life was restricted to family gatherings.

In one of her letters, Lady Montagu, wife of an English ambassador, wrote (1717-18): "The main things women do is go visiting neighbours, go to Turkish baths, spend lavishly and create new costume designs." She also told her friends in England that she liked the costumes worn by Turkish women and that she herself possessed some.

Lady Montagu, of course, meant the costumes worn by city women indoors. The clothes worn outdoors reflected the kind of secluded life led by Moslem Turkish women. Their faces were veiled and they wore a loose wrap known as a *charshaf*. A variation of this costume was the combination of the *feradje* (something like a loose-fitting overcoat) and the *yashmak* (a veil which left the eyes uncovered and which was worn especially by the women of the palace). At a later date the wives of high officials and other women who from time to time visited the palace, either as private guests or on State occasions, were compelled to wear the *feradje* and *yashmak*.

This type of costume was generally worn throughout the Moslem world but only at a later date and there is nothing to suggest that women were compelled to adopt it in the early stages of Islam.

The *Levant Herald* (England) of August 15, 1881 reported: "The officers of police are instructed to keep a strict look-out, and to make a report whenever they observe a woman daring to wear the thin veil under circumstances in which it is not sanctioned by the regulations. The report will state the name of the offending lady and the particulars of the breach of rule and will be submitted to the Minister of Police. Moslem ladies are also forbidden to drive or walk round the places of Beyazit, Shahzade-Bashi and Aksarai and to walk in the Great Bazaar and to sit down in shops.

"Moslem ladies are also strictly forbidden to gather together in groups in any public places and if the police observe any group, it will be their duty to invite them to disperse. This invitation will be addressed to the oldest lady in the group, or to the servants in attendance, at the discretion of the officer. The latter part of the regulations is devoted to prescribing the manner in which men shall behave to ladies in public. Any man who permits himself to speak to a woman or to make signs to her will be punished under Article 202 of the criminal code."

These rules, however, were not strictly applied at all times. There were even times when women enjoyed a measure of freedom. During the "Tulip Period," which coincides with the second half of the eighteenth century, women wearing light coloured *feradjes* attended open-air festivities and entertainments, as is shown by paintings and writings of that period.

From the fourteenth century until early in the twentieth century (1918), Turkish women were subjects of a Moslem Empire which spread over three continents—Asia, Europe and Africa—and covered about six million square kilometres.

But while the theocratic Ottoman State was extending its boundaries, the social position of women deteriorated. The expansion of the Ottoman Empire brought it in contact with the influence of Persia and Byzantium, and the old Turkish customs were slowly forgotten. During this period new differences of status between the sexes increased. The harem life of Persia and Byzantium was introduced into the Turkish palace. In the fifteenth century, on orders from the Sultan, the palace was divided into the *harem* (women's section) and *selamlik* (men's section).

The viziers and beys were not slow in introducing this system into their homes, and soon harem life and polygamy spread among a certain class of people and became an accepted custom.

Polygamy was practised in Arabia long before Islam and led to such a deterioration of family life that the limitation of the number of wives to four was considered to be an important reform. The Islamic stipulation that men and women are equally responsible for the honour of the family was also regarded as an advance in Arabia, the birthplace of Islam.

Thus men and women alike were expected to abide by the rules of morality and to be faithful to their spouses; but all the rules and teachings of Islam could not bring about the desired equality between the sexes even though the laws of Islam, in general, honoured women more and conceded them more rights than did the old Arabic, and perhaps even the Roman laws.

The Islamic family laws adopted by the Ottomans were concerned with marriage, inheritance and minorities. As regards marriage, women had no say in choosing their husbands who were selected by the parents of the girl or an older member of her family. Engagement was not recognized in law and, if it took place at all, it was by private arrangement between the two families. The husband had the right to divorce his wife whenever he wished merely by announcing to her, orally or in writing, "I divorce thee."

What was the situation of the slave woman of the Ottoman period who filled the harem of the palace? They were brought from the Caucasus and other parts of the empire. The leading figure in the palace harem was the sultan's mother; next came the mothers of the sultan's children; in addition to their wives the sultans could keep as many odalisques and slaves as they wished. Occasionally the sultan would give some of these women their freedom.

Although female slaves in the Ottoman period were treated like chattels, they were also given rights whereby they could acquire their freedom and become members of free society, and children of parents who had won their freedom were also regarded as free citizens. Slavery and the slave trade were abolished by a decree of 1854.

The role of country-woman in all the parts of the empire was that of the producer. In farming women supplied a great proportion of the labour and they also played their part in the economy of the home. Though polygamy was also practised in the country and men sometimes married as many as four wives it was generally for economic reasons. Country women did not dress like the city women when outdoors. Open-air life set them working alongside men and therefore they did not hide their faces behind veils or *yashmaks*. They only avoided a man and covered their faces if he was a stranger.

In the 19th century there was a movement towards western ways of life which led to considerable changes in education, art and science, as well as an evolution in social life. As a result, some progressive ideas had already been implanted in women's minds by the end of the century.

Already before 1869 the Government decided to open primary and secondary schools for girls, but because the teachers in such shcools would necessarily be male and because girls of 11-13 years of age were considered as having reached an age when they should be segregated from men, public opinion would not tolerate the idea. In 1870 a school was opened in Istanbul to train women teachers for the primary and secondary girls' schools. Although initially most of the teachers in this school were men, by 1900 women were in the majority and hence the number of women with a modern education likewise increased.

The years 1908-18 were marked by two developments: enrolment in girls' schools progressively increased, and certain men even ventured to go out in the company of their wives. The fact that Sadrasam (Prime Minister) Fuat Pasha consented to sit with his wife in the lounge of an hotel caused much comment.

A new social situation was created in Turkey when the Ottoman Empire entered the First World War. As men were called up for the army women had to be appointed to fill vacancies in the offices. During the war the first faculty for girls attached to the University of Istanbul was opened (1914). In 1921 the Arts Faculty agreed to co-educational attendance at lectures.

The passive resistance with which women, from the beginning of the twentieth century, opposed veiling and the withholding of the right to go out freely, to ride in the same carriage as their husbands and to sit next to them, eventually triumphed over the fanaticism of public opinion.

Until the end of the First World War, men and women were separated from each other on public transport by partitions. On boats sailing the Bosphorus and crossing from Istanbul to the islands, women were obliged to stay in closed cabins below decks. When women were finally permitted to remain on deck, a woman author described her feelings at being able to watch the sea in the open air during that one-hour trip with such zest that anyone would have imagined that she was crossing the ocean for the first time.

There were many changes in the status of women between 1918-23, largely brought about by the historical events of the time.

In 1918, the Ottoman Empire signed the Treaty of Mondros as one of the defeated powers, losing all rights over her Asian territories (Arabia, Syria, Palestine, Lebanon, Iraq). In 1920, the last government of the Ottoman Empire signed the Treaty of Sèvres, agreeing to the dismemberment of Turkey, and every part of the country now faced the possibility of occupation.

While the Sultan and his government accepted these terms the nation itself did not and turned its mind to the idea of liberation. To preserve the unity of the country it was necessary to bring together all the local forces.

With this in mind, Mustafa Kemal (Atatürk) assumed the leadership of the nation and his first actions as leader were to refuse to recognize the international treaties entered into by the Sultan and his government and to launch resistance against the occupying powers. In the beginning this resistance took the form of guerilla fighting, but on April 23, 1920, Kemal formed a government and a regular army and attacked the forces of the occupying powers.

In 1922 Anatolia was cleared of occupying troops and with the Treaty of Lausanne in 1923 the boundaries of the new Turkey were established. The same year, on October 29, a democracy was instituted with Ankara as the new capital. Thus monarchy in Turkey came to an end.

In the democratic State which was created in 1923, Turkish woman had at last attained the rights enjoyed by women in other modern states.

The constitution of democratic Turkey made elementary education for boys and girls compulsory, but because of the shortage of teachers and school buildings its application remains largely theoretical. Turkey's high percentage of illiteracy is thus likely to remain so for some time.

All faculties of the Istanbul University started opening their doors to girl students from 1921 and many teacher-training schools, *lycées*, and other institutes were opened for the benefit of girls. In addition, many of the existing schools introduced co-education. In 1928, the adoption of the Latin alphabet made learning much easier and as a result there was an immediate increase in the number of persons able to read and write.

Once women began to study in colleges and universities many of them entered a variety of professions and trades. But this was not always an easy matter, as was seen in the case of the medical profession. When young women wished to study law or the arts no obstacles were placed in their way. But when they showed interest in becoming doctors of medicine, public opinion was aroused and even educated parents were reluctant to accept the idea. Articles were published in the newspapers, claiming that women were not likely to succeed as doctors.

However, a small minority approved and supported women in their struggle. Encouraged by this support, seven girl students enrolled at the faculty of medicine of Istanbul University in September 1922. Because, in terms of dress, women were still bound by the old customs these first women medical students wore their veils while attending lectures with men and continued to do so until 1925, when Kemal Atatürk urged the adoption of European dress.

The first women medical students completed their studies in 1927 and, after a year's interneship, received their diplomas as fully qualified doctors. These and other women doctors who had studied in Europe or America worked only as general practitioners. When some of them wanted to become specialists, however, most of their male colleagues declared that despite their attainments as students, women would not be successful as practising doctors. In time, the difficulties were overcome and women who have specialized in different branches of medicine have once again proved their capabilities.

Today, women are found in virtually every profession. The engineer who supervised the building of the Atatürk Memorial Mausoleum in Ankara, for instance, was a woman, Sabiha Guneyman. The chief architect of the *Evkaf* (religious trusts) in Istanbul is also a woman, Cahide Tamar. The famous Rumeli Fort in Istanbul was restored by three women architects.

Teaching was the first profession open to women in Turkey and the number of women who have taken up teaching in primary and secondary schools, *lycées* and universities is still much higher than in other professions. So far, there is only a small number of women professors, although there are a good many lecturers and assistant lecturers. Those holding top positions in government departments are still far from numerous.

On the stage, women have likewise distinguished themselves, especially when it is remembered that until a quarter of a century or so ago they were kept strictly within the confines of their homes. It had always been considered against the principles of Islam for women to act. Afife Hanim was nearly imprisoned in 1921 for contravening this principle. Women had to struggle for their rights in this field just as in so many others.

The first woman joined the Turkish bar in Ankara in 1928. Since then the number has increased considerably and today, in addition, there are many women judges, commissioners of oaths, legal advisers and lecturers at the law schools.

Today, in Turkey, men and women are equal in the eyes of the law. The many social reforms introduced during the presidency of Kemal Atatürk (1923-38) always took account of women's position; many legal rights and duties were freely conceded to them.

In 1926 the Turkish Government introduced a new set of civil laws along the lines of the Swiss Civil Code. This gave Turkish women all the rights customary in modern communities.

The Turkish Civil Code, in terms of civil rights, did away with all the legal differences between men and women. It made women the equals of men, except that women were subject to certain restrictions aimed at securing permanency in marriage.

The prohibition of polygamy was one of the fundamental features of this code, which also raised the marriageable age for girls to 18, laid down certain pre-marriage formalities, and required that marriage ceremonies should take place before the municipal authorities in the presence of witnesses, and also that a marriage should be recorded both in the register and on the identity cards of both parties.

In April 1930, parliament passed the Municipal Laws Bill giving women the right to vote and to stand in municipal elections. The next step was to give women the right to stand for parliament. President Atatürk was in favour of this and often tried to induce members of the government to accept his views. In the constitution then in force, mention of franchise was always accompanied by the words "every Turkish male." On December 11, 1934 the words "and female" were added to this phrase.

Thus, Turkish women managed within a quarter of a century to overcome a fanatical opposition and thereby set an example to other women of the Moslem world.

Since they were given the right to vote both as a result of the action of political parties and their own desire to carry out their duties as citizens, a high percentage of women have participated in elections. For example, in 1954 out of 5,366,024 women voters (the total number of voters was 10,287,733), 4,741,304 used their right to vote.

In spite of all the legislation enacted for their benefit, however, Turkish women in general have not yet achieved the social and intellectual standing that could be desired. In the country as in the town, they must be educated so that they realize the meaning of all the rights conceded to them by law.

On this subject, Professor Sadi Irmak wrote in 1962: "There are four factors that undermine our efforts to bring about equality for women: ignorance, bad traditions, wrong interpretation of religious rules, male selfishness . . . " Professor Irmak analyses all these elements and emphasizes the effect of illiteracy, declaring: "we must educate women so that they, in turn, can educate our nation." It is essential that women of Turkey should realize the meaning of their rights and duties before exercising them.

The man responsible for the reforms in Turkey was Kemal Atatürk, who believed in preparing both the people around him and also public opinion before introducing anything new. Atatürk wanted his people to progress and to prosper according to the most enlightened ideas and the principles of modern civilization.

40.
One Life in Egypt

The role of the Arab woman has been changing rapidly in recent times. In 1972 a Conference on the Role of the Arab Woman in National Development met in Cairo under the sponsorship of the United Nations Children's Fund, the Arab League, and the Arab States Adult Functional Literacy Center of UNESCO. The delegates made recommendations that would greatly improve the lives of women in Arab nations.

In the following article, Mary Diamanti, writing in 1973, describes some of the changes that have taken place in the life of women in Egypt. The author writes of her visit to a settlement on land reclaimed through construction of the Aswan Dam.*

INQUIRY: After reading this article do you feel that the greatest changes were brought about by social reformers or that they were the result of technological progress (the construction of a dam, land reclamation, introduction of electricity, etc.)?

It had rained all night and the narrow street was thick with mud. A strong wind was blowing. As we approached the row of houses, a white embroidered curtain waved through a window. Nifissa stood at her door, her son Abdou on her arm and a broad smile on her face. She was of medium height, with broad hips, a dark complexion, her hair pulled back, a scarf tied around the back of her head. Standing there, looking healthy and clean, she typified the new breed of settlers who had come from overpopulated villages around Egypt to start a new life on the lands reclaimed from desert and swamps.

"Village Number 8" where Nifissa lives is outside of Abis, which is near Alexandria. It is one of the many recently built villages that have sprung up to accommodate migratory populations settling on newly created farms. Land reclamation (through irrigation systems made possible by the Aswan Dam) is one of Egypt's most ambitious and strategic programs to meet the

*"One Life in Egypt," by Mary Diamanti. Reprinted with permission from *Ms.* Magazine, 1972.

needs of its ever-increasing population—34 million in 1971, an estimated 41 million by 1981.

We were taken around this new settlement to see the school, day-care center, youth club, cooperative stores and storerooms: an impressive array of modern facilities put at the disposal of the settlers by the government, with the help of the United Nations Children's Fund (UNICEF) and voluntary programs. But I was anxious to talk to the settlers.

I was the only woman in the group, and Nifissa seemed willing to talk to me. In the past I had seen examples of appalling conditions in village huts, but as we walked into Nifissa's home I was dumbfounded, it was very neat and clean. The beds were well made with an embroidered canopy over them, and there were embroidered napkins on the tables. Up on the wall, there was even a row of sparkling glasses on a shelf—a great contrast to the old custom in many villages whereby all the family members drink from one earthenware jug. I asked Nifissa to tell me about her life. In an attractive, unaffected manner, she spoke to me in Arabic. I have put the facts in chronological order, but this is her story in her own words:

"I am forty years old. When I was fifteen, my father married me off to our neighbor, Aziz. As it is our custom in Egypt, Aziz had to give two cows to my father to get his blessing for our marriage, although it was the old man who had arranged it all with Aziz's family. We were married and lived in a village in Behera. The closest town to us was Damanhour, but I never went there.

"Aziz worked very hard in the fields from sunrise to sunset. He earned very little so we did not have much food. We lived in a mud hut. We had no water or electricity. Every morning I had to walk to the village fountain to get water, and I washed my cooking utensils and clothes in the dirty river. Not far away, water buffalo were bathing, and children were relieving themselves. Every day was the same. We women served our husbands and bore children, but often saw our little ones die.

"My first two children died, one at birth and the other at six months of age. 'It was God's will,' we said. Five more came later, three girls and two boys. They are all alive, thank God.

"One day we heard that the government was looking for laborers to work on new lands, not far away from where we were. Aziz had heard on the radio in the village coffeehouse that with the High Dam in Aswan, they were making new farms out of the desert.

"There were certain conditions to become a settler. The men had to be between twenty-one and fifty, know how to read and write, own no land, and have a family of not more than five. Our eldest daughter was already married, and our youngest son was not born yet, so we were accepted. The government gave us about three-and-a-half feddans [about 2½ acres] and a two-room house. We were taken to our new home by truck, and we were given some money on loan to buy some furniture.

"Our new home had two small rooms, a toilet with a water tap and sink, a small backyard, but no kitchen. We had running water in the house for the first time in our lives, but no electricity. This home was so much better than where we lived before, but at first I found it a little difficult the way the rooms were placed. When friends called on Aziz, it was impossible for me to go to the toilet, which was in full view of the room. I was too embarrassed to go past all those men to use it. Also, because I had no kitchen, we built a small place with mud bricks in the backyard for me to cook.

"You probably know that Moslem law allows a man to have four wives. When we moved to Abis, Aziz decided to take another wife, younger than I. He left the house and moved into a nearby village with his new bride. But he continues to spend one or two nights with me sometimes. At the beginning I was lonely, and angry that he was staying with her and not me. It was difficult also because I had no relatives here, and I had the children to care for. But it is our custom.

"We have a school close by. There is also a place where we can leave our little children when we have work to do. We have a club for the young boys where they can get together and watch television, or play games, or listen to music. There is a large hall where we grown-ups attend classes to learn to read and write. In the evening, the hall is used for watching television; it also has tables for Ping-Pong, which the men enjoy playing. And there are two rooms with sewing and knitting machines where we are taught how to sew and knit. That is where I made all these embroideries.

"My neighbors and I are now used to all these things. But at the beginning we were all very surprised when we first saw television, or when we were shown how to use a sewing machine or a knitting machine. Our children had new benches and blackboards in their classrooms. They have a big yard to play in.

"All these things were new to us. Slowly we learned to live in these new surroundings, but some of us are still set in our old ways. Some families still keep their hay on their roofs even though there are large storehouses available to the villagers. Because of this, we have had several fires, but the villagers still prefer to watch over their possessions themselves. Some people keep their children away from school to help at home or in the fields. We also have our old rituals to chase the bad spirits away.

"But we also like the new methods. Dr. Isis Wawar from the University of Alexandria comes regularly to our village. She is the one who taught us how to make soap with oil and soda we get from our cooperative, and how to prepare a salad, and how to keep our house and our children clean. She is a very nice woman and interested in every one of us. She told us how we can avoid some diseases if we make a little effort. Now I give my children clean food; I boil the milk; I bathe my youngest one three times a week. My other children would not be washed for weeks. In the old village, some of the children would lie on the floor with lots of flies on their eyes and mouths, and no one cared. You never see this in our new village.

"I go to school myself. I am not embarrassed about my age because there are other women of my age there. We learn how to read and write and how to count. I can read labels on tin cans. Maybe some day I will be able to read the newspaper!

"Those of us who have many children take pills not to become pregnant. The nurse told us how important it is to have a small family because then the mother is able to take better care of her children; they get more food, and they grow up stronger and can work better later. We cannot always obtain these pills here because the clinic does not open regularly, but we can send for them to Alexandria, although it costs us more.

"In the old village, many women delivered their babies alone, or with the help of their mother or mother-in-law. The cord was cut with a piece of broken glass or a tin cover from a can. When I had my children, the village midwife came, and she used a razor blade. My youngest son was born in the new village. It was still the midwife who delivered the baby, but she had a bag with instruments. She boiled the water and washed her hands before touching me. She had learned all this at the community center.

"There is no electricity in the village. They tell us it will come soon. We women do not go out at night, but we visit each other during the day. We talk about what we learn, and I try to encourage the other women to do all these things at home. Some of them are lazy or their husbands will not let them go to the center, so I try to show them what I have learned. It is good to share.

"I am happier now. But I still worry about my children, and my neighbors' children. They go to school and are taught many things, so they will want more when they grow up. I am more worried about my boys. Although the ladies at the center tell us that women have responsibilities, that we are important in our family and outside, I still think it is more important for boys to get an education and a skill. My grandfather said so, my father said so, and Aziz thinks so. My youngest daughter who is with me will probably get married and her husband will take care of her. But maybe she will want to work and earn money. I will let her do what she wants because I want her to be happy.

"It will still be God's will, but now I think I can also help."

41.
I Am an Arab Refugee

The plight of refugees is not a happy one in any part of the world, and, ironically, their fate is frequently not their fault. In the following reading, Abdul Fattah Mohammad Nassar, describes his life in a camp for Arab refugees.*

INQUIRY: What parallels can you draw between the lives of Arab refugees and American Indians living on reservations?

WE WERE BOMBED OUT OF OUR VILLAGE

Every morning after breakfast I leave the little house where I now live and go to look at the map where I can see the little village where

*From the book YOUNG PEOPLE OF THE MEDITERRANEAN: THEIR STORIES IN THEIR OWN WORDS by Charles R. Joy. Copyright © 1959 by Charles R. Joy. Reprinted by permission of Hawthorn Books, Inc., 70 Fifth Avenue, New York 10011.

my family used to live so happily. It makes me sad, for while it is only about fifteen miles away I cannot go back. The Jews occupy it now. I remember it very well. It is called Ishwa' and it is in the Jerusalem district about nine miles west of the city on the road to Jaffa, which is on the Mediterranean Sea. My father used to work in the quarry there, but he also had large orange groves where I used to play. He used to send his oranges down to Jaffa and then export them. We lived in a stone house in the village. But that was nine years ago.

I was only four when we had to leave our home, but I cannot forget what happened, for my father and mother have told me many times all about it. It was in 1948 that the Jews started to bomb our village which was right on the frontier between the Arabs and the Jews. There were no soldiers in our town. I could hear the bombs falling in the village and could see the houses that were destroyed. Our own house was not hit while we were there, but we do not know what happened after we left.

WE WENT TO JERICHO

Finally the whole village decided that they could not stay any longer. Everyone was afraid. The Jews did not tell us to leave, nor did any-one else, but it was too dangerous to remain. So in April or May of 1948 everybody started trudging over the roads, first through Bethlehem, where the Christians think Jesus was born, and then up the hill to Jerusalem. There the Arab forces picked us up and drove us down on the east side of Jerusalem to Jericho. For five months we stayed in Jericho, living in tents and sleeping on the ground, and wondering what was going to become of us and of our old homes. I did not like Jericho at all, though the International Red Cross probably did all they could for us. They provided the food we ate.

While I was there I visited the Jordan River where John baptized Jesus and also went to the Dead Sea, which is the lowest spot on earth and so salty that you cannot sink in it. The salt makes your eyes and nose smart, however, and I don't think that the swimming is good there. The old Jericho with the walls that they say Joshua blew down with his trumpet is not the same as the modern Jericho. It is about a mile and a half away. Not far from the modern Jericho is a well that they call Elisha's well. This is supposed to be the well whose waters were sweetened by Elisha by throwing salt in them. All the Bedouins in the vicinity go to this well to draw water in their jars. Nearby they are digging to find the old cities that used to stand in this place. They say that they are finding some very interesting things, and that Jericho is the oldest city in the world where people have always lived.

THE CAMP AT KALANDIA

In 1950 my family left Jericho for the camp at Ein 'Arik near Ramallah just north of Jerusalem. This was still a Red Cross camp and I did not like it any better than I did Jericho. I was there for a year before coming to the UNRWA camp at Kalandia, ten miles north of Jerusalem, and I have been here ever since. I am fourteen years old, but my parents do not remember the exact month and day of my birth. Most of my life I have been a refugee. There are bare hills all around us here with hardly a tree in sight, and when we think in my family of our old home and the orange trees everywhere we are very sorrowful. All we want is to be allowed to go back to our houses and lands again. We don't want money or anything else. My father says he won't accept money. We just want to go home.

MY FAMILY

My father's name is Mohammad Ahmad Nassar. He was born in this old village of ours and my mother, Jamileh Mohammad Abed Ismaiel, was also born there. My father now works as a laborer, crushing stones about a mile away from our camp. He helps to support the family in this way.

I have one brother and three sisters. The oldest is my sister Halimah, who is nineteen. She is married and lives with her husband in the same camp with us. She has one boy, two and a half years old.

Next comes my brother Abdul Rahman, who is seventeen and a student in the same class with me.

My sister Amnah is six years old, and in the first class, and finally I have a baby sister, Mariam, who is one year old. Halimah and Abdul remember our old home very well, but Amnah and Mariam have been refugees all their lives. I have been in camps for ten years now.

This camp is one of many run by UNRWA, which tries to provide homes and schools and food and medicine for about nine hundred and thirty thousand Arab refugees, refugees who are now in Jordan, Syria, Lebanon, the Gaza Strip, and elsewhere. About three hundred and sixty thousand of us are living in camps, and about one hundred and seventy thousand of the children are in schools like mine. We are all very grateful for everything we get from UNRWA, but still we all want to go home again as quickly as possible, and we believe we will go home, because Allah is just. Nothing else will satisfy us.

MY SCHOOLING BEGAN AT SIX

I began my schooling when I was six and a half years old and I am now in the last class in school in my camp. I should like to continue my education in Jerusalem or somewhere else. I have three more years to go before I can finish the fifth secondary class. I want to be a physician but I do not know whether or not this will be possible. The government does offer some scholarships, and I hope I may get one.

I study religion, Arabic, English, mathematics (arithmetic and geometry), history, geography, physics, chemistry, and botany. Of all my subjects I like religion, mathematics, physics, and English best.

Everybody in the camp gets up at five A.M. and for breakfast we usually have eggs, bread, cheese, and tea. Once a month UNRWA distributes rations for everybody in the camp, but my father works and so can buy some extra food. After breakfast I go to have a look at Ishwa' on the map before I go to school. School begins at eight. At ten we all go to the milk center to get a glass of milk. I have my lunch at home, usually lentils, olives, and bread. Then I go back to school until 3 P.M. There are seven classes.

At three I go to play soccer, volleyball, or basketball. We have twelve soccer teams in our camp, six or seven volleyball teams, and about the same number of basketball teams. There are a good many boys and girls here for the total population of Kalandia is 2,217.

I go home at four thirty and study my homework until about six thirty. Then I have supper, which may be soup, salad, meat, bread, and coffee. The coffee is the thick coffee that foreigners call Turkish coffee. About seven thirty I go to bed.

There is a center in the camp where we can listen to the radio and read papers and magazines. The older people use it a great deal, but the boys and girls go there also. Once every month a mobile cinema comes and we all go to see the movies.

FRIDAYS, SUNDAYS, AND HOLIDAYS

School is held five days a week. We do not have school on Friday or Sunday. On Fridays I sometimes go on a picnic to Ramallah or Jerusalem with some other boys. I am a Moslem and I usually go to the Al-Aqsa Mosque in Jerusalem in the great square of Haram esh-Sharif. This is a very holy place for both Jews and Moslems. There is a big rock there on which Abraham, who was the friend of God and the first Moslem, prepared to sacrifice his son Isaac. From this great rock also Mohammed, who is our great prophet, went up into heaven. The very beautiful Dome of the Rock has been built over it, and close by is the great mosque where I go to worship. Of course the Moslem is supposed to pray five times a day, but I do not pray in this way when I am in school.

Sundays are like Fridays except that I do not go to the mosque. I read a great deal, and I like Arabic history. At home I often play a game called trictrac, which is played with dice and round men. I know how to swim, but there is no place where I can go.

We have certain holidays during the year when our Mohammedan feast days come. During Ramadan, we are supposed to fast every day until seven in the evening, but at the end of this period there are three or four days of feasting. Ramadan sometimes comes in the summer and sometimes in the winter. Two or three months after Ramadan comes Bayram, when we have five days of feasting. The school closes during the first day.

There are spring and winter vacations of ten days each and then the long summer vacation of three months. During the summer I get a job with a contractor who is working in the camp. I work from 6 A.M. to 6 P.M. and get about twenty piastres a day (about fifty-six cents). I turn this money over to my father and it helps us in our home.

I have been in Amman, the capital of my country, and I have seen the King and his palace. The King is a good man and he wants to help his country. I have also been to Zerka, which is a large town about five miles from Amman. I have friends and relations there. In 1953 I went to Damascus in Syria to attend the fair. I went with some friends in a car and stayed with the Arab refugees there for about fifteen days.

I speak Arabic and I am beginning to speak English.

42.
The Kibbutz in Israel

The first kibbutz, or communal living arrangement, was begun in 1909 along the Jordan. The Zionists from Eastern and Central Europe who gave rise to the idea were interested in welding a socialist and Jewish heritage for a future Jewish state. The kibbutz was organized for cultural, political, and educational activities as well as to provide physical and financial protection. The kibbutz also provided a rural setting for the absorption of immigrants to Palestine, and later Israel. The kibbutz was to be self-sufficient, with everyone engaging in farming or related activities.

The following selections are from a booklet by Muki Tsur, a member of Kibbutz Ein Gev. The author gives a current appraisal of the meaning of kibbutz life, describes the function of direct democracy, and makes an interesting comparison of the kibbutz and American communes.*

INQUIRY: Israel has developed a large urban, industrial population, and members of the kibbutzim are a minority. What changes can you predict in kibbutz life as urbanization and industrialization increase in Israel? How do you think members of a kibbutz might react to these changes?

KIBBUTZ AS HOME

What is a kibbutz? For a bored tourist, a kibbutz is a collection of slides, a few strange faces and some blurred memories. For an economist, the kibbutz is a rural and industrial community whose members share the means and results of production. For a housewife, a kibbutz is a community in which every woman works and in which the children sleep in their own separate children's houses.

For statisticians, the kibbutz is only 3.5 percent of the population of Israel. For the historian, the kibbutz is an active movement which took a decisive role in the formation of Israeli society.

For the dreamers, it is an attempt to create a new society. For the cynics, it is one of many attempts to change man, and will inevitably fail.

But for us, members of the kibbutz, the kibbutz is something we can't explain. Statistics, historical implications and abstract concepts are aspects of the truth, but they are frozen pictures which cannot accurately describe our changing life.

A kibbutz is our home. Can one explain what a home means? It is a landscape of the present and memories of the past, a belonging and a basis for revolt. The kibbutz is a way of life with which we struggle.

Those who decided to join a kibbutz from the outside remember the decision as a major change in their lives. Many of us never made this decision; we were born in a kibbutz. For us the kibbutz was always home, a

---

*From WHAT IS KIBBUTZ? by Muki Tsur. © 1972 by Muki Tsur. Published by the Federation of Kibbutzim in Israel. Reprinted by permission of the author.

way of life built by our parents, a world we accept and reject, want to change and to rebuild.

The kibbutz of today is a conscious community which endeavors to live by defined principles without forgetting the human needs and life of its people. It is, above all, a creation of these 100,000 people—a reality and a dream with roots in the past and aspirations for the future.

DIRECT DEMOCRACY

The second basic ideological concept of the kibbutz is its belief in direct democracy. The kibbutz was founded by people who had revolted against the idea that individuals may control the lives of other individuals. Thus they chose the "town meeting" form of direct democracy and instituted the general assembly as their only governing body. Each member had a right and obligation to participate in the life of the community through the general assembly, and he was expected to participate in discussion and decision, confession and judgment, voting and election as well as special work in various social, cultural and economic fields.

Today the kibbutz is run by a complex network of committees on the various aspects of kibbutz life, including education, social problems, planning, culture, health, work, etc. The committees are responsible to the general assembly and are run by people who work in specific areas of agriculture, industry, or education.

Direct democracy has to be practiced in work teams which operate in various areas of production. These teams share decisions and manage different aspects of everyday work as well as propose long-term plans for developing their branch.

The system of direct democracy has encountered many problems in the course of the technological development of the kibbutz. In the beginning, work did not demand a strict division of labor, specialization, or learning, but the foundation was being laid for the very complex system of production which now exists.

The problem of direct democracy lay in determining which issues were to be presented to the general assembly for decisions, and whether or not the members would be capable of deciding upon them. In what way is it possible to insure that a member of a work team feels capable of planning the work? Would a situation eventually develop in which the general assembly merely approves suggestions by specialist members? Or, conversely, could it continue to deal with every subject individually regardless of its relative importance or triviality?

Though the rules and laws of the kibbutz are formulated by the community at large, there is no formal punishment for those who disobey. The censure of their peers is the only pressure—though a heavy one—which can be brought to bear on erring kibbutz members in official positions, or those members who fail to fulfill their obligations or refuse to accept communal decisions. A telling result of this situation is the common practice during kibbutz electoral campaigns for the candidates to try to convince the public not to elect them. This custom has its roots in the kibbutznik's fear of alienation from the group by undertaking the role of taskmaster in order to motivate the group to achieve things that are needed but which members are not inclined to do. The kibbutzim often undergo crises due to individuals who do not accept their responsibilities to hold positions as secretaries, treasurers, heads of committees, etc.

The general assembly serves not only as a decision-making body but as a means of expressing involvement in communal life. Those who want to assert their identification with the society come to the general assembly. As the society of the kibbutz has grown highly complex, however, fewer members feel it necessary to display their identification in this way.

From its inception, members who clashed with the rest of the society left the general assembly. They might remain active and involved in areas of work and even in social committees, but they ceased to attend the general assembly.

Originally, general assemblies of the kibbutz served as the prototype of today's encounter groups. Personal problems were dealt with, members judged each other, revealed themselves and dealt with the most intimate questions. As time passed, many kibbutzim concluded that this process was more damaging than beneficial, for it incurred too much pressure on the individual. The general assembly could not serve as an encounter group if members intended to live together for a lifetime. Many individuals were hurt and left the assembly or even the kibbutz.

Today, emotional and psychological problems are dealt with confidentially by the social committee. This development reflects the change in the social composition of the kibbutz. The kibbutz starts as a creation of a monolithic group of young people with the most intense personal and ideological life. Paradoxically, if the kibbutz succeeds, the society enlarges to encompass many generations and many groups. The only kibbutzim which remain young are those whose members constantly leave. This necessitates the arrival of a new group, which must then rebuild the society completely.

The consequence of these developments is the partial decline in the importance of the general assembly. Even today, however, it meets several times a month and continues to deal with all the important areas of kibbutz life. An average of 30-40% of kibbutz members participate regularly in the general assembly, but this varies from kibbutz to kibbutz. The general assembly serves as the highest decision-making body and is far more structured today than it was in its original form.

The evolution in kibbutz life has created the need for a less structured way of individual communication between members on a closer, more individual level, not only for the purpose of coming together to make decisions regarding the organization of the kibbutz. On some of the oldest or largest kibbutzim members may know each other only superficially. Attempts have been made to organize informal talks in small groups. The kibbutz movement is in constant contact with social psychologists and sociologists who are looking for new means of achieving communication between people, and who find the kibbutz a unique chance for experimentation within the framework of a life term experience and a structure striving for direct democracy.

Direct democracy is still a challenge more than an achievement. The kibbutz continues to search for new means, though troubled by old problems, and emphasizes only the questions that are being asked. Solutions are yet to be discovered.

COMMUNES AND KIBBUTZ: A COMPARISON

The development of communes in America today calls for a comparison between the kibbutz movement in Israel and the commune. There are those who see the commune as a very different phenomenon from the kibbutz while others consider it to be a development which parallels that of the kibbutz. Neither view adequately analyzes the actual differences or similarities between the two respective societies in which the commune and kibbutz function, and therefore, fails to establish a valid comparison.

The commune in contemporary America is a new happening, distinct from the religious communes of early America. Contemporary communes are societies in the making, their future character as yet undetermined. Any attempt to define them will be inadequate because of their embryonic stage of development. In many respects it is unfair to attempt a comparison between the present-day kibbutz and the commune—one is old; the other is new. It would be more valid to compare and determine what the original kibbutz had in common with the present-day commune.

Both the kibbutz and commune are results of ideological motivation. It may be said that both arose as an expression of revolt against existing social conditions. Their founders expressed growing feelings of alienation from their own societies and a sense of urgency in founding a new social environment. The founders of both the kibbutz and the commune were survivors of political movements which surrendered or were crushed by circumstances.

The ideology of a radical, new society was not popularly held by many of the early founders of the kibbutz. Most of those among the early groups of settlers who came to Israel from 1905-1914 and founded the communes and *kvutzot* were ready to give up their utopian dreams or be content with expressions of despair and alienation. There was a basic difference between the commune of those times and the *kvutza*. The former consisted of a group of 3 to 12 individuals who worked as a group or separately, did not hold ownership of the means of production, but consumed collectively. In the *kvutza*, the communal life was not only based in consumption, but the workers owned and were responsible for production as well. Production was also organized communally. Both types of collectives exist today in the commune scene in America.

Economically, neither the early kibbutz nor the present day commune was self-sufficient. Both received financial aid and both strived to maintain their independence.

In the commune of today, as in the original kibbutzim, the members are students and intellectuals who identify with oppressed and working people.

In both the kibbutz and commune, the problems of the second generation, education, and the roles of men and women were and still remain crucial problems, all prone to radical solutions.

The creation of a new form of human relationship was the primary goal of some kibbutzim, while the creation of a new social order was at the center of others. Some considered their main task to be the education of a new type of person, while others considered the political aim as primary. Tension between these two centers shaped the ideological development of the kibbutz, a tension that is present significantly in the communes in America today.

Wide differences exist between the American communes and the Israeli kibbutz. The nature of both respective countries provides a basic reason for these differences. The kibbutz was formed in a developing country—in a country which could not be built economically without extraordinary effort. The ideology behind this developing economy was a thorough-going socialism which included control of the methods of production as well as distribution. On the other hand, the American commune was established in a country which had a most advanced system of production. The commune in America was conceived of as a revolt against a consumer society, and hence, the value of work to produce goods was questioned in many communes. This is in sharp contrast to the socialist notion of work and production: the workers are persons who have successfully overcome alienation by participating in the means as well as results of their labor.

Another difference between the kibbutz and commune is in the attitude of the rest of the community toward them. The early settlers of the kibbutz were pioneers who had the moral support of the entire community. Politically, they were centers for the Jewish community because they represented islands of Jewish sovereignty. The American communes, on the other hand, find little sympathy from outsiders and frequently are paralyzed by deep hostility and suspicion which threaten their continued existence as independent entities.

The kibbutzim were built by people who were refugees, many of whom had fled religious and political oppression. To them, kibbutz was not only a spiritual refuge or political instrument, but a home. They were prepared to resolve the problems of education, death, and illness, within the framework of the community. From a tradition of wandering in exile, they had come home. The communes, on the other hand, were created by people dissatisfied with the security represented by home. They were seeking a new stage of wandering. The commune served as a means of striving for a new life experience, without the trappings of bourgeois security and stability.

Many of the problems facing the kibbutz are a direct consequence of its attempt to offer a life-long home for its members. Many decisions to depart from the original model and format are a result of the natural development of the kibbutz society, one that now can look back on several generations, and which today exists within a wealthier society with highly developed means of production.

The communes have as yet been unable to determine whether they are an experimental society which serve as a temporary life experience to transient members, or as a permanent society intended to take responsibility for the life-span of its people. The kibbutz itself went through a stage in which it had to make similar decisions. The first kibbutz was not based on the idea of home. After the second year, members had to decide whether to leave it or to remain. The decision to remain in the kibbutz was perhaps no less decisive than the one to live communally. Large numbers who entered the kibbutz movement left after a short time. Thousands have passed through the kibbutz while relatively few have remained. Yet the kibbutz was and remains determined to build a permanent structure, based on the values of equality, freedom and democracy. What the basis will be for the future of the communes remains to be seen.

43.
The Villages of Lebanon

Lebanon is a land that has supported human life since very ancient days. This was the homeland of the Phoenicians who were skillful artisans, enterprising merchants, and daring sailors. Not all turned to the sea to trade and to explore, however; many stayed behind in villages where they carried on the timeless work of shepherds and farmers. All people are eventually touched by currents of change, but the links to the ancient past are stronger and more enduring in the countryside.*

INQUIRY: With increased industrialization, do you think village life will be changed in Lebanon? Which aspects of life described in this article might be changed most by industrialization?

What a different world! Only five minutes out of Beirut, the air turns cool, the gently swaying palm fronds and rustling banana trees are replaced first by orange groves in the valleys, and then, a little farther on, gnarled olive groves appear on the slopes. The steep highway curves its way up the mountains between deep gorges and craggy cliffs where boulders seem to have burst out of the earth. Scrubby evergreens mingle with umbrella pines, and the mountain air exudes a sweet and spicy fragrance. As far as one can see, the mountain sides have been arduously terraced from the deepest valley to the topmost peak. On these terraces, fig and apple trees as well as grape vines cling to the narrow rows for their very existence. Here and there small villages bask lazily in the sun. Looking over the hills and vales, one sees below Beirut sprawling out to the sea and is startled to find that bustling capital so close yet so far from the serene setting. A certain stillness spreads over the mountains, and one feels an eternal quality—a strong sense of continuity with the past that gives a restoring peace and beauty.

On observing the scene a bit longer, one is struck by the location of the villages. They appear to be placed in the most inaccessible and remote nooks and crannies. What factors determined these village sites? The most basic one was the availability of water. The snow accumulates on the mountain tops, seeps through the layers of rock and soil and gushes out in abundant springs to supply each village with its water. Another determinant was a location with a good defense potential, a practical requirement anxiously sought by religious minorities. Present-day villages date back to ancient times when such basic considerations were essential for survival. The antiquity and stability of these villages is amply attested, and in living memory no one is known to have founded a new village. Of the 1500 village communities in Lebanon, more than 400, judged by their names, date from the days of the Phoenicians.

---

*From the book THE LAND AND PEOPLE OF LEBANON by Viola H. Winder. Copyright, ©, 1965 by Viola H. Winder. Reprinted by permission of J. B. Lippincott Company.

The villages, clean and attractive, vary from one hundred to about six hundred houses. The neat, rectangular dwellings are built out of limestone garnered from the immediate surroundings. The houses may be one or two stories high, and the smaller ones have flat roofs used to dry apricots, almonds, figs and grapes—the latter to be transformed into the most moist and flavorsome raisins. The larger houses have pitched red-tiled roofs, and arched casement windows opening inward, framed by bright green wood shutters kept closed at night and in the winter to keep out the cold. Steep winding garden paths lead to wide porches partially enclosed by leaning trellises heavy with vines. Sweet marjoram, basil and geraniums grow in large clay pots stuck around at random. Close by the houses, intensely colored zinnias, hollyhocks, jasmine and roses thrive in the nourishing sun. A larger plot is set aside for garden vegetables such as tomatoes, parsley, onions, lettuce, cucumbers, peas and beans. Often an enclosure adjacent to the house harbors chickens, pigeons or rabbits and sometimes a lonely sheep. Unmortared natural stone walls about three feet high, reminiscent of the Connecticut countryside, demarcate property lines and furnish a sunny hangout for an odd chameleon or midget-sized lizard who lies perfectly still until the slightest disturbance startles him into scurrying out of sight. Beyond the central group of dwellings, individually owned orchards, vineyards and fields extend in all directions.

So cheerful and friendly under the noon-day sun, the village takes on a different aspect with the fall of night—a certain eeriness envelops it. No lights shine anywhere except in the windows and most of them go off by ten. The solid blackness is broken only by an occasional villager, flashlight in hand, groping his way over a tortuous cobblestone path. The darkness is dense and hushed. Later on in the dead stillness of the night, the jackals frisk, and their weird distant calls echo and resound through the mountain passes interrupted only by the hooting of a not-so-distant owl. For a visitor, sleep may not come quickly among such unfamiliar calls of the wild magnified by the all-pervading silence.

To generalize about the villages and their inhabitants presents a problem, because each community has its own very individual character and customs based on its religion, size and distance from Beirut. Well over half the communities are scattered along the western ridges and slopes within forty miles of the capital city, and these have been noticeably touched by the twentieth century. In fact, some of the larger ones have built modern hotels, restaurants, cabarets, swimming pools and other facilities to attract well-to-do vacationers. In smaller settlements, summer residents, mostly from Beirut, Baghdad or the Persian Gulf area have put up European-style villas surrounded by large gardens and high stone walls heavily draped with bougainvillaea. The more isolated and distant villages live much as they did in the past. Those of Druze or Muslim population particularly retain the conservative and traditional customs. Except in the southern communities, electricity, sometimes perversely unpredictable, and piped water have penetrated most homes. In smaller villages, telephones are still not standard equipment, and one of the village shopkeepers often pinch-hits as switchboard operator. Between talk and sales, he gladly takes messages for those without phones. Telephoning from Beirut, however, may involve difficulties unless the call is made before the proprietor goes home—a variable hour depending on the season of the year and his mood. Even in the daytime the few lines are apt to be busy, and actually driving to the village may be less frustrating and quicker than telephoning. Cars and radios run rampant. Men and women now wear European clothes. Only a few old men still wear the traditional baggy trousers with tight legs below the knee, collarless shirt and European jacket. The village women usually wear skirts, blouses and sweaters. They have rejected slacks and shorts as wholeheartedly as their city counterparts have adopted them. Nearly gone are the long full-skirted dresses with tight bodices and knit shawls, the women gracefully carrying water from the village fount in jugs hoisted on their shoulders, young girls balancing large, round trays of bread on their heads as they walk from the community oven, and almost gone are the traditional feasts. The quaint old-world ways are quickly passing into oblivion. Although much that was picturesque, external and superficial has disappeared, the basic fundamental culture still lives. The long, rich cultural heritage of the mountaineer is too vigorous to have been superseded.

Their cultural heritage is not the only distinguishing feature of the inhabitants of these mountain hamlets. They also do not resemble modern twentieth-century city dwellers. They look as mountaineers do—rugged, husky, ruddy-faced, and as if life had been hard. Yet their friendliness, good humor and pleasant self-confidence belie their appearance. While working outdoors, the men sing old folk songs, and nothing amuses them more than telling jokes and pulling pranks on each other. Such activities add zest to their simple lives.

Their diet is as uncomplicated as other aspects of their daily routine. Bread, coffee and olives unfailingly accompany every meal. The lightest repast of the day is lunch when yogurt is usually served. Milk is preferred in this form, because in its preparation the milk must be boiled, a substitute for pasteurization. Dessert most often consists of fresh or dried fruit and nuts. Dried figs, cooked with sugar and lemon to a sticky, thick consistency, one of the favorite desserts or snacks, keeps well throughout the winter. During most of the year an abundance of fresh fruits and vegetables are available, but throughout the short winter the villagers' diet is more limited. On certain days of the week the butcher, one of four or five skilled workmen essential to every village, hangs a side of sheep on a hook in the middle of his shop, and on other days a side of beef. The village, however, cannot feed itself completely and must depend on the outside for food staples. Bread remains the staff of life. In former days baking bread in the community oven was common practice, but in recent years more and more women buy it from the stores. Some villages, however, still have not closed down their ovens. The dough is made at home, separated into flat disks, arranged on a round straw tray, covered with a white cloth and toted to the oven. At one end of the small one-room structure stands a large, rectangular masonry oven with an opening above the floor of a shallow pit where the baker stands and deftly pushes long boards dotted with dough into the oven. Then he nimbly tosses the double-crusted, flat loaves into big bins nearby. Half a dozen housewives work comfortably on a raised concrete counter, chatting, laughing and sometimes singing to the accompaniment of the rhythmical slapping of hands and dough on stone.

If the women meet socially at the oven the men meet at the village coffee house. There they exchange news and views over cups of coffee and tric-trac (backgammon). The most frequented place for both men and women are the local stores where they while away the time discussing prices, the weather and other subjects of interest just as nineteenth-century American country folk used to meet over the cracker barrel in the general store. The Lebanese proprietor keeps a tric-trac table and cards handy so his friends will be tempted to sit and linger over coffee and a game or two. Village stores all seem to carry the same goods at the same prices on a cash and carry basis. Flour, rice, grain, dried peas and beans, as well as sugar, coffee beans and nuts sit on the floor in four-foot high white flour-like sacks with the open end rolled back, and the price per kilogram marked on a tag lying in the middle. Fresh vegetables and fruits are arranged in rows of heavy wicker baskets while eggs in wire baskets invariably hang from the middle of the low ceiling. Along the sides of the wide counter tops, large glass jars hold chewy and hard candies. Writing paper, pens, pencils, hair pins, combs, toothpaste, soap and flashlights look out at the customer from wall shelves climbing up to the ceiling. Larger items such as furniture and clothes are usually bought directly from Beirut as the village seamstress and carpenter could cope with only a small porportion of the work involved.

By seizing every possible opportunity for a simple social gathering, the village folk apply the principles of hospitality in their daily lives. Most entertaining takes place in homes where evenings slip pleasantly by in conversation and games. In the Near East, board games are traditional, and the most popular in Lebanon is backgammon. Bridge, pinochle and word games are also played. In such social groups, men and women inter-mingle freely and equally. The women do not suffer from undue segregation and actually have a much greater influence than assumed by many out-siders. They occupy a relatively high status, and many have won the respect of all members of the community. In Muslim and Christian villages alike, boys and girls attend the same school. The whole social structure is equali-tarian. Individuals may be rated on a scale of values from excellent to worthless, but such judgments do not extend to groups of people. The fact that no one has been a tenant on someone else's land may explain this attitude. Notable prosperity or poverty are attributed to luck. The villagers' sociability and generous hospitality encompass strangers. As a visitor walks along, the village byways resound with *ahlan wa-sahlan* (literally, you have come to your family, and there will be no difficulties; welcome) fol-lowed by invitations to stop in for lunch or at least a cup of coffee. Conver-sation, especially with a stranger or visitor, is a real joy in the villager's life. On hearing English spoken, someone might well call out to ask what state the visitor hails from, and then go on to tell how many years he had spent in the "States" or inquire about a relative there.

As much a part of their heritage as hospitality is the high value placed on education. These mountaineers have traditionally been brought up with a respect for schooling, and this long-standing emphasis on education has resulted in almost universal literacy, 90 per cent. For the sake of educating the younger members of the family, parents, uncles and older brothers often make real sacrifices. The existence of English, French and American schools, a good distribution of public elementary and numerous private Lebanese schools have provided good educational opportunities for all. The effect of these schools and the foreign cultures they represent is so extensive that English and French language magazines and paperbacks circulate in the villages and are passed on from one person to another.

Being literate and having a relatively high standard of living have helped the country folk become conscious of their civil rights, and vitally interested in domestic and foreign politics.

More important, however, than either politics or education is religious faith. Christians and Muslims alike take their religions seriously. In this connection, it should be remembered that the three principal monotheistic religions, Judaism, Christianity and later Islam all originated in the Near East. With religious traditions reaching back as far as early human history, the people of that part of the world have quite naturally always been highly religion-conscious, and the villages of Lebanon are no exception. Christians, Muslims and Druzes are localized geographically with one sect dominating each village. Within each community people are strongly bound by a single faith. An ancient and deep-seated institution, religion has permeated with emotional force into all aspects of life. The iman or priest is a member of the community, takes an active part in its affairs, is chosen by the people and is ordained by higher religious authorities. Known to all in the village, the priest is expected to remain their priest for his lifetime. The villagers donate the land and erect the church or mosque which becomes the cultural and physical center of the village. The church is stable and identifies with the community rather than with any outside hierarchy. In Christian homes, religious pictures hang on the walls, and crosses and medals are often worn around the neck, whereas Muslims, especially the children, tend to wear miniature Korans and amulets to ward off evil and bring good luck.

As unchanging, deep-rooted and powerful a force as religion is the strong attachment to the land. The village farmer and his ancestors before him have patiently and assiduously cultivated the difficult terrain, blasted the rocks, terraced the slopes to make room for growing trees, vines and grains. The mountain has also provided a refuge from persecution and oppression. Year in and year out, the villagers have depended on the same plots of land to produce crops and raise livestock. To the mountaineer it has been a source of life. The binding tie to the land has contributed essential stability and continuity to the national character, especially in times of crises and change. Even when he emigrates abroad, the villager does so with the hope of returning some day, and should that hope fade, many still refuse to sell their land back home faraway in the mountains. Evidence of the deep-rooted love of the soil is also borne out by the fact that the most frequent and bitter disputes arise from the question of land ownership. In spite of the mediation of older influential men of the village, quarrels concerning property may pass on to the second generation. Basically, however, life is peaceful, and policemen are not a part of the village scene. The towns do have police headquarters, and they are summoned when necessary. Serious crimes seldom take place.

The lack of violence and vice may be explained by the deep roots the mountaineers have for their land, their all-pervasive emotional religion, and also by their strong sense of loyalty to the village as a whole and to each other. The relationship between land, religion and kin creates an equilibrium that gives vigor to the community's sense of integrity and strengthens it in facing the outside world. The villager, conscious of his membership in a certain community, never forgets that the village is his own preserve. It gives him a sense of security and a feeling of belonging not based primarily on economic factors.

politics

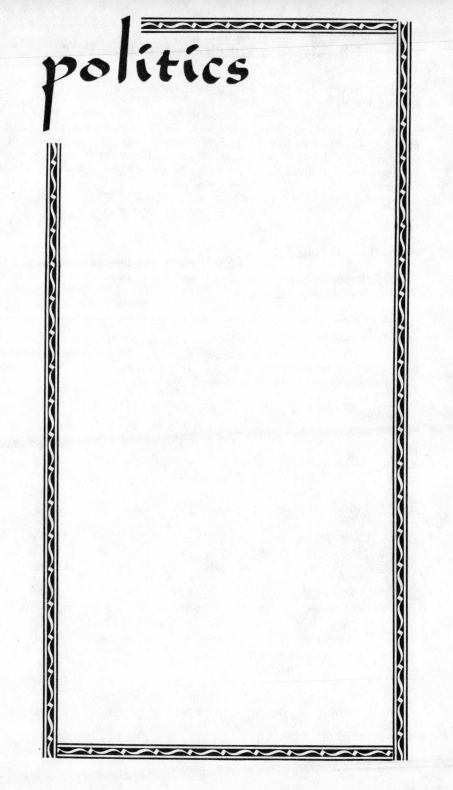

44.
The Jewish Question and the Plan

In the year 70 A.D. Titus, who was later emperor of Rome, destroyed much of the city of Jerusalem and burned the Temple. In 135 A.D. the Roman emperor Hadrian forbade the Jews to enter Jerusalem. Since that time the Jews have been living dispersed in various parts of the world. This dispersion is called the *Diaspora*. Many Jews believed they could never return to their old homeland until the coming of the Messiah. A few among them did not think they needed to wait for the dawn of this indefinite day before returning home.

The movement to make Palestine a homeland of the Jews came to be identified by the name Zionism. This movement was given greater life and vigor by the publication of a pamphlet and other writings by Theodor Herzl during the latter part of the nineteenth century. In 1897 Herzl and others met at the First Zionist Congress in Basel, Switzerland. This Congress decided that Palestine should be a homeland for the Jews and stated the principles upon which Zionism would be based. These principles are expressed by Herzl in the following article.*

INQUIRY: How does the situation of the Jews, as expressed in this article, compare with that of other peoples who have been removed from their homelands, such as the American Indians and the blacks brought forcibly to America as slaves?

No one can deny the gravity of the Jews' situation. Wherever they live in perceptible numbers, they are more or less persecuted. Their equality before the law, granted by statute, has become practically a dead letter. They are debarred from filling even moderately high positions, either in the army, or in any public or private capacity. And attempts are made to crowd them out of business also. "No dealing with Jews!"

Attacks in Parliaments, in assemblies, in the press, in the pulpit, in the streets, on journeys—for example, their exclusion from certain hotels—even in places of recreation, become daily more numerous, the forms of persecution varying according to the countries in which they occur. In Russia, impositions are levied on Jewish villages; in Roumania, a few human beings are put to death; in Germany, they get a good beating when the occasion serves; in Austria, Anti-Semites exercise terrorism over all public life; in Paris, they are shut out of the so-called best social circles and excluded from clubs. Shades of Anti-Jewish feeling are innumerable. But this is not to be an attempt to make out a doleful category of Jewish hardships; it is futile to linger over details, however painful they may be.

I do not intend to awaken sympathetic emotions on our behalf. That would be a foolish, futile, and undignified proceeding. I shall content myself with putting the following questions to the Jews: Is it true that in

*Theodor Herzl, A JEWISH STATE, 3rd ed. (New York, Zionist Organization of America, 1917), pp. 8, 11-12.

countries where we live in perceptible numbers, the position of Jewish lawyers, doctors, men of science, teachers, and officials of all descriptions, becomes daily more intolerable? True, that the Jewish middle classes are seriously threatened? True, that the passions of the mob are incited against our wealthy representatives? True, that our poor endure greater sufferings than any other proletariat?

I think that this external pressure makes itself felt everywhere. In our upper classes it causes unpleasantness, in our middle classes continual and grave anxieties, in our lower classes absolute despair.

Everything tends, in fact, to one and the same conclusion, which is clearly enunciated in that classic Berlin phrase: "Juden raus!" (Out with the Jews!)

I shall now put the Jewish Question in the curtest possible form: Are we to "get out" now? And if so, to what place?

Or, may we yet remain? And if so, how long?

The whole plan is in its essence perfectly simple, as it must necessarily be if it is to come within the comprehension of all.

Let the sovereignty be granted us over a portion of the globe large enough to satisfy the reasonable requirements of a nation; the rest we shall manage for ourselves.

The creation of a new State is neither ridiculous nor impossible. We have in our day witnessed the process in connection with nations which were not in the bulk of the middle class, but poorer, less educated, and consequently weaker than ourselves. The Governments of all countries scourged by Anti-Semitism will serve their own interests in assisting us to obtain the sovereignty we want.

The plan, simple in design, but complicated in execution, will be carried out by two mediums: the Society of Jews and the Jewish Company.

The Society of Jews will do the preparatory work in the domains of science and politics, which the Jewish Company will afterwards practically apply.

The Jewish Company will see to the realization of the business interests of departing Jews, and will organize commerce and trade in the new country.

We must not imagine the departure of the Jews to be a sudden one. It will be gradual, continuous, and will cover many decades. The poorest will go first to cultivate the soil. In accordance with a preconcerted plan, they will construct roads, bridges, railways, and telegraphs; regulate rivers, and build their own habitations; their labor will create trade, trade will create markets, and markets will attract new settlers; for every man will go voluntarily, at his own expense and his own risk. The labor expended on the land will enhance its value, and the Jews will soon perceive that a new and permanent sphere of operation is opening here for that spirit of enterprise which has heretofore met only with hatred and obloquy.

* * *

Let all who are willing to join us, fall in behind our banner and fight for our cause with voice and pen and deed.

* * *

Shall we choose Palestine or Argentina? We shall take what is given us, and what is elected by Jewish public opinion. The Society will settle both these points.

Argentina is one of the most fertile countries in the world, extends over a vast area, has a sparse population and a mild climate. The Argentine Republic would derive considerable profit from the cession of a portion of its territory to us. The present infiltration of Jews has certainly produced some friction, and it would be necessary to enlighten the Republic on the intrinsic difference of our new movement.

Palestine is our ever-memorable historic home. The very name of Palestine would attract our people with a force of marvellous potency. Supposing His Majesty the Sultan were to give us Palestine, we could in return pledge ourselves to regulate the whole finances of Turkey. We should there form a portion of the rampart of Europe against Asia, an outpost of civilization as opposed to barbarism. The sanctuaries of Christendom would be safeguarded by assigning to them an extra-territorial status, such as is well known to the law of nations. We should form a guard of honor about these sanctuaries, answering for the fulfilment of this duty with our existence. This guard of honor would be the great symbol of the solution of the Jewish Question after eighteen centuries of Jewish suffering.

45.
The Balfour Declaration

During the First World War another champion of Zionism, Chaim Weizmann, won British approval for his cause. This approval was expressed in a declaration by Arthur J. Balfour, the British Foreign Secretary, when he formally recognized in writing the historical connection of the Jews and the land of Palestine. The Balfour letter was written November 2, 1917.

INQUIRY: Balfour states that "nothing shall be done which may prejudice the civil and religious rights of existing non-Jewish communities in Palestine." Do you think it would have been possible to establish the state of Israel in such a way that there would have been no Arab refugees and no conflicts between Jews and Arabs? How might this have been done?

Dear Lord Rothschild,

I have much pleasure in conveying to you, on behalf of His Majesty's Government, the following declaration of sympathy with Jewish Zionist aspirations, which has been submitted to and approved by the Cabinet:

"His Majesty's Government view with favour the establishment in Palestine of a national home for the Jewish people, and will use their best endeavours to facilitate the achievement of this object, it being clearly understood that nothing shall be done which may prejudice the civil and religious rights of existing non-Jewish communities in Palestine, or the rights and political status enjoyed by Jews in any other country."

I should be grateful if you would bring this declaration to the knowledge of the Zionist Federation.

Yours sincerely,
Arthur James Balfour

46.
The Words of Atatürk

Mustafa Kemal Atatürk (1881-1938) exemplifies the modern enlightened nationalist in the Middle East. The following selections from his writings and speeches reveal his aspirations.*

INQUIRY: How does Atatürk express a concern for the position of women in Turkish society? Why do you think he was especially concerned with international relations as well as internal reforms?

"We want nothing else but to live free and independent within our national frontiers. The Turkish people and the Turkish Grand National Assembly and its government, definitely persist in their demand for the recognition of their right to existence, freedom and independence, like every civilized nation and government. This is our cause."

* * *

"In the world the existence, value, right and freedom, and independence possessed by every people is proportional to its deeds."

"To go forward and succeed on the way of civilization is a vital condition."

"At the meeting of the sublime power of civilization with medieval societies, nations trying to carry on with primitive superstitions are condemned either to destruction or to being at least subjugated and debased."

* * *

"We cannot shut our eyes and suppose that we live alone. We cannot put a fence round our country and live without connection with the world. On the contrary, as a progressive reforming nation, we shall live in the field of civilization."

"Which nation that desires to enter civilization has not turned to the West?"

---

*"The Life of Atatürk," TURKISH DIGEST, Vol. 3, No. 11 (November 15, 1967), pp. 4-5.

"We must have our equity and justice at the same degree as equity and justice altogether in social civil life. To fulfil these conditions we shall form this point of view of reform, reinvigorate and renew our existing laws and practices."

"The civil laws of all existing civilized states in the world are very close to one another. Our nation and our government, in the idea and conception of justice, is inferior to no civilized people. History perhaps bears witness to our high level in this respect. Therefore it is not permissible that our existing legal code should be inferior to the collected laws of civilized nations as a whole."

* * *

"If a social organization is content to meet contemporary requirements with only one of the two sexes, that social organization loses more than half its strength." "The reason for the lack of success of our social organization originates from the neglect and defective attitude we have to women. Human beings have come into the world to live as long as fate decrees. To live means to be active. Therefore if, while one element of a social organization is active, the other is idle, that social organization is paralyzed." "One of the necessities of today is to ensure the rise of our women in every way."

* * *

"We want nothing else but to live free and independent within our national frontiers. We want Europe and other nations not to grudge us our rights or to trespass on them.

"In our foreign policy there is no attack on the rights of any other state. We are defending and shall defend only our rights and our honour.

"Our Assembly and the government of our Assembly is far from being bellicose or given to adventure. On the contrary it prefers peace and tranquillity. In particular it is exceptionally in favour of the attainment and realization of humane and civilized ideals. Within these principles it seeks with the worlds of the East and the West always good relations and friendly ties.

"I am, however, the merciless enemy of a nation that wants to enslave my nation, until it relinquishes that desire."

* * *

"If in the world and between the nations of the world there is no peace and good relations, whatever a nation does for itself, it has no tranquillity.

"We cannot know that an event which we consider quite remote will not one day affect us. For this reason we must regard humanity as one body and a nation as part of this.

"Pain in the finger-tip of the body causes all the other members to suffer.

"If there is an illness in some part of the world or other, we must not say 'What is that to me?' If there is such an illness, it must concern us exactly as if it were among us. However remote an incident may be, we must not depart from this principle. It is this idea that saves nations from selfishness. Whether selfishness is personal or national, it must always be regarded as bad."

* * *

"There is no such thing as a line of defense. . . . There is only defense in depth and defense of surfaces. . . . That depth, that surface is the whole country."

"Victory can never be the ultimate aim. . . . Victory is a means to a greater aspiration. . . . Victory can have meaning or value when it helps to achieve an ideal."

* * *

"There are two meanings of conquering: One is the sword, and the other is the plough. . . . The nation whose only means for victory is the sword will be ultimately defeated. The real conquest is the one achieved by the plough. The plough and the sword—of these the second has always been defeated by the first."

"Peace at home, peace in the world."

* * *

"If war were to explode suddenly, like a bomb, nations would not delay joining their armed forces and national potentials to prevent it. The fastest way and the most effective measure is to establish an international organization which would prove to the aggressor that its aggression would not pay". (1935)

"The whole of humanity should be considered as a body, and a nation one of its organs. We should not say, What do I care if there is trouble in a remote corner of the world. If there is such trouble, we should be concerned with it as if it were our own. . . . If everlasting peace is desired, international measures should be taken to improve the conditions of the human masses. The prosperity of all humanity should replace hunger and misery. World citizens should be brought up far away from envy, greed and hate."

47.
The Revolution in Egypt

On June 18, 1953, Egypt was proclaimed a republic with General Mohammed Naguib as the first president. In 1954 Colonel Gamal Abdel Nasser became prime minister, and in 1956 he was elected president. In 1958 Egypt joined with Yemen and Syria to form the United Arab Republic with Nasser as its president. The UAR dissolved in 1961, but Nasser continued as president of Egypt until his death in 1970.

President Nasser thought of himself as the leader of a social and political revolution, not only for Egypt but for the entire Arab world. He believed strongly that in the hearts of most Arabs there existed a spiritual impulse toward solidarity which rests upon their shared religion, language, culture, and history. He insisted that the Arabs could never reach their full potential in the political, economic, cultural, and social areas until there was a close and voluntary relationship among all Arabs.

The article presenting the Arab point of view about President Nasser's revolution was written by a staff member attached to the Permanent Mission of Egypt to the United Nations.*

INQUIRY: Compare the words of Nasser with those of Atatürk in reading 46. How are the two men similar in their attitudes? How are they different?

When the Revolution did come, the old regime was actually in a state of chaos. Premier Nasser's group of Free Officers began to clean up the corruption in evidence throughout Egypt. The first task was to rid Egypt of the presence of British occupation forces in the Suez. This was accomplished October 19, 1954. Seven days after the British agreed to evacuate the Suez Canal Zone, Nasser faced a cheering crowd in Alexandria. As he rose to make his speech, a man stood up in the audience and fired eight shots at him. Nasser remained standing and all eight shots missed. His first cry was, "Arrest that man." Then he stepped to the microphone and spoke: "Oh, my men, stand in your places. Oh, free men, stand! I revolted for your sake. I brought you dignity and self-respect. Oh, my citizens, my men, I brought to this country dignity and freedom, and I fought for your sons. Oh, free men, stand! Raise your heads, brothers, because the days of feudalism and colonialism are past." The panic subsided and at that moment perhaps Egypt truly became a republic of free men.

Premier Nasser, in planning the Revolution, had a positive aim to fulfill certain goals which may be summarized as follows:

1. Getting rid of imperialism and its henchmen, because imperialism gained a firm foothold in Egypt only when it co-operated with the traitors of the Mahamed Aly family and their opportunist adherents.
2. Shattering feudalism.
3. Eliminating capitalist domination over those in authority.
4. Establishing social justice.
5. Creating strong national armed forces.
6. Establishing sound democratic life.

Premier Nasser's Revolution did not envisage a final ideology styled after any pre-existing ones. To be realistic, as he is, conditions in different countries cannot be made to accept transplantation. He has a practical positive sight in mind and that is to meet the needs of the people, achieve these goals and entwine them with the tradition and background of Egypt. *"We began our Revolution with principles, not a program,"* he once said. *"We find that sometimes we have to change our methods. I have read much about socialism, communism, democracy and fascism. Our Revolution will not be labeled by any of those names. . . . We are not trying to copy anybody else's ideology.* We are a country of 22.5 million; 18 million are poor farmers

---

*Abdel-Mawgoud Hassan, THE TRUTH ABOUT GAMAL ABDEL-NASSER (Press Bureau of The Permanent Mission of Egypt to the United Nations).

. . . deprived of personal liberty for 5,000 years . . . under the domination of landlords. Only when they are liberated from this will Egypt be truly free."

In the short time that the new regime has been in power, Premier Nasser has made great strides toward achieving his goals of a free and prosperous Egypt. On the historic day of January 16, 1956, he presented to the people the promised Constitution guaranteeing "the establishment of social justice," and ". . . a sound democratic society."

In addition to this great advance in the young republic's development, negotiations for the High Dam project are now approaching fruition under Premier Nasser's careful and diligent guidance. The Dam will give Egypt ten times as much electric power as she now has and will increase the area of cultivated agricultural land by almost one-third. Of the Dam, Premier Nasser has said, "Ancient Egypt constructed the pyramids as memorials to the dead, but modern Egypt is venturing upon a monument much more imposing and useful for the living." This will indeed be a great step forward for the Republic of Egypt.

Among many other accomplishments is the land reform which dealt a death blow to feudalism. Also, the Revolution has fixed rent value at seven times the land tax. It has issued laws for the workman's protection and the raising of his wages.

The Revolution has, in addition, made great strides towards the execution of economic plans drawn up with a view toward providing every citizen with food, clothing, medicine, dwelling, and the right to education. It has carried out schemes for the expansion of vast areas of cultivable land by reclamation of waste land and for the increase of production by creating a considerable number of industrial enterprises and obtaining a considerably greater share of mineral wealth.

An end has been put to injustice and favoritism in appointments in the Civil Service. Social laws and regulations have been issued. Millions of workmen and their skills have been mobilized for the rebuilding of the Fatherland on sound economic basis, for the increase of the national income and with a view to ensuring welfare and prosperity to the people of Egypt.

To point out the unswerving dedication, self-denial, and lack of self-interest of this leader, it is to be recalled that when the Revolutionary Command Council decided to make General Naguib head of the government, they did so with nothing else in mind but to serve the cause of their country. Although Naguib was not and never had been a member of the original Revolutionary group, it was felt that being a man with appeal for the masses, he would best be able to ease the country over difficulties likely to come up with a new regime. Unfortunately, however, it later became evident that Naguib did not fully understand the goals of the Revolution and was using his power and influence in a manner detrimental to the achievement of these goals. The members of the Revolutionary Command Council also found that Naguib was constantly associating with members of the old regime and with leaders of political parties that had been proven corrupt. Consequently, the steady progress the Council had expected was faltering. This situation caused a great deal of unrest in the Council and they decided by majority vote to request that Naguib withdraw. The choice of Gamal Abdel Nasser to succeed Naguib was unanimous by all members of the Council since he was looked up to as the leader of the dedicated cause.

The avowed policy to which Premier Nasser is dedicated is one of prosperity and progress for his country. He has said, *"Our policy is one of non-alignment. I believe in an independent personality for Egypt and the Arabs. I want strength for the army of my country and prosperity for her national economy. It is with this conviction that I plan my policy of cooperation or non-cooperation with this or that bloc."* If this is the axiom by which he is judged, misinterpretations as to his pro-West or pro-Eastern tendencies may be more easily understood. The well-being of Egypt lies in its fostering friendly relations with all nations, a position which will help Egypt attain its desired goals. This cannot be achieved if Egypt accepts the accommodation of foreign political influences. The traditions and mode of living of the Egyptian people embody their religious and cultural heritage, and these must be cared for so that the Republic of Egypt may continue to exist and flourish in the future.

The answer to the plight of the Egyptian people which had for so long been sought was found in the determination and strength of this man who was one of them, Gamal Abdel-Nasser. Here was a man they could easily understand just as Abraham Lincoln was understood by his fellow Americans, someone who had been subjected to the very same abuses and discontent as they. In him they have found a leader who grasped the opportunity and with that fulfilled a promise that was destined to be the new Egypt.

48.
The League of Arab States

The formal expression of Arab unity is the League of Arab States, which was formed at the end of World War II. Although harmony has not always been achieved among the various states belonging to the League, it still managed to survive and grow. In 1966, the Arab Economic Council was formed to aid trade among the Arab states as well. In the following article Mohammed Abdel-Khalek Hassouna, Secretary General of the League, speaks about its purposes and activities.*

INQUIRY: Do members of the Organization of American States all have in common the same cultural, linguistic, and political histories that members of the League of Arab States have? How might nations in other regions join together in leagues based on such historical ties? Why are such alignments of nations an advantage to the members?

The League of Arab States is the second oldest continuously existing, inter-governmental, regional organization of its kind. Only the Organization of American States has a longer history. When the League

*ARAB WORLD, Vol. XIII, No. 3 (March 1967), pp. 3-4. Reprinted by permission.

was formed at the end of World War II, its membership consisted of Egypt, Iraq, Syria, the Lebanon, Transjordan, Saudi Arabia and the Yemen. Not only has the League survived, but it has flourished so that its membership was almost doubled between 1945 and 1962. Since 1962, and upon declaring independence, the Sudan, Libya, Morocco, Tunisia, Kuwait and Algeria have also joined the League.

* * *

The League is the working embodiment of a formula for bringing Arabs into a closer relationship. . . . "the League was created for the development of Arab countries, united by their cultural, linguistic and political histories, and by having borne the former yoke of colonialism."[1]

The Arab League has been the agency through which the member states have consciously confirmed their own national sovereignties and secured their regions from external control. The liberation movements in North Africa graphically illustrated this function.

Throughout most of its history, the organization has provided emergent Arab states with an increasingly effective institutional framework within which they have synthesized national and regional goals and objectives. Within the League, revolutions become constructive evolutions of national identity. The constitutional organs, specialized agencies and affiliated groups of the League provide a diversified regional apparatus, its influence embracing most aspects of contemporary Arab life.

The Arab League states have effectively maintained peace in their own regions during most of the League's history. The Lebanese crisis of 1958, which threatened to become an issue for the United Nations, was eventually settled within the Arab League family. In 1961, the League's handling of the Kuwait incident was prompt and efficient. Most internal threats to the peace of the region have been settled amicably before they could become inflamed, usually by means of arbitration and mediation, and often by the personal mediation of the League's Secretary-General.

. . . the members of the Arab League Council—which is composed of the representatives of the member states of the League, with each state having a single vote, irrespective of the number of its representatives—have no direct veto power. Technically, a dissenting member can refuse to implement the decision if it is otherwise approved by the majority, but it cannot block all action. In practice, the League seeks unanimity. Either opposition is reconciled before the matter comes to a vote, or, if the opponents are adamant, the vote may never be taken.

---

[1] Mohammed Abdel-Khalek Hassouna.

49.
Israel's First Decade

Jews were migrating to Palestine before the Balfour Declaration. Attacks against Jews in Eastern Europe and in Russia resulted in a migration to Palestine of around fifty thousand Jews between 1903 and 1913. Among this group was David Ben-Gurion, a Polish Jew, who became the first prime minister of Israel. A strong figure in Israeli politics since its founding as an independent state, Ben-Gurion in this article reviewed the achievements of Israel and its hopes for the future.*

INQUIRY: Compare this reading with reading 44. How do the actual events described by Ben-Gurion compare with predictions made by Herzl? Did the development of the new state take place in the way that Herzl expected and described?

No small number of new countries have arisen in Asia and Africa during the past decade, but Israel differs from them all, both in the origins of her rise to independence and in her history during the first decade of her existence.

* * *

The circumstances in which Israel's independence was proclaimed were also different from those which applied to the other young states. All the other new countries were established with the agreement—willing or enforced—of their foreign rulers. The midwife of Israel, however, was the U.N. General Assembly. Over two-thirds of the members of the U.N., headed by the United States and the Soviet Union, decided on Nov. 29, 1947, on the partition of Palestine and the establishment of a Jewish state in one part of the country and an Arab state in the other. Then, in defiance of this U.N. decision, Israel had war declared on her even before she was established.

* * *

On May 14, 1948, I announced Israel's independence in Tel Aviv. (According to the Hebrew calendar, the tenth anniversary of that date is April 25; since that is a Sabbath, the anniversary will be observed on April 24.) Eight hours later, at midnight, the British authorities left the country and the armies of five Arab states—Egypt, Jordan, Syria, Lebanon and Iraq—invaded Israel with the aim of wiping the revived Jewish state off the face of the earth.

* * *

. . . The Arab armies were defeated and expelled, the area of Israel was increased, and the new Jerusalem again became the capital of Israel, as in the days of King David.

But Israel's most distinctive feature is the fact that during the first decade

---

*David Ben-Gurion, "Israel's First Decade—And the Future," THE NEW YORK TIMES MAGAZINE (April 20, 1958), pp. 9 ff. © 1958 by The New York Times Company. Reprinted by permission.

it has trebled its population. At the end of 1957 Israel had a population of 1,976,471, including 1,762,471 Jews and 214,000 Arabs.

* * *

Of the three great achievements of these ten years—the renewal of the Jewish state after more than 1,800 years of exile and wandering, the amazing victory of the Israel defense forces over the Arab armies in the war of independence and the immigration of a million Jews in the course of the decade —there is no doubt that the last was the most important and difficult. . . .

The immigrants who reached this country before the Second World War came mainly from Europe, endowed with capital, education and vocational skills. The great majority of immigrants who have arrived since the establishment of the state, however, came from impoverished and backward countries, without capital, vocational training or education.

The young state, subjected to military siege and economic boycott by its Arab neighbors, was compelled to find housing for the immigrants, to teach them trades, to give them work, to settle them on the soil, to help them to acquire a new language and to educate them to live as free and equal citizens of a democratic and freedom-loving state. It is doubtful whether this could have been achieved without the devoted assistance of the Jews of the world and especially of American Jewry. Valuable aid was also received from the Government of the United States.

More than a half million rooms have been built in the course of the last nine years; the state invested over $721,500,000 in building alone during the period. About a quarter of a million immigrants settled on the soil and became diligent farmers, although only a few among them had tilled the land before their arrival in Israel. About 500 new agricultural settlements were established, and the cultivated area was increased from 195,000 acres to 950,000 acres, while the irrigated area rose from 63,000 acres to 275,000 acres.

The greater part of these villages were established by immigrants from Asia and Africa who had had no agricultural training of any kind before their arrival—and yet within a few years they became transformed in Israel into a constructive and creative force, providing the town population with most of its food and, together with the Israel defense forces, maintaining the security of the country's borders. Most of the immigrants were absorbed in industry, communications and shipping—mainly in vocations in which they had never engaged before settling in Israel.

And just as there was a far-reaching transformation among the million immigrants in the cultural, economic and social spheres so there was also a profound change in the appearance of the country.

Agricultural and mining settlements sprang up in wastes that had been desolate and uninhabited for centuries; bare and lonely mountains and hills were covered with forests and orchards. Millions of trees were planted on the sand dunes on the hills and by the roadsides up and down the country. The extensive and pestilential Hula swamps in the north were drained, and thousands of acres of good and fertile land were reclaimed for new settlement.

There have also been cultural achievements on a large scale in the course of this decade. In September, 1949, a law was enacted providing for compulsory and free education between the ages of 6 and 14. In 1949 there were 180,844 pupils (including 6,780 Arabs) in the elementary schools; in 1958 the number had risen to 404,900 (including 27,500 Arabs). There was a considerable expansion in secondary, vocational and agricultural education.

The Hebrew University in Jerusalem and the Technion (Israel Institute of Technology) in Haifa became fertile sources of scientists and technologists of a high standard; the Weizmann Institute in Rehovot has become one of the finest scientific institutions in the world. About 1,200 new Hebrew books are published in Israel every year, which is no small number in proportion to the size of the population and bears witness to the spiritual energies of the young state of Israel.

There has also been important progress in the field of health during the first decade. The infant death rate, which was 52 per 1,000 in 1949, had fallen to 36 per 1,000 by 1957. In 1949 the average expectation of life was 65 for males and 68 for females; in 1957 it had risen to 68 and 72, respectively.

The main feature of the last three years of the decade was the more intensive development of the South and the Negev. A railway was built to Beersheba, and a road was laid from Beersheba to Elath, thus joining our country's two seas—the Red Sea and the Mediterranean—by a network of roads. After the Sinai campaign an oil pipeline was laid from Elath to Ashdad on the Mediterranean coast. These three undertakings opened up the Negev for settlement and development, which will be one of our central tasks in the second decade.

* * *

If the Arab states understood the benefits to be obtained from peace and cooperation between neighbors, Israel would be ready to cooperate with them in the political, economic and cultural fields on a basis of equality and mutual assistance. I am convinced that not only would this be an important contribution to world peace, but it would be of advantage to the Arab peoples.

What these peoples need above all is development, education, health and the enhancement of the dignity and value of man. In these fields Israel has shown her capacity during the past ten years, and she would gladly give her neighbors the benefit of her experience. Nor would she limit cooperation only to the economic and cultural sphere. She would also be ready for political cooperation on the condition that it should be aimed at fostering peace in the Middle East and in the world.

In the meantime, Israel is determined to strengthen her military preparedness and to persevere in her work of rebuilding and redemption; to bring in Jews from the lands of oppression and misery; to conquer the desert and make it flourish by the power of science and the pioneering spirit, and to transform the country into a bastion of democracy, liberty and universal cultural values based on the teaching of Israel's prophets and the achievements of modern science.

50.
Arab Point of View—Israeli Point of View

Unfortunately the past few decades have witnessed considerable tension and conflict in the Middle East over the founding of the Jewish state. The emergence of a strong and vigorous Israel on the ancient land of Palestine has been bitterly resented by the Arabs. The result has been innumerable border skirmishes, terrorist activities, and sometimes full-scale warfare.

Great power rivalries in this region make this tension dangerous to the world. The following article, "The ABC's of Middle East Crisis," sums up the Arab and Israeli points of view on their common problems. Reprinted from U. S. News & World Report (October 30, 1967).

INQUIRY: If portions of North America were returned to their original Indian owners, would a conflict exist such as that in the Middle East between Israel and the Arab states? Do you think any of the same arguments expressed in this article would be used? Why do you think the Arabs argue that the world would be a "madhouse" if lands were returned to their ancient owners?

THE ARAB POINT OF VIEW

This is how the Arabs see Israel:

• Virtually all Arabs feel that the creation of the state of Israel in 1948 perpetrated injustices against the Arab peoples who lived in the land taken over by Israel.

• Virtually all Arabs believe that the policies of Israel for the past 19 years have added to these injustices.

• Virtually all Arabs see the continued existence of Israel as a continued danger to them. Israeli policy of bringing in as many Jews as possible, Arabs believe, will in the long run require Israel to expand its territory once again.

Origin of the injustices claimed by the Arabs is rooted, they say, in the period after World War I when hundreds of thousands of Jews were moved into a territory inhabited mainly by Arabs for 2,000 years. This was done first under British protection, then clandestinely—and without the consent of the Arabs who lived there. Then a state was created—again without Arab consent—which gave the Jews political control over most of the territory. This resulted in the displacement of hundreds of thousands of Arabs to make room for newly arrived Jews.

. . . Arabs know that Palestine was the Jewish "promised land" of the Bible, but they reject the idea that the Jews were only "returning" to a land they left long ago.

"How can they lay claim to a land that other people had lived on for two millenniums?" asked an Arab voicing an argument common to his people. "If you follow that theory, the American Indians could take over New York

City. You would have to reshuffle people all over the globe. The world would be a madhouse."

* * *

On May 15, 1948, as Israel came into being, the Arabs attacked. As the Arabs see it, the Israelis were the real aggressors because they had brought in their immigrants and were setting up a state without Arab consent.

The Israelis won that war. Arabs today note that Israel at this time bought arms from Communist nations nearly a decade before Arabs were criticized by Western nations for buying arms from the same source.

As a result of this first war, Israel kept 77 per cent of all Palestine compared with the 54 per cent allotted to it by the U. N. This new territory was incorporated into Israel. During the war, and after, more than 1 million Palestinian Arabs fled their homes into adjoining Arab nations. The Arabs say they fled because they feared for their lives.

. . . Israeli terrorism, the Arabs insist, predated and exceeded Arab terrorism starting even before Israel became a state. The Arabs cite the case of an Arab village in Palestine called Deir Yassin. In April, 1948, an Israeli terrorist organization attacked Deir Yassin and killed 250 inhabitants. This attack, the Arabs agree, was publicly deplored by Israeli leaders, but they cite the writings of the Jewish leader of the terrorists who later declared: "There could not have been a state of Israel without the victory at Deir Yassin." Arabs agree.

* * *

. . . The property these Arabs left behind was substantial. A 1951 report by the U. N.'s Palestine Conciliation Commission estimated that more than 80 per cent of Israel's total area and more than two thirds of its cultivable land was abandoned by Arab refugees during and after the war. One third of Israel's Jewish population was living on refugee property. Nearly one third of the new Jewish immigrants settled in urban areas abandoned by the Arabs.

Israel's own "Custodian of Absentee Property," the Arabs say, stated that, of the 370 agricultural settlements established between 1948 and 1953, 350 were on Arab property.

Nearly all the olive groves, nearly half the citrus groves and about 10,000 shops and businesses in Israel were left behind by Arab refugees, say the Arabs.

What particularly irks the Arabs is that the United Nations, first in December, 1948, and almost every year since then, has called on Israel either to allow the displaced Palestinian refugees of the 1948 war to return or to compensate them for their property losses.

* * *

Why don't the Arabs accept the existence of Israel as the fact it is, forget the past, negotiate face to face?

For the Arabs there seems no point in negotiating with a state that continues, in their view, to be operating on a policy of growth at the expense of its neighbors. Intelligent Arabs can cite chapter and verse of quotations from Israeli leaders on this policy of an "ingathering of the exiles" from all over the world.

What worries all Arabs are official Israeli statements such as those which have appeared in the official Israeli yearbook over the years. One such declared that Israel today "has been established in only part of the land of Israel" and that independence exists only "in a small part of our country."

* * *

THE ISRAELI POINT OF VIEW

This is how the Israelis see the Arabs:

• Virtually all Israelis believe the Arabs have no right to deny them a homeland in which Jews have lived for more than 3,000 years.

• Virtually all Israelis feel that Arab policies for 20 years have been devoted to the eradication of Israel.

• Virtually all Israelis see the Arabs as people who won their independence in lands they shared with Jews, but who now insist on denying this same independence to the Jews. Mideast peace is possible, the Israelis say, when Arabs want it.

For the Jews of Israel, the origins of their state are rooted neither in the Balfour Declaration of 1917, nor in the Nazi persecution of the Jews of Europe.

The modern movement of the Jews back to the land they all called "home" began to grow as far back as the middle of the nineteenth century when the country was under Turkish rule.

Jews have always lived, say the Israelis, in the territory which now is Israel. One Israeli, voicing an argument often put forward by his conationals, said this:

"We are the only people in the Middle East which can say of itself that its children speak the same language in the same place that their ancestors did more than 3,000 years ago. No Arab of the area can say the same."

. . . The Israelis say that the Jews of Yemen, Iraq and Egypt were among the first to return to the land of Israel in the nineteenth-century immigration. Right of the Jews to a homeland of their own, Israeli leaders note, was recognized both by the League of Nations in 1923 and by the United Nations in 1947.

The Israelis did not evict the Arabs from their territory, they say. On the contrary, they insist, it was the economic growth of Palestine under the British mandate, sparked largely by Jewish enterprise, which increased the Arab population of Palestine by "substantial" immigration. Much of this Arab immigration, the Israelis contend, was illegal just as the Jewish immigration of the time was illegal.

Arab immigration and emigration involving the area of Palestine "flowed like the tides" through history, say the Israelis. Before World War I, there was a flow of Arabs out of the area. After the war, this movement was reversed and Arabs went back into Palestine.

. . . Arab concern about Jewish immigration is what Israelis call the "more-Jews, more-land myth." This argument, they say, is raised by Arabs constantly, but they insist the whole theme is without foundation in fact.

* * *

. . . If Israel has land enough, then why is there any question about the return of conquered Arab lands to the Arab nations? Israelis not connected with the Government tell you that they intend to keep Jordan's share of the city of Jerusalem—"our Holy City which we will keep open to others"—but all the rest of their conquests from the Arabs in the [Six-Day] war is "definitely negotiable—an economic liability required for defense only as long as the Arabs are out to wipe Israel off the map." Government officials, more cautiously, echo the same policy.

"It all boils down to the fact that we would be happy to give the Sinai Desert and the Gaza Strip to Egypt, the Jordan West Bank to Jordan and the Syrian highland strip to Syria in exchange for face-to-face negotiation which would leave us in a mutually satisfactory peace with our neighbors."

* * *

. . . Much of the blame for the Arab-refugee problem, say Israelis, falls on Arab leaders who ordered Palestinian Arabs to flee. In Haifa, in 1948, say Israelis, Arab leaders asked the British for transport for evacuation. The Arab Higher Committee in Beirut, say the Israelis, assured Palestinians that they would be brought back to their homes in a few weeks—after the expected Arab victory.

As for the terrorist activities of the 1947-48 period, the Israelis insist, the Arabs are selective. Israeli historians say that long before the Deir Yassin incident, 35 young Jews in the Judean hills were slaughtered by Arabs who left their bodies mutilated. After Deir Yassin, where Israeli terrorists killed Arabs, Jewish civilians on their way up to Hadassah Hospital on Mount Scopus had their convoy shot up and burned by Arabs. These incidents and others including the dynamiting of homes on Ben Yehudah Street in Jerusalem, say the Israelis, were not only never denounced by Arab leaders, but were held up as examples for other Arabs.

. . . The Israelis also call attention to what they call "the other refugee problem"—the question of Jewish refugees from Arab nations.

* * *

Said an Israeli observer:

"We can hardly accept that attitude. Israel's existence does not depend upon Arab recognition of Israel's existence. It depends on the attitudes and actions of Israel's people themselves.

"We feel we have the right to be where we are. We feel this right has been acknowledged by the international community. We feel we have a greater need to live as a country and as a people than anyone's need to kill us and remove our country from the scene of history."

. . . Step by step, the Israelis trace this Arab drive to eliminate Israel through their history. They give this picture:

In 1947, the Arabs rejected the partition agreement.

In 1948, the Arabs attacked Israel—and lost.

In 1949, the Arabs refused to turn the armistice agreement with Israel into permanent peace treaties.

In 1956, the Arab border raids on Israel "forced" the Israeli attack in the Suez-crisis war. A U. N. cease-fire order ended hostilities, and Israel pulled back to prewar frontiers—"reluctantly," say Israelis today, "because we had only half-hearted guarantees of the great powers, no direct talks with Arabs. We knew they would attack again."

From 1948 to the present, say the Israelis, the Arab countries have maintained they are in a state of "belligerency" with Israel. They have used diplomatic hostility, economic boycott, blockade and, finally, elaborately prepared military aggression up to the June war of 1967—all in an effort "to drive us into the sea."

As for Arabs' charges that they cannot afford to resettle their refugees from Palestine, the Israelis note that they have repeatedly offered to negotiate their financial contribution to such an effort, but that the Arabs refuse to negotiate on this or anything else.

* * *

. . . On terrorism, say the Israelis, the Arab thesis seems to be that it is all right for the Arabs to give official support to their terrorist groups against Israel, but it is not all right when the Israeli retaliate in kind.

* * *

. . . The Israelis feel strongly that the future of their country is bound permanently to better relations with their Arab neighbors and to mutual development of the whole Mideast area in which they live.

51.
Golda Meir Speaks to the World

On June 5, 1967, full-scale war erupted between Israel and her Arab neighbors. In a period of six days, the Israelis virtually destroyed the Egyptian air force, army, and military equipment, advancing up to the Suez Canal. The Israelis also took Jordanian territory up to the west bank of the Jordan River, and captured the Golan Heights where Syrian guns had long harassed them. It was a fantastic victory for the Israelis and a crushing defeat for the Arabs. It did not settle anything, however. The continuing hostility blocks any form of cooperation between Israel and her neighbors and holds back social progress within each nation.

On October 21, 1970, Golda Meir, Prime Minister of Israel, spoke at the United Nations about her world, her region, and her country. She spoke realistically about freedom of speech, freedom of worship, freedom from want, and freedom from fear. She spoke about the problems that continue to obstruct healthy progress in the region of the Middle East.*

INQUIRY: Mrs. Meir states that "cooperation with . . . neighbors in the solution of regional problems is essential." How have Israel and the Arab states cooperated? Why is cooperation difficult between nations that do not share common aims? How does concentration on military aims retard social progress?

Mr. President,

Rising now to look upon a quarter of a century in the life of the United Nations Organization, I cannot help but recall that the United Nations will always be linked, in the mind of our people, with the signal role this Organization played in the emergence of modern sovereign Israel. The Organization put the seal of international recognition upon our historic process of return, ingathering, liberation and development—and this we cannot forget. Neither can we forget that the United Nations came into being after the overwhelming tragedy of the Nazi holocaust which the United Nations' predecessor, the League of Nations, proved unable to prevent.

World War I was the war to have ended all wars. Those of us who were in their teens then believed this. The entire world wanted it to be true; the League of Nations was to be the guarantee that this would be so. And we were all witnesses to, and victims of, its failure.

The reason for the failure, I am convinced, was not lack of a sincere desire for peace but a lack of determination to act for its preservation. We need only recall the moving words of the Emperor of Ethiopia when he appeared before this Organization in 1962, warning against a recurrence of the international inaction which had opened the way to aggression against his country and thus endangered the peace of the world.

It is in the light of the League's tragic failure that we must judge the achievements and shortcomings of our Organization which came into being after the shattering experience of World War II had made absolutely clear the need for a world body capable of international action to prevent World War III.

Even before the adoption of our Charter, in the midst of World War II—in 1941—President Roosevelt had in four famous phrases outlined a program which, if implemented, would have saved the world from the agonies of these decades.

Almost thirty years later and after twenty-five years of the United Nations Organization, what is the fate of the Four Freedoms?

Freedom of Speech: Millions of people in the world, are denied this elementary freedom. Sadly, we seem to have become accustomed to this situation, as though it were normal for human beings to be denied the right to express their ideas, and in some places, to be denied even the freedom to

---

*Courtesy of the Permanent Mission of Israel to the United Nations.

think. To a lesser degree, *freedom of worship*, too, is drastically restricted in many a human community.

Freedom from Want: To see how we have failed in achieving this freedom, we need only compare the immense increase in wealth since this principle was enunciated, with the horror of want and consequent degradation among hundreds of millions of people in various parts of the world.

Freedom from Fear: During the last twenty-five years there have been almost constant so-called "local" wars: there were very few in which major powers were not indirectly involved. And today no country in the world, no matter how large and powerful, enjoys absolute freedom from fear of war. One might almost say that the only factor which has prevented a new world conflagration is the fact that the major powers have reached a state of mutual fear. Not freedom from fear but a balance of fear has made it possible for civilization to survive at all. Is it an exaggeration to say that at best our Organization has been able to stop some wars—perhaps temporarily, while actually it has hardly prevented any? The most serious aspect of this situation, it seems to me, is the fact that those who commit aggression and those who are its victims have equal status in the United Nations—and even on the Security Council.

Bleak as the picture is, there is also a record of which we in this hall can be proud.

There can be little doubt that the supreme historic achievement of the Organization has been its role in ending the era of colonialism and inaugurating, in its stead, the age of national liberation. Close to seventy nations have gained freedom and independence. This phenomenal transition has changed the face of the globe, rectifying the historical injustice which for centuries had acknowledged national freedom for the few and denied it to the many. It has set in motion vast forces which lay dormant and suppressed over centuries. The concept of the Family of Nations now has authentic meaning and with this the dignity of the individual is enhanced. And though there are still millions of human beings on the globe who because of color, race, religion, are denied national or individual self-expression, this condition has become the exception to the rule, rather than the rule as it had been only two decades ago. If the United Nations had achieved nothing more, its existence would be justified by the fact that so many millions, once subjugated, are today the masters of their own destiny. This liberation is primarily the result of effort and struggle by the emerging peoples themselves. But the United Nations has encouraged it at every stage; and it is through membership in the United Nations that liberated countries express and celebrate their new dignity and equality.

A notable result of the great movement of national liberation characteristic of our century, a movement in which the United Nations played so creative a role, was the rebirth of the State of Israel in its historic homeland. This rectified an ancient wrong within the framework of international law and in accordance with the principles of international justice.

Mr. President,

The emergence of new, independent countries has been followed by economic and social cooperation between the advanced, developed and developing countries. Programs of international aid which only decades ago would have been considered Utopian, have been undertaken in large measure under the aegis of this Organization. Great strides have been made in deepening communication between peoples, lending validity to the essential truth that freedom and welfare are indivisible, and that no nation can find ultimate fulfilment within its frontiers so long as others, no matter how remote, are denied liberty and progress. We know too well that the world is still divided by the tragic gap between the haves and the have-nots. It is by now a truism that only a very small percentage of the world's expenditures for armaments could have liberated the African and Asian continents from fear of want and brought them into an era of greater development. The fact is that part of the world is growing richer, while much of the rest is as poor as before. In relative terms the gap has widened.

National independence is not the mere assertion of a new political reality, it is a framework within which the improvement of society and the betterment of the individual must take place. It is the creation of the instrument through which the society must strive for new heights of social justice and economic well-being. . . .

The whole Middle East is a dramatic demonstration of the emergence of peoples into national independence. Once the domain of colonial powers, it is today an area inhabited entirely by independent and sovereign countries. The Middle East, however, is an area in which national independence has unfortunately not been accompanied by peace, stability and resultant prosperity. Rather it is an area of strife and struggle, within the shadows of which lurks an even greater danger to the peoples of the area—the danger of the loss of their long fought for right to determine their own fate and their own future course of action.

The question we all face—Israelis and Arabs alike—is whether we forfeit our right to decide our own destiny. That question will only be resolved in the measure that the people of the Middle East succeed or fail in making peace among themselves and by themselves without hindrance or intervention of any outside Power. Recent events in the Middle East have proven yet again that resort to substitutes and alternatives for direct peaceful solution of the conflict creates fertile ground for breaches of promise and mutual suspicion.

This brings me to another basic question which vitally affects the prospects for peace in the Middle East. Unfortunately, the Middle East has for twenty-two years been the scene for the cynical flouting of solemn agreements. International order, the integrity of the United Nations itself, depend upon the scrupulous observance of international obligations. Unless the members of this august body respect the sanctity of agreements, no treaties can be binding and no pacts can be maintained.

The authority of the United Nations rests primarily on moral not physical force. Any member state that disregards the Charter and agreed covenants imperils peace as well as the United Nations. For this reason, though I have no wish to engage in the polemics of the General Debate, let me recall the sad record of broken covenants in the Middle East. From the initial violation of the Charter of the United Nations by the concerted Arab invasion of the new state of Israel, to the present day, the sequence of events follows the same disastrous line of agreements made and instantly broken.

The Arab states violated the armistice agreements of 1949, they nullified the arrangements concluded in 1957, they unilaterally destroyed the cease-fire resolution of 1967 by embarking on a "war of attrition" against Israel, and now Egypt is undermining the American peace initiative by flagrantly violating the cease-fire standstill agreement.

It is these violations which have halted all progress towards peace despite Israel's earnest commitment towards its quest. As long as the present breaches continue there can be no hope for the resumption of meaningful negotiations. Agreements can only be reached if those making them enter upon them in mutual trust and in the assurance that they will be honorably executed. Until the situation obtaining at the time when the cease-fire went into effect is restored Israel cannot be expected to take part in the Jarring talks. Israel seeks to resume negotiations; it wants the Jarring talks to be fruitful, but it cannot renew its participation in them, until it is demonstrated that agreements that have been concluded are faithfully observed.

The 1967 cease-fire Security Council resolution, unanimously adopted and accepted by all parties, is not limited in time and is unconditional. I hereby announce on behalf of the Government of Israel that we are prepared to continue the present cease-fire without a time limit.

In an atmosphere in which a callous breach of faith between nations is touted as a virtue, and aggression against a peaceful neighbor is acclaimed as a sacred cause, no hope for peace can prosper. Yet, despite what has happened, we still trust that for the sake of all our peoples, the Arab leadership will join with us one day in guiding our area from the present turmoil to the horizons of peace. I therefore call from this rostrum, in the presence of the representatives of the entire community of nations, upon the leaders of the Arab nations of the Middle East and especially upon the new leadership of Egypt to recognize once and for all that the future of the Middle East lies in peace and this must be achieved by Israelis and Arabs themselves. It will only be achieved by the building of faith and not the breach of faith; by honoring commitments solemnly undertaken and not by undermining them; by negotiation and not by evasion; by talking to each other and not at each other; in short, by the confrontation of peace and not of war.

It has been the fate of my country that peace has been denied us by our neighbors since the very emergence of Israel. Has Israel alone been the sufferer? No. All those around us, as well as Israel, have paid the terrible price of endless warfare.

Billions of dollars have been spent on armaments instead of on war against poverty, disease and ignorance. There are now deserts of death where there could be blooming fields.

I say this today not in rancor but in sorrow. I am convinced that all of us in the Middle East will continue to exist as sovereign states. None of us will leave. But we may choose whether we will continue in the sterile course of mutual destruction, whether we will go on hurting each other to no one's benefit, or whether we will venture on a constructive course, and build our lands separately and together.

For each of us to attain the best for his people, cooperation with his neighbors in the solution of regional problems is essential. Our borders not only separate us but are bridges between us. No people is an island. We are bound to each other by the problems of our region, our world. We can make of these ties a curse or a blessing. Each nation, each land must decide.

52.
Statement to the Nation

A war of words continued to characterize the Arab position with regard to Israel. Although President Anwar El Sadat of Egypt speaks, in the following speech, of 1971 as a "decisive year for peace or war," no full-scale war started then, nor in 1972. But Sadat kept the idea of revenge in the minds of his people while he stored up war materièl.*

INQUIRY: How would you feel, as an Israeli, about Egypt denying use of the Suez Canal to Israel? How would you feel, as an Egyptian, about Israeli occupation of the land adjoining the Canal?

September 16, 1971

In the name of God,
Fellow Citizens, People of Egypt,
Brothers and Sisters,
    . . . I have previously spoken to you; especially when I spoke on May 1st I said that if we did not make the defeat which took place in 1967 a starting point from which to embark upon building a new state—even if we gain victory in the war we are facing today—we should be wronging ourselves and the coming generations.

We cannot possibly afford to lag behind, I said that many countries had passed through the same experience before. In 1941, the Germans who were at war with the Soviet Union, were at a distance of 15 kilometres from Moscow, and more than one-third of the Soviet Union's industry, its agricultural production as well as its basic production had fallen into the hands of the Germans. The Soviet Union had not then attained a high level of industrialisation. The revolution, as you know, took place in 1917 and the Soviet Union began to build up and develop its country, but it was still passing through the stages of industrialisation. It received a blow in 1941 which was by far more violent than the one we received in 1967, more severe from every point of view. However, the Soviet Union made this defeat a starting point from which to build up the new state.

---

*Reprinted by permission of Ahmed Tawfik Khalil, Minister Plenipotentiary, Egyptian Interests Section, Washington, D.C.

Today, the Soviet Union is one of the two states in the world which they call the Big Powers, from the point of view of development, science and technology. This is why I say that if we do not make the 1967 war a starting point from which to build up a new state, we shall not be able to end today's battle, nor shall we be able to face our responsibilities towards the coming generations to which we are accountable.

* * *

The war of liberation today and tomorrow is our life and our hope; our honour and dignity depend upon it. Our enemies should not imagine that during the past months we have neglected the war of liberation and over-looked it, being preoccupied with domestic affairs; or that we no longer want the war of liberation or that we are ready to give up. We have set the house in order from within. We had to make order within. We had to prepare ourselves and prepare our new structure and our new State in Arab Egypt.

* * *

I promised you in a previous speech to talk to you about the stand of the United States. I must talk to you about it today not only to you, but also to the entire Arab World and to the whole world, because we are back again to the methods of twisted politics and deception.

* * *

On July 6, . . . the Director of Egypt's Office in the U.S. State Department came to me, . . . with a message from President Nixon and from Rogers. In that message, the U.S. President said he had decided to adopt a definite attitude towards the problem.

Good! That is what we have been asking for a long time. Just tell us your attitude. As for that middleman affair, he said that he would stop it and would now work out a definite attitude . . . but that he had a few questions to put to me.

I said I was ready to clear up any point. He asked: Do you agree to America defining her attitude?

I said that that was what I had been asking for a long time and that I actually wanted America to define her attitude.

Then he asked whether the Soviet-Egyptian treaty had made any change in our relations or had any impact. Of course, according to his conception, he wondered whether or not our will was our own free will.

I told him that the Egyptian-Soviet treaty had not altered our position. The Egyptian-Soviet treaty embodied Egyptian-Soviet relations . . . but our will is free . . . it was free, it is now free, and it will remain free for ever, God willing. This is our problem with the whole world, or with Western imperialism in particular . . . that we are determined to maintain our free will. Well, they said that Sisco was going to Israel on July 26, after that he might either return here, or return to the U.S. Anyhow America was going to define its attitude, after Sisco's return, in a clear paper. It was to be a clear declaration. Well, I said, that is good! We were ready and waiting . . . This . . . was on July 6, 1971. From that day—July 6—to this very day, September 16, namely, two months and 10 days, there has been no communication from America. Then we broached the American authorities and asked them what had become of the Sisco visit. They sent a memorandum saying that Sisco had gone to Israel, had held three long meetings with Mrs. Meir, Allon, and Eban together, as well as a separate meeting with Eban to discuss bilateral relations . . . and that Mr. Sisco, in his talks, had concentrated on the following items:

1. The relation between the settlement in stages and the comprehensive settlement.
2. The question of Israel's use of the Canal.
3. The nature of the ceasefire.
4. The question of the Egyptian presence at Sharm El-Sheikh and the Suez Canal.
5. The range of the Israeli withdrawal area.
6. The nature of the means control.

Sisco held these three meetings and considered all these items. But what is the attitude of America?

What are the declarations of Israel?

What is the viewpoint of America regarding the settlement and the decision of the American President to end the role of middleman, and adopt a definite attitude? There was no communication concerning all this; in other words, two months and ten days ago contacts between us and America ceased completely. At the beginning of my speech I said that I had discovered that the problem before the world and the Arab world, and before our people, is lending itself to camouflage and deception. Why? America is announcing everywhere that contacts with Egypt are continuing, that there is room for optimism and that there is a solution on the way. In fact, America went further than that; it said that Egypt had accepted the partial solution and had communicated her decision to the Soviet Union. The delegate representing America at the Big Four meeting in their final conference said that which signified that they had better relax and not bother any longer because America was in contact with Egypt and Egypt was co-operating and a settlement was near. He indicated that contacts were being pursued and that the solution was on the way.

Here I announce to our people, that as the most interested party to the Arab world, as an interested party, and to the entire world that contacts between America and ourselves completely ceased two months and ten days ago. We have come to no agreement, America has not revealed its attitude to us, neither has it proposed anything definite. Our position is what I said it was, and America's position is merely concerned with Sisco's visit to Israel and his talks about six points.

I consider that the six points constitute a descent from the position we had attained with Rogers and Sisco when they visited Egypt. We defined matters concerning the first stage of withdrawal in a specific manner. Now, in the chat Sisco had with Israel, they began to talk, once more, of the relation between a settlement in phases and a complete settlement. Our viewpoint is clear. Rogers has rescinded and knows that we do not accept a settlement in phases without a complete settlement, or as part of a complete settlement.

The second point—Israel's use of the Canal—is rejected until she implements all the commitments stipulated in the Security Council Resolution. The U.S. knows this. The nature of the ceasefire—they know and we told them that we do not accept a continuous ceasefire. I am saying here even if they deny it there in America, that they agreed with us and considered it our right, not to accept a ceasefire for an indefinite period as long as one foreign soldier remained on our soil. They may deny it, but I am stating this as a fact. I said that I should not accept a continuous ceasefire for an indefinite period as long as there was one foreign soldier on my land and they said: "You are right." Rogers and Sisco may deny it today, but that is what happened. Today, they are still repeating some old things. I explained to them our attitude concerning the question of the Egyptian presence east of the Canal. They know that there is no discussion about it. East of the Canal is Egyptian and not a part of Israel; it is Egyptian territory and there can be no discussion about it with Israel. The Egyptian presence east of the Canal is our right.

The range of the withdrawal area, the nature of the means of control—all the things Sisco just went and simply talked about; this means that America not only did not define her role, as she said she would, but also gave up the role of middleman. Now Sisco goes and talks there in Israel, while America does not send us an answer for two months and ten days.

Therefore, I declare to our people, to the Arab world to the whole world and the U.N. which will meet in a few days that the United States has resorted once again to deception and misleading. There have been no contacts between us and the United States for two months and ten days. There is no agreement any paper defining her attitude. Then what is the reason behind the information that the United States is spreading all over the world about having contacts with us and why should her delegate to the Big Four state that Egypt has agreed, or almost agreed, with America? Why should they go and tell the Soviet Union that Egypt has accepted a partial settlement? All this talk has no basis at all—it is intended to mislead and deceive, it is in the interest of Israel in order that 1971 may pass and then 1972, the election year, also, and we find ourselves entering upon another ten years, or in order that the day may come on which we might face the *fait accompli* and surrender to Israel's conditions. Today, while declaring this they say as they used to say that it was calm diplomacy not to talk or declare anything. I agreed to that before and we remained silent, saying to them that we should not declare anything or talk while we were putting the house in order from within. But today, and in face of the campaign of misrepresentation and deception which the United States is launching throughout the world, I must declare the truth to our people, to the Arab world and to the whole world, to the Big Four and to the U.N. which will meet in a few days.

* * *

. . . Whatever there is between the United States and Israel, will definitely be revealed one of these days. All the facts and the conspiracy will come to light. The farce, which we have before us, of the United States asking Israel's permission to send Sisco, and then of Israel telling her that she will see, whether or not she will agree, is a farce before the whole world because the world knows that the United States is a great state. The United States provides Israel with everything from a loaf of bread to the Phantom. Without the United States, Israel cannot live for two months. We have overlooked many things; because we have been speaking of peace. Unfortunately, this is the United States' attitude and I am putting it before the whole world, before our people primarily before our Arab world, before the entire world, before all the international communities so that the United Nations, the Security Council, the U.N. Secretary-General and Gunnar Jarring may shoulder their responsibilities. I asserted, in a previous speech, and otherwise, that 1971 will be a year of decision; either there will be war or peace. I asserted this on the basis of the true interest of the cause, not at all because we are biased towards somebody or because our patience has come to an end. No. On the basis of our comprehensive study regarding interests of this nation, we must not neglect our cause today, as the United States and Israel desire. They want it to remain in the United Nations for twenty years, until, as was the case in Berlin and concerning the Oder-Neisse borders, it becomes a *fait accompli*—they remain east of the Canal and the story ends. The Israelis want it that way. However, I do not care very much what Israel has to say. What I cared for, in the first place, was that the United States, as a great nation, should define its attitude and I had great hopes that President Nixon was going to keep his word.

1971 is a decisive year either for peace or for war. The cause can no longer brook delay. We have organised our home-front and we should now start to prepare ourselves to face the responsibilities of the forthcoming stage.

I must tell you that everything depends on us. This war of liberation is ours, it does not belong to the U.S. or to the Soviet Union or to anyone else. It is our war of liberation according to our will and our determination. For this reason, we should prepare ourselves to show the resolution and decisiveness which the coming stage requires.

Our will is one and as long as our home-front is one, then no weapon in the world can conquer the will of the people. The best example before us is that of Vietnam.

The entire U.S.A. arsenal consisting of the most up-to-date and electronic weapons, which are all employed in Vietnam, have not been able to defeat the will of a determined people, with their national unity and one objective.

After reorganising our home-front our national unity is now stronger; our target is one and the same and our will is unified. We are never afraid; we will pay a high price and on this occasion the U.S.A. should know that Israel will also pay a high price. When I say violence for violence, napalm for napalm, an eye for an eye and a tooth for a tooth, I mean exactly what I say.

When I say that I am willing to sacrifice a million lives for our independence and for the liberation of our land, then America should, in turn, tell its spoilt pets in Israel that they, too, should be ready to sacrifice a million lives. For I will never sacrifice a million lives without making them pay with a million lives, too no matter what the cost.

* * *

Despite all difficulties, I have deep faith in God Almighty that He will grant us victory as long as we have one will. Our will is one, our front is one and the will of the people is the voice of God Almighty.

May God guide your steps and may God's peace and mercy be upon you.

53.
Cease-Fire, 1973

On October 6, 1973, Egypt and Syria attacked Israel. In the first few days of the war, it appeared that Israeli forces were being beaten. However, Israel rallied and drove into Syria almost to Damascus and invaded the west bank of the Suez Canal. Supplies and men from other Arab countries failed to help the Egyptians and the Syrians. When the Soviet Union began resupplying the Arabs, the United States stepped in to help the Israelis.

The following resolution of the United Nations Security Council called for an end to fighting. However, the fighting continued for several days as both sides tried to improve their military positions at the bargaining table. The UN sent an emergency force to the area to police the uneasy peace as negotiations began.*

INQUIRY: Evaluate the Resolution of 1967 in light of reading 50. What do you think are the possibilities for a lasting peace between Israel and the Arab countries? for continued sporadic fighting between the sides? What basic changes in attitude and demands do you think are necessary for a lasting peace?

RESOLUTION 338 (1973)
OF 21/22 OCTOBER 1973

The Security Council

1. Calls upon all parties to the present fighting to cease all firing and terminate all military activity immediately, no later than 12 hours after the moment of the adoption of this decision, in the positions they now occupy;

2. Calls upon the parties concerned to start immediately after the cease-fire the implementation of Security Council resolution 242 (1967) in all of its parts;

3. Decides that, immediately and concurrently with the cease-fire, negotiations start between the parties concerned under appropriate auspices aimed at establishing a just and durable peace in the Middle East.

* * *

---

*Courtesy of the United Nations.

RESOLUTION 242 (1967)
OF 22 NOVEMBER 1967

The Security Council

Expressing its continuing concern with the grave situation in the Middle East,

Emphasizing the inadmissibility of the acquisition of territory by war and the need to work for a just and lasting peace in which every State in the area can live in security,

Emphasizing further that all Member States in their acceptance of the Charter of the United Nations have undertaken a commitment to act in accordance with Article 2 of the Charter,

1. Affirms that the fulfilment of Charter principles requires the establishment of a just and lasting peace in the Middle East which should include the application of both the following principles:

  (i) Withdrawal of Israel armed forces from territories occupied in the recent conflict;

  (ii) Termination of all claims or states of belligerency and respect for and acknowledgement of the sovereignty, territorial integrity and political independence of every State in the area and their right to live in peace within secure and recognized boundaries free from threats or acts of force;

2. Affirms further the necessity

  (a) For guaranteeing freedom of navigation through international waterways in the area;

  (b) For achieving a just settlement of the refugee problem;

  (c) For guaranteeing the territorial inviolability and political independence of every State in the area.

  through measures including the establishment of demilitarized zones;

3. Requests the Secretary-General to designate a Special Representative to proceed to the Middle East to establish and maintain contacts with the States concerned in order to promote agreement and assist efforts to achieve a peaceful and accepted settlement in accordance with the provisions and principles in this resolution;

4. Requests the Secretary-General to report to the Security Council on the progress of the efforts of the Special Representative as soon as possible.

Further Readings

GENERAL

THE ANCIENT NEAR EAST SUPPLEMENTARY TEXT AND PICTURES, J. Pritchard, ed. Princeton University Press, 1969. Collection of photographs and text to 1700 B.C.

THE ARAB COLD WAR 1958-1970 by Malcolm Kerr, 3rd ed. Oxford University Press, Inc., 1971. Deals with the politics of Gamal Abdel Nasser and his rivals from 1958 to 1970. Paperback.

THE ARAB WORLD TODAY by Morroe Berger. Doubleday & Company, Inc., 1962. Good introduction to modern life of the Arabs. Paperback.

HISTORY OF ARABS by Philip K. Hitti, 10th ed. St. Martin's Press, Inc., 1970. One-volume study of Arabs from earliest times to the fall of the Ottoman Empire in 1917. Paperback.

ISRAEL by Chaim Bermant. Walker & Company, 1967. Covers political, social, cultural, and economic conditions of Israel to middle sixties.

ISRAEL: YEARS OF CHALLENGE by David Ben-Gurion. Holt, Rinehart and Winston, Inc., 1963. Treats the conditions of Jews in Palestine up to the proclamation of the state of Israel.

THE LAND AND PEOPLE OF EGYPT by Zaki Naguib Mahamoud, rev. ed. J. B. Lippincott Company, 1972. Revised edition brings this introduction up-to-date.

THE LAND AND PEOPLE OF ISRAEL by Gail Hoffman, rev. ed. J. B. Lippincott Company, 1972. Introduces the country in clear language.

THE LAND AND PEOPLE OF TURKEY by William Spencer, rev. ed. J. B. Lippincott Company, 1972. Introduction to the Turkish people.

MODERN IRAN by Peter Avery. Praeger Publishers, Inc., 1965. Good treatment of modern Iran.

NEW LIGHT ON THE MOST ANCIENT EAST by V. Gorden Childe, 4th ed. W. W. Norton & Company, Inc., 1969. Discusses the beginning of civilization in the Middle East. Paperback.

POLITICS IN LEBANON by Leonard Binder. John Wiley & Sons, Inc., 1966. Lebanon's response to the modern forces of change.

THE PYRAMIDS OF EGYPT by I. E. Edwards, new ed. The Viking Press, Inc., 1972. The pyramids are monuments to the mighty dreams of the Pharaohs.

MUSIC, LITERATURE, ART, TECHNOLOGY

LETTERS FROM MESOPOTAMIA by A. Leo Oppenheim. University of Chicago Press, 1967. These letters are original translations. They frequently suggest style and content of letters today.

BIOGRAPHY AND SOCIETY

A VIEW OF THE NILE by Elizabeth W. Fernea. Doubleday & Company, Inc., 1970. Personal narrative of a young American family's life in Egypt from 1959 to 1965.

EVERYDAY LIFE IN BABYLON AND ASSYRIA by Georges Contenau. W. W. Norton & Company, Inc., 1966. Fundamental to understanding human life during this period. Paperback.

EVERYDAY LIFE IN EGYPT by John M. White. G. P. Putnam's Sons, 1967. Very interesting portrayal of cultural and daily life of old Egypt.

EVOLUTION OF URBAN SOCIETY by Robert M. Adams. Aldine-Atherton, Inc., 1966. Comparative study of early urban societies of Mesopotamia and Pre-Hispanic Mexico.

THE LIFE OF ATATÜRK. Turkish Ministry of Broadcasting and Tourism, 1961. Definitive biography of the father of modern Turkey.

PEOPLES AND CULTURES OF THE MIDDLE EAST by Louis Sweet. Vols. I and II. Doubleday & Company, Inc., 1970. Volume I *Depth and Diversity* focuses on the historical heritage of the area. Volume II *Life in the Cities, Towns, and Countryside* concentrates on the effects of urbanization and change on traditional institutions. Paperback.

PICTORIAL HISTORY

CONSTANTINOPLE, CITY ON THE GOLDEN HORN by David Jacobs and Cyril A. Mango. American Heritage Publishing Co., Inc., 1969. A clear and well-illustrated description of an ancient and important city. It is now known as Istanbul.

GREAT AGES OF MAN SERIES by various authors. Time-Life Books, A Division of Time Inc. Relevant titles are: *Cradle of Civilization, Ancient Empire, Byzantium, Early Islam, Classical Greece,* and *Imperial Rome.* Excellent illustrations and readable content.

LIFE NATURE LIBRARY by various authors. Time-Life Books, A Division of Time Inc. Relevant titles are: *The Desert* and *The Land and Wildlife of Eurasia.* Well-illustrated.

"THE MARVELS OF EGYPT'S PAST." A series of articles in *Life* Magazine from April 5, 1968 through May 1968.

MILESTONES OF HISTORY SERIES by various authors. Newsweek, 1970. Relevant titles are: *Ancient Empires* and *The Expanding World of Man.* Good pictorial essays.

ROYAL CITIES OF THE OLD TESTAMENT by Kathleen Kenyon. Schocken Books Inc., 1971. Many photographs and drawings.

WONDERS OF MAN SERIES by various authors. Newsweek. Relevant titles are: *The Pyramids and Sphinx, Hagia Sophia,* and *Dome of the Rock.* Beautifully illustrated and clearly written.